# Elderberry Wine

## Vintage 2010

# Elderberry Wine
## Vintage 2010

Writings from the Clark College Mature Learning Program

Edited by DEBORAH GUYOL, EDITOR

Order this book online at www.trafford.com
or email orders@trafford.com

Most Trafford titles are also available at major online book retailers.

Printed in the United States of America.

ISBN: 978-1-4269-5274-6 (sc)
ISBN: 978-1-4269-5276-0 (hc)
ISBN: 978-1-4269-5275-3 (e)

Library of Congress Control Number: 2010919489

*Trafford rev. 04/11/2011*

 www.trafford.com

**North America & International**
toll-free: 1 888 232 4444 (USA & Canada)
phone: 250 383 6864 ♦ fax: 812 355 4082

# ELDERBERRY WINE

By Elizabeth Wilson

Sit with us a little time
Taste the fullness of our wine
Breathe the bouquet it exudes,
Through words, their many moods.

Joy and lightness, gloom and doom,
Bravo, evil all have room
On the pages of this book.
Take it to your fav'rite nook.

Hang a sign, "Please don't disturb."
And read what Helen, Ron and Herb
And all these other authors wrote
Of life and dreams, of fears and hope .

Read our writings line by line,
Drink deep of Elderberry Wine.

# FOREWORD

Ara Serjoie, MPA, CFRE
Vice President of Development, Clark College Foundation

This issue of Elderberry Wine–full of expression that provokes reflection–was made possible through a generous and thoughtful contribution by an anonymous donor. A creative publication like this one demonstrates the importance of philanthropy for providing the margin of excellence in education

Dr. Alfred Apsler, distinguished and beloved history and philosophy professor at Clark College, championed the Mature Learning cause in 1972. This occurred at a time when such efforts were considered novel and innovative, even by the most progressive standards in the country. Nearly 40 years later, the Mature Learning program at Clark College is considered a model for colleges and universities everywhere.

Courses, activities, seminars and travel opportunities spanning a spectrum of interests bring hundreds of seniors and retirees in our community to their college. Mature Learning is a tremendous service offered by Clark College for the venerable members of our community. In turn, participants learn of ways they can help support the college and its unparalleled impact on the economic vitality and livability of the community.

The literary offerings of our Mature Learning students in this publication are an intermingling of contemplative and joyful discourse nurtured by Clark College. We are all graced by the synchronicity between a thoughtful donor and the mutual investment of time, talents and treasure that make Elderberry Wine a cherished cornerstone of our program.

# FOREWORD

Tracy Reilly Kelly

Corporate & Continuing Education
Continuing Education and Mature Learning Program Manager

Elderberry Wine is indeed of a superior vintage–like a fine wine, this anthology celebrates a magical chemistry displayed through quality ingredients, age, set and setting. And the appellation of wine is a fitting one for the alluring Creative Writing classes at Clark College Mature Learning, still going strong after 33 years of continuous, superior programming. Unafraid to shout out our age, the elder writers of Mature Learning exhibit inspired writing under the gifted instruction of editor and instructor Debbie Guyol.

From its beginning in 1977, the creative writing community at Mature Learning has attracted accomplished instructors for its treasured studio environment, including Elizabeth McPherson, Elaine Limbaugh, Charles Deemer, Bill Aull and Sharla Yates. Longtime instructor Debbie Guyol has brought a masterful ability to work with students at whatever level of ability they present and to carefully shepherd their progress as they improve. Debbie is an accomplished editor and this edition attests to her exhaustive time and expertise. These writings, representing the diverse contributions of our students, exhibit humor, pathos and originality which guarantee a delighted reader.

In 1999, instructor Charles Deemer came up with the concept of an anthology of student writing, and worked with the first two editions. Vintage 2000 was edited by Deemer, and Vintage 2001 by Barbara Hamby. There was an enormous effort brought to these editions by volunteers and our small Mature Learning staff. This fine new edition could not have been produced in its higher quality format without the generous support of donors to the Clark College Foundation. Our whole program is assisted by this kind of support, which cannot exist with just student fees and state support. I am grateful for this support from the deepest reaches of my heart–it allows our remarkable vision of lifelong learning to flourish here at Clark College, for students now, and as this legacy anthology exhibits–for the future.

# INTRODUCTION

Deborah Guyol, Editor

When I started teaching in the Mature Learning Program I worried just a bit about the broad definition of the course: Creative Writing–not Poetry, or Short Fiction, or Essay and Memoir. How could I help aspiring poets improve their verse AND convey the elements of a successful piece of fiction AND introduce students to the wonders of creative nonfiction all in one ten-week course? It seemed, I confess, overwhelming.

What I've learned since then has helped my own writing as much as the writing of my students. It's the power of the various, of cross-fertilization–call it hybrid vigor. The prose writer can learn from the meticulous word-choice of the poet; the poet can appreciate the role of character (mainstay of fiction) in poems, including those that appear to simply contemplate nature. The memories and meditations that fuel the work of the essayist inspire poetry and fiction as well as essays. It all works together beautifully.

Which brings me to Elderberry Wine. Like the Creative Writing class it springs from, this vintage ranges far and wide. Its offerings include not only the expected reflections on life and death and love and loss, but fictional ventures into other–sometimes bizarre–worlds, and meditations–often poetic–on the fantastic as well as the everyday. Let's change the metaphor and call it a banquet.

We have time travel: adventures in 1920s Mexico, a swampy town in the American South in the 1930s, the lair of a drug lord in the 1980s Caribbean. We have the natural world–rivers, lakes, fish, spiders, dolphins–and the lives of houses. We have cats and dogs and a guinea pig. We have recollections of childhood, rueful reflections on the aging process, and anticipations of the future. Yes, death is there too, lurking benignly, malevolently, even playfully.

The only requirement for participating in this anthology is having been part of Clark's Mature Learning Creative Writing class. Every student who wanted to contribute could do so. This inclusiveness, to my mind, makes the banquet all the more delicious. There is something here for everyone. So take a seat at the table with a glass of wine–or a cup of tea–and feast. Bon appétit!

# TABLE OF CONTENTS

# JANE AUSTIN

Jane Austin (aka "Famous Jane") describes herself as an old lady who relies heavily on her intuitive senses. She is also practical and intelligent and spends her days keeping her whack job husband from wandering in front of a speeding train, falling off a cliff or leaping tall buildings in a single bound. She helped raise a small gang of children and has managed to learn a secret or two about life and love.

# GRANDMA'S BED

It was there in Grandma's extra bedroom, this beautiful bed made of oak with posters carved into pineapple finials. On the bed sat a doll wearing a white dress with red polka dots. Grandma sewed the dress with scraps from a costume she made for my dance recital when I was five. On every trip to Grandma's house to get fresh eggs, I would go into the spare room and stare at the bed. If I asked politely, I could hold the doll while Mom and Grandma visited. I would sit quietly and play with the dolly – carefully, as she was very fragile. I would stare at the beautiful bed and imagine it in a different room with lacy curtains and a ruffled bedspread.

Both of my parents had died by the time I was 16. At 17 I went to live with my grandmother. This was a shock to my teenage bones—a teenager moving in with an 85-year-old deaf grandmother and my 65-year-old bachelor Uncle Wally, who had emphysema. Wally had lived with Grandma all his life, except for a few years when he was in the Army. I was a quiet and well-behaved teenager, but living with a deaf grandmother and an uncle who growled and grunted like a huge bear with every breath was an adjustment. I had been basically on my own and now Grandma wanted me to call her and let her know anytime I was to be late coming home. This always turned into an Abbott and Costello routine:

"Hi Grandma it's me."

"Who is this?"

"Jane."

"Jane's not home."

"I know. This is Jane."

"I don't know where Jane is."

"I won't be home for dinner."

"Yes, she should be here by dinner."

3

"Grandma, it's me."

"Call her later."

Grandma put me in the extra bedroom. The beautiful pineapple bed was mine to sleep in. This made the whole idea of being there tolerable. I did my homework on the bed, read books on the bed. It was my safe haven.

Not long after graduating from high school, I married a Navy man and moved on, living from one end of the country to the other. Grandma died when my son was about 18 months old. I was glad she had lived to see her first great-grandchild. My uncle growled on for not much more than a year without Grandma, and then he died. The house and its belongings were inherited by Grandma's only living son, my Uncle Val and his wife Mary.

As Uncle Val and Aunt Mary cleaned out Grandma's house I asked them about the pineapple bed. Their response was a non-answer of babbles and gobbledy gook, giving me the distinct impression I was not to ask about it again. One day, with great ceremony, Aunt Mary did present me with a milk glass butter dish that belonged to Grandma and a set of dime store glasses. Both of these had been gifts from me to Grandma.

Years passed and my kids were grown. Now I was the Grandma, Uncle Val had died and Aunt Mary was old. On one visit I again questioned her about the pineapple bed. She replied with indistinct babbling and non-answers with a hint that it had been sold along with all the other family heirlooms.

The phone call came in the spring 2004. Aunt Mary had fallen; she was in a nursing home and would not be able to return to her home. Someone had to deal with this situation: sell her home and belongings and pay her bills. I took a deep breath and said I would travel the 1500 miles and do the job. My brother and sister-in-law did not want the responsibility themselves but said they would help me clean out the house.

I had decided that to get the job done in a reasonable amount of time, I needed to stay at Aunt Mary's house. Before my arrival, my brother had a plumber make the water in the bathroom work and my sister-in-law cleared a path through the house and bought new sheets and a blanket for the bed. It was early spring and still chilly. I took the rotten curtains off the windows and kept the windows open as much as possible. The walls seemed to thank me for letting them see the sun after so many years of darkness.

Aunt Mary had been a widow for 15 years. During those years the walls kept moving in. My brother would try to remove all the old newspapers and magazines he could get in his grasp without being noticed. My sister-in-law would remove stale food from the kitchen as best she could until Mary would snarl, "What are you doing out there? Leave things alone. Get out of my kitchen."

Aunt Mary had Meals on Wheels come each day. Each day there would be a container of fruit on the tray. Each day Mary put the fruit cup in the refrigerator. Mary never ate the fruit but she kept the fruit because it was hers. The cups multiplied in the refrigerator until my sister-in-law managed to grab the ones with the most hairy growth and sneak them out the back door to the garbage. We had tried to tell Mary there were mice in her midst, but she insisted they never had mice before and so they didn't have mice now. At one point an opossum crawled in through a dirt opening under the basement stairs and made his way upstairs. It was dusk when she saw it run across the living room and called her neighbor to chase it outside. She would admit an opossum got into the house, but would never admit a mouse could!

Aunt Mary's back bedroom was off limits. If anyone even mentioned the back bedroom, Aunt Mary would freak out. "There is nothing in there! Besides, it's a mess." We used to make jokes about what might be in the back bedroom. We knew my uncle had been cremated or we would have figured she kept his body back there with all the other "stuff" she kept. I know what you are thinking, and no, she didn't have his ashes on the mantle. On the mantle were the ashes of her dog.

My sister-in-law and I started cleaning and sorting in the kitchen and worked our way through the house. Bleach was our best friend.

Aunt Mary had lived in this small house for 54 years. Every nook and cranny had something stashed in it, including the rafters. Every time we found some dish or trinket we thought might be of some value, it was broken or cracked. Many things had been destroyed by the mice. A beautiful collection of old 78 records had been nested in and urinated on. The giant organ my uncle used to play took up most of the living room. It was a haven for mice. They chewed wires, nested and urinated inside it, making it nothing more than an enormous tchotchke.

My brother began sorting in the garage and the basement. You could not walk into either one; you had to dig your way through the mess of boxes and junk. Boxes and boxes of "stuff" – all sorts of stuff: boxes of moldy linens, boxes of utility bills from the 1970s, boxes of boxes. It seemed never-ending. When I cleaned out a bedroom closet, I found my Grandma's doll tucked away in a box. She looked exactly as she always had and was happy to be removed from her dark tomb.

We didn't look forward to tackling the back bedroom. You could not open the door more than a few inches. Finally I had no choice but to venture in. Slowly I worked my way through the stuff stashed, piled and thrown in the forbidden room. Right inside the door was my bachelor uncle's antique dresser with the unmistakable sounds it made when the drawers opened. Aunt Mary's sewing machines that had not seen use in 20 years, racks of clothes, fabric, books, papers—you name it—had been forgotten in the back bedroom. Her desk drawers were full of old papers, mouse nests and treats the mice had stolen from the bags of snacks she kept on the floor by her chair in the living room. The forbidden back bedroom had not been forbidden or forgotten by the mice. The exterminator had come the day after my arrival to make the house saleable and not so creepy for me to sleep in. Even though there were no cases of the hanta virus in the Midwest, we always wore gloves and were careful cleaning not to make dust. We ate only fast food while we were at the house and we put our clothes directly in the washer at the end of each long day.

In the corner of this spare room, covered with a white sheet, was an old mattress rolled up and sitting on top of old bed springs. I slowly dug my way to the corner. All flat surfaces were covered with mouse droppings. I carefully removed the sheet, keeping the droppings rolled inside. When I turned back from stuffing the sheet into a garbage bag I was amazed. I could not stop my tears. Why would she hide it like this? What was her logic? I could only surmise I was to wait my turn to inherit it.

It is here now in my extra bedroom with lace curtains and a ruffled bedspread. A beautiful bed made of oak with posters carved into pineapple finials. On the bed sits my Grandma's doll wearing a white dress with red polka dots. Grandma sewed the dress with scraps from a costume she made for my dance recital when I was five.

# BIG BROTHER

My parents, Ruth and Marshall, had been married five years when my brother, John, made his entry into the world in March 1939. When they brought John home to meet the family dog, Silver, any fear they had that the dog would not accept the baby was put at ease. Silver saw the tiny critter as another job to be done. Silver protected John and never left his side. When John was learning to walk, he would hang on to Silver's hair and the dog would help him walk about the room. When John mastered walking alone, Silver took charge and carefully kept his eye on the little tyke, herding him away from trouble. Trail Creek was just across the street and down the bank. Dad, John and Silver made many trips down to the creek to play by the water.

The family lived in a 600-square-foot house that became known as the "little house." It was out in the country on Johnson Road. The tiny living room of the little house was overwhelmed by a fireplace that took up one entire wall. The only real function of the fireplace was to allow access for Santa. The one and only fire my parents built in it toasted the clothes in the closet behind the fireplace. It seems the firebrick was left out when the house was built.

My parents decided to move into town, and in 1944 they moved to Ohio Street, a predominantly Polish Catholic neighborhood filled with colorful characters. Compared to the little house, this house was gigantic. It had two large bedrooms, a formal dining room, a full walk-up attic and a full basement. John's bedroom was decorated with tan wallpaper accented with trains, boats and cars. What a great room for a small boy.

In the fall of 1944 Mom and John ventured off to visit Garfield School and enroll John in kindergarten. Entering the wide front doors, John captured his first glimpse of school.

Before him in the hallway stood a woman dressed in a long black skirt, ruffled white blouse and black vest. Her strange black shoes looked like something to be worn on Halloween. A pair of glasses dangled round her neck, suspended on a beaded chain. She introduced herself as Miss Florence Coffin. John took a step backward as she cackled, "I bet you are excited about coming to school?"

"No."

Mom quickly stepped in with, "Of course he is."

"No."

Miss Coffin ushered them into an office. John was amazed as Miss Coffin walked in front of him. She leaned so far forward as she walked it was as if she defied gravity. She plopped down behind a huge desk that dwarfed her frail body and quickly began the paperwork. All the while John studied her: dark red lipstick, dyed black hair pulled back in a loose bun. The glasses were now perched on her hooked nose allowing the chain to drape precariously on each side of her skinny face.

He glanced at mother; she seemed quite at ease answering each question this peculiar woman put forth. Didn't mom read me a story about this woman and a house of gingerbread?

John sat bolt upright as Miss Coffin swiftly dislodged the glasses off her face and let them go, allowing the chain to plop the glasses onto her flat chest. Peering over her hooked nose, her beady eyes looked straight at him like an eagle ready to pounce on its prey.

"Come John, I will give you a tour of the school."

"No."

"Sure John—it will be exciting," Mom coaxed.

"No."

As they toured the school, John never let go of Mom's hand. Miss Coffin babbled about how wonderful the school was and how much fun kindergarten was. John's eyes kept darting about as they walked around. He took notice when the Eagle pointed out the side door into the school. It was next to the kindergarten room, making it easy for mothers to drop off the kids and make a quick exit. As they finished the tour, the Eagle again peered at John, this time from over the top of her glasses. She wasn't leaning from the waist, she was tipping from her funny black shoes so far forward, he was sure gravity was going to win.

"Isn't it nice, won't this be fun?"

"No." He couldn't stop watching the chain from her glasses wobble back and forth against her sunken cheeks.

"It will be fun and you will learn things," Mom injected as she gave his arm a tug as a silent warning.

"No."

Against his wishes John was deposited in the kindergarten room on the first day of school. He attended for several days and Mom was pleased that he had adjusted. Then the phone rang.

"Mrs. Carpenter, John is missing."

Mom jumped in the car and started toward the school. The school was eight blocks down Ohio Street. About half way to the school she saw him. There was John casually walking down the sidewalk. Relieved but distraught she got out of the car.

"What do you think you are doing?"

"Going home!"

"Why?"

"I have things to do."

"Get in the car."

John was made to realize that no matter what, he was going to school. To him school was a world with rules you were to follow no matter how stupid you thought they were. He had trouble with non-parental authority. He also found that sitting still while listening to someone with a God complex drone on endlessly about all they knew was excruciating. He was a get-to-the-point-and-move-on kind of guy. He had to go to school but he didn't have to like it.

Teachers seemed to be a problem during all of John's school years. Most teachers he butted heads with were spinsters whose only life seemed to be the classroom. Most of these spinster teachers could be made into comic-strip characters with ease. Miss Coffin, without exaggeration, could be the main character in a whole series of books. It turned out I had these same comic-strip characters for teachers when I went to school, including Miss Coffin. Add to this mix that for most of our grade school years, Mother was PTA president. She was constantly at the school and knew all the teachers well. John was doomed. I made it through classes taught by the same teachers by being a sweet little thing who was not John.

The one good thing that came from his school experience was that John made a wonderful friend. In kindergarten he met Henry, a buddy to ease the dull and monotonous boredom of this thing called school. He and Henry went all through school together, had the same interests and remained good friends for over 50 years, until Henry's death.

There was to be an addition to the family. John was going to have a brother or sister. In the first grade things were still boring, but at least he was learning to read about Dick and Jane. Look, look and see. See Jane. See Jane run. It was then John announced to his mother he was going to have a sister and her name was Jane. John wouldn't budge on the name choice or even consider that it might be a brother. When the baby girl was born—me—she was named Jane. I have always been thankful my brother didn't fancy the dog Spot or Puff the cat.

For my first five years I slept in a crib in my brother's room. I remember my brother sleeping across the room in his big bed. He seemed so big, so smart. I was just the dumb little sister. To improve the sleeping arrangements, our parents decided to add a dormer on the upstairs and make a bedroom for John. The stairway to the upstairs was in the kitchen and he was old enough to venture off in his own space. This project meant plaster and paint and I was small, but I got to slap paint around on a wall thinking I was doing a great job. John's new upstairs room was painted blue and I was now alone in a room with walls covered with boats, trains and automobiles.

Along came a paperhanger, Mr. Karr. Mom didn't mind when he painted the outside of the house but she didn't like the strange man being in the house. Dad said it would be fine. I realized years later that although he was an actual painter and paperhanger, he was also a drunk. I picked out pink and grey wallpaper in a speckled pattern and Mom chose white paper for the ceiling. Mr. Karr proudly put pink paper on the ceiling for me. I loved it. Pink, a girl's room, no trains, boats or automobiles, I was in heaven. Mom put Priscilla curtains at the window, the final touch to make it truly feminine.

Once John moved upstairs, he seemed to disappear from the family. He had his own private retreat. Santa had brought John's first drum set down the chimney of the little house when John was two. When he was older he played drums in the school band. His private retreat housed a large drum set and the sound of drum beats echoed through the house.

John was fascinated by radio and even had his own radio station when he was about 14. There were speakers, turntables and microphones all over his room. The fascination with radio stayed with him. Although he spent many years working with my dad at the gas station, John went on to work at radio stations in some form or other, announcing, advertising, managing, etc. He still has a business that measures the frequency of radio stations to be sure they are on track. Radio has treated him well.

School was always John's downfall. He never found it challenging and he was bored. Today he would have been a good candidate for the Montessori school system. My brother is very intelligent and sought out things that were interesting to him and what he needed to know to make a living his way. My dad was the same, having lots of smarts, just not necessarily from formal schooling. I was lucky with school. I had teachers who would give me extra work to keep me busy. I didn't find school challenging, but I didn't find it boring either. I just sat still, listened and regurgitated what I heard.

Because John was almost seven years older, he was always off doing things that I was too little to do. Once he was old enough to drive he was never home. He was rarely around for family gatherings or family dinners. I remained the dumb little sister. Once in a while he would take me with him. He took me skin diving with his friends. I was the one in the boat counting heads and making sure everyone was accounted for. I am not sure if was a necessary job or just something to make me think I was an important part of the expedition. Once he tried to get me to dive off the boat and see how much fun it was. After an afternoon of coaxing, I jumped in the water for the first and last time. The only way I was going to swim with the fishes was by the hand of some Godfather and cement shoes.

Mother died when I was 14 and Dad when I was 15. My brother was my legal guardian until he ran out of deferments from the Navy and went on active duty. I went to live with my Grandma Carpenter who lived a few blocks from the "little house." Walking to the bus stop I would pass by the little house and imagine what it was like when my parents lived there.

The little house still stands, recently purchased by a distant cousin. She has remodeled inside and out and transformed it into a charming bungalow with lots of flowers about the yard. My parents would approve. A few years ago I was able to walk through the Ohio Street house while it was being upgraded after a fire. I touched every corner.

From the time John could ride his bike he was always away from home exploring. Except for the Navy, though, he never left town. He moved from Ohio Street in 1972 to a brick house in a wooded area of town. He still lives in this house with his drums, a boat, his trains, and a collection of automobiles.

As for me, it took a long time but I finally graduated from being the dumb little sister.

# CHARLEY

It was Sunday morning, my day off. That didn't mean much since I was on call 24 hours a day 7 days a week. The police dispatcher could only tell me that a family was being attacked by their dog and they were trapped in various rooms of their house. Usually Sunday calls were routine and my kids would ride along with me. This time they stayed at home.

As the only Animal Control Officer for the City, these were the calls that made me shudder. An out-of-control animal can be unpredictable when confronted. With very little equipment for dealing with the situation and even less information to go on, why do I think I can handle this crazed dog?

My thoughts went to previous calls. The Saint Bernard the court took away from his owners. He had broken his chain and attacked a woman walking down the sidewalk. He had torn open her arm and was quarantined at the shelter on death row. His kennel of doom was in a confined area and while the attendant cleaned his kennel she allowed him to roam free. Considering him friendly she begged to be allowed to adopt him. I knew she had small children and because of his background I kept refusing her request. When his final day was upon him, I agreed she could show me how she interacted with the dog. I was in a secluded hallway storage area and she came in with the dog on a leash. She showed me how well-behaved he was and told me how much she liked him. As we talked I moved backward and knocked over an empty metal garbage can, making a loud clanking noise. As I tried to catch my balance, the Saint Bernard went for me. In an instant my eyes were looking down his throat as the attendant pulled on his leash with all her might. She pulled him back less than an inch from his teeth tearing off my face. I stood up straight, looked at her and said only two words, "Dead Dog!"

I got a cold chill thinking about the Saint Bernard as I switched on the yellow bubble gum light on top of the ugly red Animal Control truck. I rarely used the light since it was really only a caution light and I had no authority to go over the speed limit. I felt like more of a show off than someone important when I used the light, but a feeling of power gets mixed in as drivers curtsey to the right and let you through.

Upon arriving at the scene, I saw the whole neighborhood was in attendance. Usually it is nice to have the neighbors come out to help bring in a stray or point which way he went. This time I felt like they were just going to watch while I made a gigantic fool of myself.

I remembered the audience I had while picking up a dog that had been hit by a car. Even though I had tied his mouth shut, he still managed to bite my arm. I finished loading the dog into the truck while holding my heavy winter coat sleeve tight around my wrist. I didn't want the blood I felt running down my arm to be seen. One audience member asked if I had been bitten and I mumbled about a close call. After driving away, I took a look at my arm. It didn't need stitches, but I still have the scar.

Overall I was lucky; I had been on many strange calls and survived with only minor bites, scrapes or bruises. Here I was again, facing the unknown.

I walked up to the police officer in charge. He advised me the dog had gone crazy: barking, snapping and chasing anyone who came in sight. The dog had grandma trapped in the bathroom, momma was trapped in her bedroom and the kids were in another bedroom. Dad had dashed outside where he managed to get a neighbor to call 911. Once the police verified that everyone inside was safe, I was called.

The police were willing to shoot the dog, but were not thrilled to shoot him with people watching. They also didn't like shooting the dog with the kids present or on momma's nice new carpet. Great! Now I am the bad guy if we get momma's carpet bloody.

At the back of the house, a tall outside staircase led to the kitchen door. My heart pounded as I began the climb. Equipment for dog catching is not exactly high tech. I only had a leash and a metal noose in my hand. It is not easy to get a noose on an angry dog. If you get the noose on and the dog still fights, you just keep making it tighter and tighter until he surrenders peacefully, passes out or breaks his neck. What would be the fate of this crazy dog?

Behind me was a cop with his gun drawn, ready to be a hero and save me from attack. The staircase seemed to go on forever. At the top of the stairs I looked through a window in the door. I could see right through the kitchen into the living room. There he was, on the sofa, barking out the front window at people in the yard. He jumped down and ran to the hallway to check on his captives. Back to the sofa to continue the furious bark out the window. I turned and smiled at the cop. I opened the door and stepped in.

"Charley, what the hell are you doing? "

The cop took aim. Charley spun around and ran toward me. Instantly his whole demeanor changed. Charley was so glad to hear a voice he recognized and thrilled to be rescued. His barks of anger, confusion and fear were now yaps of welcome.

"Come on Charley." I snapped the leash on his collar. "Let's get out of here."

We walked down the steps to slight applause and smatterings of laughter. The vicious dog was under control. As the neighbors stood there bewildered, I played it up a bit. Rather than put Charley in the back, I opened the door and allowed him to sit in the front of the truck with me while he wagged his tail and licked my face. The vicious attack dog was nowhere to be seen. I started the truck and drove away.

All the way to the shelter, I told him how disappointed I was.

"Charley, you really blew it. What a stupid thing to do. Those people wanted you over all the other dogs at the shelter and look what you've done."

At the shelter I fixed him some food and found him a kennel. I checked on the other animals and went home to my kids.

Adopting a pet is a large responsibility. People don't understand how hard it is to place animals in new homes. They are often willing to give up an unruly pet, thinking it will have no problem finding another home. Many people bring in whole litters of puppies expecting they will find homes because they are so cute. Shelters always have more cute puppies than they can adopt out. People need to have their pets spayed and neutered.

When Charley first came to the shelter he was not like most dogs, he was special. He came from a family with a lame excuse but he was beautiful and would find a home quickly. You couldn't help but rub your hand through his soft gray fur. Someone would look into his beautiful eyes and want him to be part of their family. We knew Charley would not last the weekend without a new home.

On Saturday, two hours before closing, I left for home. Nine dogs had been adopted out, making it a good day for all concerned. Charley was still sitting patiently in his kennel. Everyone was amazed he was not the first dog adopted.

Just before the shelter closed, a mom, dad, grandma and two kids came in to look for a dog. The family walked past several kennels and when they came to Charley they fell in love. Charley was brought out to the front area and he greeted each family member with licks and wags. As the family drove off with Charley, the shelter staff was very pleased he didn't have to spend another night in a kennel.

Saturday evening was a joy for Charley and his new family. They played with him, fed him and brushed his soft gray coat. When they went to bed, Charley found a spot on the floor in the little girl's room. Their family was complete.

On Sunday morning, Grandma got out of bed and headed to the bathroom. Charley heard this and ran out into the hall barking and snapping. Grandma managed to get herself into the bathroom, but Charley would not let her out. It seems Charley forgot all about the night before. He woke up with no idea where he was; he didn't recognize any smells and he was scared. His barking and Grandma's screams now had everyone awake. At the slightest noise, Charley would charge the bedroom doors keeping everyone trapped. The father, wanting to save his family, rushed out into the hall after Charley. That tactic only frightened Charley further and he snapped furiously at the father. Charley did great with the bark and snap but he could not quite get a good grip on the father as he dashed down the hall and out the back door.

When the police arrived and tried to enter the house, the petrified Charley greeted them with bared teeth before the door opened more than a few inches. The mother was talking to the police through an open bedroom window. Everyone was more than willing to stay put until police said it was safe to come out from their hiding places.

On Monday morning I took Charley from his kennel.

"Charley, I am so sorry. You did this to yourself. Now you are unadoptable."

Charley stood quietly while I gave him an injection. I kept running my hand through his soft coat. Almost immediately Charley, the little gray poodle, closed his beautiful eyes for the last time.

# RON AUSTIN

Ron Austin describes himself an old man who spends his time dragging his wife around North America by boat, plane and recreational vehicle. Along the way in life he picked up a bachelors degree in psychology and a masters degree in criminal justice; he also held down numerous jobs to help raise a small gang of children. His primary dysfunction is an inability to understand that anything must be done with a sense of urgency.

# REBECCA IS WAITING

The sun rose slowly over the mountain range, broke through the tops of the firs and rushed through the window of the cabin to fill the single room with light.

Morning exposed a sagging bed, surrounded by the clutter of an old man who had lived without a woman for years. An old black Labrador with a gray muzzle slept peacefully on a decaying rug beside the bed.

The morning light signaled something deep in the man's mind and he began to return from his sleep. Slowly he stretched, yawned, and rubbed his chin. He smacked his lips and reached unconsciously for the dog beside the bed.

"Good morning, Pup."

Feeling the familiar hand between his ears, the old dog raised his head. His legs strained to raise his aged body.

"Well, we can't stay here all day, can we Pup? Rebecca would have been up by now and had the fire going."

Rising from the bed, he removed his pants and shirt from the end of the bed and pulled them over his gray wool underwear. "There," he said with a small sense of triumph. "Lucky you. Just wear your clothes all the time. Wish I could do that. Sure would be easier."

"Well, let's see what we have for breakfast. First we'll make some coffee, huh. What do you say to that Pup? Right after I build a little fire."

He took cedar kindling sticks and dry fir from the wooden box beside the stove and carefully arranged them on a piece of wadded-up newspaper inside the stove. After lighting the paper, he shut the isinglass door and opened the damper all the way. "There, that'll be hot in a minute. Now, for some coffee." He measured grounds into an aluminum percolator and added water to the pot before placing it on the stove. "Not as good as Rebecca's coffee, but it'll have to do."

"That takes care of the coffee, Pup. Now let's see. I don't think I'll eat breakfast today, but how about you?"

The old Labrador looked up from beneath his sagging eyelids, seeking only the approval of his master, moving only when necessary, no longer fighting the stiffness of his joints.

"That's what I thought. You're hungry, huh? Well, let's see what we can scrounge up." He went to the squeaking refrigerator. "Hmm, what have we here? One sirloin steak! You know what that is, Pup? Not used to that, are you? Think that would be better than your usual dog food? Well, I can't cook it like Rebecca could but let's give it a try, huh?"

The old man took a large cast-iron skillet from the cupboard, poured some grease into it from the can on the counter. "Let's let it heat up a bit first, Pup. Think your old teeth can handle it? You don't chew much better than I do anymore."

The old man put the meat into the hot pan and seared it on each side before moving the pan to the side of the stove to let it finish up more slowly. "Ahh, it's just fine now," he said after awhile.

"It'd be a good day for a cougar hunt, wouldn't it, Pup? Just like we used to do. Eighty-five dollars for the bounty, fifty-five dollars for the hide. Those were the good old days.

"Say, I think the coffee's done now," he said, picking up the pot and pouring coffee into an old cup on the counter. "Nothing like a hot cup of coffee first off in the morning."

The old dog looked up, pleading for an opportunity to please, moving his head slowly as the old man scratched him between the ears.

"There we are now, all done. A nice steak, if I do say so. But I think you will like it better if it cools a bit and I cut it up real small." He put the steak on a plate and began to cut it with a knife.

"Sure would be a nice day to go after a cougar! Never did understand why they took the bounty off them critters. You know how many deer them cats kill? One every week. What a shame. That's a deer every week could be in some man's locker.

"Here, it's cool enough now, Pup. See how you like that."

The old dog raised his head and searched his master's eyes to understand the reason for this strange delicacy.

"But when they passed a law against killing them critters, that was just too much. They had no business doing that at all. That was just plain stupid!"

The old man squatted next to his friend while he drank his coffee and the dog ate his breakfast.

"How was that meat, huh, Pup? Pretty good? Well, it's no more than you deserve. You've been a good friend for a long time."

"It's time to get started Pup," the old man said as he took the 30-30 Winchester down from its rack on the wall. The varnish had long been sanded off and the stock rubbed lovingly with linseed oil. The bluing was badly scratched from trips through the brush, except for bluing that was on the new four power scope the old man installed as his sight worsened.

"Let's go Pup!"

The old man helped the dog down the front steps of the porch. As he stepped off the porch he picked up a small shovel that was leaning against the outside wall of the cabin.

Slowly, the two walked down the well-worn path toward the big tree, stopping once while the old man adjusted the heavy copper wires that he wore around each wrist to help fight his rheumatism.

They stopped just before reaching the big tree. The old man sat on the ground and held the dog's head in his lap. As he had so many times before, he told the dog what a fine woman Rebecca was and how, before the dog was even a puppy, he and Rebecca had built the cabin with logs they dragged in from the woods with the help of a little donkey. And then he talked about the big cougar the dog had chased up that tree, and how he shot the big cougar with his .22 rifle.

Then there was talk of the bounty for the cougar and how they had sold the hide.

When he was done talking, the old man sat looking up into the big tree imagining how the dog had treed the cougar. He could almost see the nervous critter jumping from limb to limb while the dog barked down below.

They walked to the tree. "This is where we bagged the big one, Pup. You remember? He gave us quite a chase! You treed him right here and I got him with the old .22. We sure got a lot of cougars in our day, didn't we?"

While the old man dug a hole under the branches of the big tree, the sun warmed the fir needles that had fallen on the ground; a deer ate leaves by the edge of a clearing and chipmunks cut fir cones to bury for their winter food supply.

For a moment it seemed as if the sun stopped being warm and time refused to pass. The old man did not hear the sound of the rifle, he only felt it jerk in his hands as it had so many times before when he pulled the trigger. A deer heard the shot and bolted into the vine maple. The chipmunks stopped their harvest.

The old man filled the grave with the fresh earth and then smoothed the surface with his hands and his tears. The chipmunks resumed cutting their winter harvest. The deer went back to eating the leaves at the edge of the clearing. The sun warmed the fallen fir needles.

The second shot rang out.

# THE SWEET LITTLE GIRL

Once upon a time there was a pretty young girl who lived with her mother and her father in a pretty little cottage in the forest by a river.

The pretty young girl loved to wear her beautiful new gossamer gown. It was fine lace and when the sun's rays touched it the outline of her nearly perfect body was clearly visible.

Actually, the beautiful gown was made for her by her mother from the drapes that had hung in the front room window until they started to fade. And the river? It was just a big creek.

The pretty young girl loved to dance in the field in front of the house while an orchestra played in her mind. She would twirl and leap like a ballerina, the sun streaming through her gown. Sometimes she would leap so high, so gracefully, it seemed as if she stayed in the air longer than gravity allowed. Sometimes she would land and instantly go into a beautiful pirouette.

Actually, she was well into the awkward stage and her dance was not as graceful as she believed.

One early evening she was in the field dancing and twirling, the light shining through her dress. Her mother poked her head out of the cottage door and yelled at her. "Now mind you what I said about dinner. And don't be wandering off to where that half-monster lives."

Actually, the half-monster was not a monster at all. He was half wolf and half man. In truth he was also part coyote, but his family was embarrassed and would never acknowledge coyote blood. His father used to say, "If there was any coyote blood in me I would cut my throat and let it run out."

The half-monster spent most of his time in the swamp. He was born in the swamp and he loved it there. Usually he was down on all fours looking for lizards and bugs and mice. Lizards and bugs were all right, but he preferred warm-blooded animals. And he liked to catch them and eat them while they were still warm and alive. It's not that he was a bad half-monster, it's just that, well, half-monsters have to eat too. And things taste better when they are fresh.

Sometimes the half-monster hung out down by the river. There he would pretend he was a man. He would walk upright, sort of, and look for fish. But he still preferred the warm-blooded food.

On this particular day, the pretty young girl got so wrapped up in what she was doing that she completely forgot what her mother had told her about dinner and about the half-monster and she went off skipping and twirling into the forest. She skipped and she twirled and she danced until eventually she found herself down by the river.

Her arrival did not go unnoticed by the half-monster. When she came twirling down the bank, sun shining through her gossamer gown, he was hiding in the vine maple by the river.

She leaped from a giant boulder the river had unearthed, landed on another boulder and went into a beautiful pirouette, her gown spinning like a wheel. It was magnificent.

The half-monster was excited. Well, at least he was curious.

Then the pretty young girl entered the giant cave by the side of the river. Really it was just a place where the river had pushed three or four large boulders together during the winter runoff. But it was big enough for a half-grown girl to crawl way down inside.

The half-monster was hot on her tail. That is, he followed to see what she was doing. She had disappeared. Slowly he crept over a big boulder and peered down into the cave. No one in sight. Gradually he made his way toward the mouth of the cave. Obviously she had gone into the cave. With stealth he crept on. Silently, slowly, on all fours. His mouth was wet with saliva—but then it always was. Suddenly, there she was, her back to him. He crouched, still on all fours, ready for fast action. Slowly, ever so slowly, she turned to face him. She was smiling sweetly, knowingly, hungrily. Then he saw the great long fangs that protruded from the upper part of her mouth.

Mother would certainly be angry. She had warned her daughter. "Now mind you what I say. Don't you go off and spoil your dinner. And if I've told you once I've told you a thousand times to leave that half-monster alone and stay away from the river."

And to top it all off, not only had the pretty young girl disobeyed her mother, but she got a big red stain all over her beautiful gossamer gown.

# A NEW ASSIGNMENT

"Wake up Bill! Wake up!"

"Aaaah. Hi Cindy. Where are we?"

"By a big beautiful waterfall. In a park I think. Maybe Yellowstone."

"Oh wow! I feel kind of funny. Where have I been?"

"You've been in oblivion. We always feel that way when he wakes us up. I'm just starting to feel normal myself."

"So you just woke up too?"

"Just a few minutes ago. Wow! Just look at this place."

"Any idea why our writer brought us back? Did he get a new assignment?"

"He must have or he wouldn't have wakened us. I hope we get good parts this time. Maybe you and I can be lovers again."

"Yeah. We were even married once. But that didn't work out. You fooled around on me and I had to kill you–and your lover."

"That story doesn't count. No one read it except the writer."

"It counted to me. I had to live through it."

"Look! Ted and Alice are coming up the trail. Our writer will have to use some narrative now so the reader can keep track of who is talking."

"Probably," said Bill. "Hi Ted. Hi Alice. How ya doin'? Are you fully awake yet?"

"Hi Bill. Hi Cindy," Ted said with a wry smile. "Yeah, we're awake. He woke us up first."

"Why the wry smile, Ted?" said Cindy.

"Why have you got one boob bigger than the other?" said Ted with a wry smile.

"I don't know. It must have something to do with the story our writer is telling."

"Same here. I think I will be saying everything with a wry smile in this story," Ted said with a wry smile.

"Other than that Cindy has one large breast and one small one, and that Ted says everything with a wry smile, does anyone know what this story is about?" said Bill.

"I do . . . "

"He said with a wry smile," said Cindy, Bill and Alice in unison.

"What are you doing?" Ted said with a wry smile.

"We're tired of hearing about your wry smile. Maybe that part could be dropped," said Bill.

"And while we're at it, maybe we could not discuss the size of my boobs," said Cindy.

"Of course, it's not up to us," Alice said. "We'll just have to see how it goes."

"So Ted, what do you know that we don't? How do you know what the story is about?" said Bill.

"I hacked into his email," said Ted. "I know what the assignment is."

"Boy! Way to piss him off. You could spend a whole story with your head stuck where the sun don't shine," said Bill.

"He'll never find out," said Ted. "I'm smarter than he is."

"Well what is the assignment?" they all said, in unison again.

"It's a tragedy. One of us, or maybe all of us, will have a tragedy befall us."

"Oh my God!" said Alice. "And out here in this wilderness. We could fall off that waterfall. Or get eaten by a bear or a mountain lion. What shall we do?"

"Now listen everyone, while I tell you this with a wry smile. It's okay. Sure we will have a little tragedy but we're just characters. When the story is over we'll go back to oblivion until we're needed again. Then we'll be back for a new story, good as new. Well, one or two of us may come back with a funny-looking breast, but, by and large, we'll be good as new."

"I don't know about you," said Alice, "but I'm scared."

"Me too," said Cindy. "Let's all be on the alert for bears or mountain lions."

"First let's get some big sticks to hit them with if we have to," said Alice.

"And don't go near the water," said Cindy.

"Look," said Bill, "Look at that star. You can see it plainly, right in the middle of the day."

"Oh, it's just a satellite," said Ted.

"Do you think we're going to find a baby in a manger?" asked Alice.

"Maybe it's not our tragedy," said Cindy. "Maybe something wonderful is going to happen. Yes, I can feel it. Something wonderful will happen. The tragedy belongs to someone else."

"Yes! Yes! I can feel it too. It's going to be wonderful," said Alice.

"It's just a satellite," said Ted. "Nothing wonderful is going to happen."

"Well, the satellite is getting bigger," said Bill.

"It's just the atmosphere," said Ted. "As it gets later in the day we see it through more atmospheres and it looks bigger."

"I still think something wonderful is going to happen," said Cindy.

"Me too," said Alice. "Ted is so negative."

"I'm just realistic."

"It's really big now. I don't think it's a satellite," said Bill.

"Oh my," said Ted. "That's a meteor. And it's headed straight for us."

"Maybe one of us has superpowers! Do any of you have superpowers? Or maybe the Bat-mobile is parked in a cave near here," said Alice.

"It's not that kind of story," said Ted. "Our writer wants to kill us off quickly so he can get back to swilling his tea."

"Not very imaginative though," said Bill. "With just a few more pages, he could have killed us off after we out-foxed a mountain lion or a rabid bear. We might have tricked the animal into falling over the waterfall or we might have rolled a big stone on it. Some of us might have survived. Bloodied but alive."

"Then it's no use?" asked Alice.

"I'm afraid not," said Ted. "Our writer has decided to take the easy way out. He always has been lazy."

"Bill, I'm frightened!" said Cindy. "Will you hold me the way you did when we were married? Hold me until the end? I'm trembling all over."

"Of course I will, Honey."

Alice wandered off toward the waterfall.

Ted sat, a wry smile on his face, watching the approaching meteor.

Cindy and Bill stood clutched tightly together, waiting for the end.

SATISFIED THAT HIS ASSIGNMENT WAS COMPLETED, THE WRITER LEFT HIS KEYBOARD AND WENT TO THE KITCHEN FOR A POT OF EARL GREY. IN THE FREEZER HE FOUND A FRESH BLUEBERRY MUFFIN THAT HIS WIFE HAD PUT THERE ON THE PREVIOUS EVENING. THE WRITER KNEW THAT IF HE ATE HIS WIFE'S BLUEBERRY MUFFIN SHE WOULD BE ANGRY. BUT THE WRITER ALSO KNEW HOW DELICIOUS THE BLUEBERRY MUFFIN WOULD TASTE WITH HIS EARL GREY. THE WRITER POPPED THE BLUEBERRY MUFFIN IN THE MICROWAVE AND SET THE DIAL FOR THIRTY SECONDS.

THE END

# A TALE FROM
# THE EDGE OF THE SWAMP

## A love story

My editor, Mr. Barker, was hesitant to send me down to get this story. He said that the people in this little town were descendents of Scottish and Irish immigrants and they don't care much for outsiders. He said revenuers and newspapermen who cause trouble in this part of the country tend to disappear.

"Be especially careful to not mess with their women," he said. "Mess with one of their women and then don't marry her and they take you for a boat ride in the swamp. They tie a rock on you before they throw you in because these swamp people are real partial to catfish. Catfish live on the bottom and they want you to stay down there where the catfish can get their fair share before the alligators eat what's left."

Mr. Barker has a sense of humor, I think, but I couldn't tell if he was kidding. Either way, I could not help thinking about what he said as I drove into the little town.

(May 4: Copy to Mr. Barker.) It was a little southern town, surrounded by family farms, built on the rich soil created as the swamp receded. On summer nights the humidity was high and the heat was unbearable. It was heaven for mosquitoes.

On the road through the little town, wagon wheels had long since kneaded black chewing tobacco spit and horse manure into a hard surface. A once-stately mansion leaned toward the alley and the general store leaned toward the jail. While less impressive buildings had lost their luster, the church, with its lingering aroma from the days it was a saloon, remained straight and strong and newly polished in whitewash.

I parked my Model T by the general store and walked across the hard-packed street to the sheriff's office.

(May 4: Copy to Mr. Barker.) The sheriff's office was a sturdy building that had never known paint. The exterior walls were made of wide vertical planks with small planks covering the gaps between the larger ones. The sign on the door read "Sheriff Tater."

Inside, I was greeted by a big, smiling, rugged man in overalls. "Welcome stranger. I'm Sheriff Tater but everyone calls me Sheriff Taterhead. You can do that too if you like." He picked up a can from the desk and spit a little juice into it, revealing a gap between his blackened teeth. Then he motioned me to sit in a big wooden chair.

(May 4 Copy to Mr. Barker.) Sheriff Tater presented himself as a man of integrity, charm, good looks and insight. Dressed in local attire, his only vice appeared to be that of all men living in this area: he chewed tobacco. No gun or badge was visible.

"Where you from?" he asked.

"From the city," I told him, thinking about the catfish. "My name is Allen. Allen Forsby. I'm a reporter for the Herald. I'm here to do a bit on that thing with the missing kid."

"The kid in the swamp thing, huh? You sure about that son? We got us some real good catfishing in these parts. You sure you wouldn't rather write about that?"

"No. No," I said, trying to not appear nervous. "I have to do what my editor tells me to do. My editor acts like a real bear. I just do what I'm told."

After a short pause and a spit into the can, Sheriff Taterhead said, "Why don't you just stay here in town for a while, Allen? Sheriff Taterhead will look into this whole matter for you and make some arrangements. Meanwhile, Madame Butterfly can show you what real southern hospitality is all about."

"Madame Butterfly?" I asked, still nervous.

"Well son, we got only one place in this town for visitors to stay and it's right down the street. Madame Butterfly's Finishing School for Girls."

"They put folks up in a finishing school for girls?" I asked.

"It's a whorehouse, son. It's kinda run down too, but it's all we got. A finer woman than Madame Butterfly you'll never meet. And she does take in a boarder now and then. The food is good and Madame and the girls really do spoil their guests. Don't be so scared son, nobody's going to bite you. Tell you what, son, I'll walk you down there 'cause I need to talk to Madame for a minute anyhow. But you just leave the whole matter of this story about the girl up to Sheriff Taterhead. I'll make all the arrangements."

We must have been a sight, the big smiling sheriff in his overalls and the little city dude in his Sunday best and small brimmed hat, walking down the street to the mansion. This mansion leaned toward the alley.

Sheriff Taterhead didn't stop to knock. In the foyer of the mansion a radiant middle-aged woman dressed in linen and lace rushed to greet us. "Welcome, welcome, welcome," she beamed, taking my elbow and pressing it against her breast.

The Madame led me into a dimly lit room with large windows covered in lace. The room was crowded with fine furniture suitable for an eighteenth-century English queen.

On one of the love seats sat a lovely girl, her smile gracious, her posture erect. Like a lady-in-waiting to the owner of the furniture, I thought.

"You just sit right here with Miss Louise and have a good talk," Madame Butterfly said. "I'll say goodbye to the sheriff and then we'll get you all fixed up."

(May 4: Note to Mr. Barker) Suitable lodging located. Rates reasonable. One of the old mansions in this charming little town has been converted to a comfortable boarding house. The proprietor is a most genteel woman.

When she came back, Madame Butterfly explained that if I agreed to stay a week I would be entitled to one free poke with the hostess of my choice. I looked over at the firm breasts and creamy thigh on Miss Louise and thought, Oh what the hell – I've got an expense account. "Sure," I said. "Maybe even longer than a week."

Each morning would start the same. Miss Louise would give me a hot bath and massage my sore muscles and then Madame Butterfly would bring us a fine breakfast of steak and eggs.

Modesty forbids that I tell you about the rest of the day, but it is probably fortunate that I strained a groin muscle on that first day. Without some pain, I would have surely believed I had died and gone to heaven. Fortunately, those hot baths loosened up the groin muscle real well.

(May 7: Note to Barker) Injured muscle while doing location interview. See expense account regarding treatment. This story may take longer than anticipated due to reluctance of the locals to trust outsiders. The only catfish seen so far were nicely cooked and on a plate. Ha ha.

One warm evening, Sheriff Tater arranged for me to interview the brother of the lost girl. His name was Jimmy and his little sister was named Mary. Jimmy introduced me to his wife, who brought us glasses and then left. After introductions Sheriff Tater left, promising to return for me in two hours. I was invited to sit on the porch and relax with Jimmy in true southern style including white lightning and cigars.

Jimmy lives on some fine farmland in a fine white house with a porch that goes all the way around. Large columns make the place look kind of Romanesque. The paint and the bushes around the house have suffered neglect recently.

Jimmy held out a lighted match for the cigar he had handed me and then poured whiskey in the glasses his wife had brought us.

(May 10: Copy to Mr. Barker) The sweet smell of cigar smoke wafted gently off the porch and was caught in a gentle breeze.

Jimmy and I sat puffing lightly on our cigars and sipping some of O'Sullivan's brutal but pleasant whiskey.

This whiskey will challenge your testosterone to a duel. This whiskey will say, "Are you man enough to take me on? I'll tear open your testes and leave you lying on the ground yelping like an injured girl. When I'm done with you, you'll have breasts. Only a real man can drink me and walk away whole."

Jimmy asked me what I had written so far so I showed it to him. He read it and said, "I don't know what wafted means and I sure as hell don't know what a testosterone is. What I do know is that if you sip O'Sullivan's whiskey slowly you can have a really mellow evening. If you swallow it right down, it will eat a hole in your stomach and come rushing out around your belly button."

I thought, that's pretty funny and I may use it in my story somewhere. If I survive drinking this stuff! Anyway, after a couple more drinks, Jimmy told me about the community and his friends. Here is what he said.

# WHAT HAPPENED - Jimmy's story

Right here on the edge of the swamp, my parents had this nice farm with a nice house and this nice porch. They died and left the farm to me and my little sister, Mary, right at the worst of the Depression. My little sister should have been a grown woman by now, but she just never seemed to grow up. That's why I always called her Munchkin. She was so small she had to buy kids' clothes or make her own. She liked to smoke cigarettes she rolled herself. I told her it was not lady-like but she said I should mind my own business.

(May 10: Copy to Mr. Barker) Mary (also known as Munchkin) was a lovely young girl who made many of her own clothes. She was known to be feisty and independent. Like many kids around here, sometimes she sneaked cigarette tobacco.

[NOTE TO SELF. I'M TOO DAMN DRUNK TO WRITE ANYMORE AND I FEEL WET AROUND MY BELLY BUTTON. FINISH THE COPY LATER IF STILL ALIVE.]

Three of us guys grew up together. There was me, and Billy, who grew up to marry my little sister Munchkin and become my brother-in-law. And of course there was Tater. His real name was James Elroy Tater, but we called him Taterhead. Even his parents called him Taterhead.

When we were young we didn't let Taterhead hang around us much because we didn't think he was too bright. But we liked him okay I guess.

Now we had an old Indian guy who was sheriff for a long time. He was even sheriff when my daddy was a boy. He was a good sheriff who didn't bother nobody much. But he finally got old and died so we needed a new sheriff.

The main job of the sheriff in our town was to host a good poker game on Saturday night. We would sip some local whiskey, smoke a cigar or two and play a little stud or five card draw. We knew that Taterhead was good at all of those things so we got together and made him sheriff. After that we decided to get respectful and so instead of calling him Taterhead, we called him Sheriff Taterhead.

If you drank too much at the poker game, Sheriff Taterhead would let you sleep it off in the jail. Once, Joe Bob Coons got so mad because he lost his money in the poker game that he threatened to kill us all. We put him in a cell and actually locked the door. He yelled and called us names for a long time and we laughed and threw pennies at him until he fell asleep. In the morning he was the same old smiling Joe Bob.

Billy and my sister used to drop by my house a lot. And after I married a pretty, sophisticated girl named Ann, Munchkin was always bugging Billy to bring her over so she could confab with my wife.

And that is when it happened. During one of those confabs. We were all sitting on the porch just listening to the crickets. Me and Billy were enjoying a sip or two of whiskey and smoking a cigar or two. The girls were drinking wine and Munchkin was smoking her roll-your-own cigarettes.

Suddenly a gator rushed up on the porch, grabbed Munchkin by the foot and dragged her into the swamp. Of course we followed, at a safe distance, to see if we could get Munchkin back. All we had for light was the matches we used for lighting the cigars. After a while, we ran out of matches so we gave up and went back up on the porch. Billy and I relit our cigars. Ann poured the wine from Munchkin's glass into her own glass.

(May 10: Copy to Mr. Barker) YES DRUNK BUT HEAR WHAT I KNOW. LARGE FIENDISH ANIMAL SHE CLAMPED IN POWERFUL HER JAWS AND RIPPED APART BY A CATFISH OR A STORK LIKE IS WAS NIGHT HORROR EATEN. (Translation: We shall never know the horror that girl must have felt the night she was dragged by that large fiendish animal, clamped in his powerful jaws, ripped apart and eaten as if she were a stork or a catfish.)

After a while of listening to the crickets, Billy admitted, "You know I never did like her that much no how." But he did look a little sad about the whole thing.

But Ann was crying. "You bastards," she yelled at us. "You bastards. Here we are stuck in this God-forsaken swamp. And who do I have to talk to now?"

"You've always got me Honey," I said, trying to reassure her.

"You! You! You are both disgusting smelly drunks," she yelled and went in the house without even finishing her wine.

"Women," I said.

"Yeah," agreed Billy.

"So I guess we better tell Sheriff Taterhead about this in the morning," I said and took a little puff of my cigar and a sip of my whiskey.

"Well we just might have problem with that," Billy said.

"How's that Billy?"

"Most everybody in these parts knows that gators ain't aggressive. Who's going to believe what happened here tonight?"

"Let's just say it was a croc then," I suggested.

"We can't do that," he said. "Everybody knows there ain't no crocs around here."

"What do you suggest?" I asked.

"Well," he said, "I was thinking that we could say she ran off with the Electrolux salesman."

"Sure," I said. "Everyone knows she always was a kind of a slut. Everyone knows about her and that swamp guy."

Well we decided that was the way we would play it. So the next Saturday we went to the poker game at the sheriff's office and after about an hour of five card draw, three bourbons and one cigar, I said in my most innocent voice, "Gee, Billy, I'm really sorry about my sister running off. That must be real tough on you."

"That slut run off with the chicken thief again?" Sheriff Taterhead asked.

"No," I said, "this time it seems to have been that Electrolux salesman that came through a while back."

Then we both looked over at Billie and he was almost crying. "Oh, I'm sorry," Sheriff Taterhead said. "I'm really, really sorry. I didn't mean no disrespect. And I didn't mean to insult your sister neither," he said looking at me.

"Oh, it's okay, Sheriff. You just said what's true."

[NOW I KNOW WHY THE SHERIFF SAID HE WOULD PICK ME UP. I'M SEEING DOUBLE AND MY LEGS NO LONGER WORK. IN THE MORNING IT WILL FEEL AS IF A RAILROAD SPIKE HAS BEEN DRIVEN THROUGH MY HEAD. OH GOD, TAKE ME BACK TO LOUISE, MY ONE AND ONLY LOVE.]

# WHAT REALLY HAPPENED

## Mary's (aka Munchkin's) story

That story my brother just told you, about how a gator grabbed me by the foot and dragged me into the swamp? Well, that just ain't the way it happened. There weren't no gator at all. There was only a dashing Frenchman.

But first, let me tell you about that "sophisticated girl" my brother married. Her name was Ann all right. She came from a little town sorta like ours only about thirty miles down the road. Her mama had long since run off and her daddy died leaving her with no real kin. Madame Butterfly took her in just as she did all of the unclaimed girls around here. Madame Butterfly let Ann work in Madame Butterfly's Finishing School for Girls as a whore and made sure she went to school. She also taught Ann to have manners and sit in a chair like a lady and bought her nice clothes.

Now Ann was my friend and she never called me Munchkin the way my brother and his friends did. They just called me that because I'm little and because they are mean. My real mane is Mary LaRosa McBroom and I am of fine Scottish stock. Ann always called me Rosie.

By the way, my brother never told you his full name. It is James Thomas McBroom. I always called him Squirrelhead.

But back to what happened that night. You see I've been having this romantic relationship with a handsome Frenchman that some call The Swamp Guy. They call him that because they can't pronounce his real name which is LaPierre.

When LaPierre talks to me in French I get all goose-pimply. He'd say things like "Vouly vou a couchy avec moi." I have no idea what that means but it makes my heart melt.

So me and Ann and my beloved LaPierre made a plan. LaPierre waited for me in the bushes by the house. Me and Ann got some dandelion wine she had made and we sat on the far end of the porch and I smoked some cigarettes. Squirrelhead and Billy were on the other end of the porch smoking cigars and drinking that awful white lightning that Ray O'Sullivan makes. That stuff will work just fine for starting a fire when your kindling is wet, but to drink it is just plain crazy.

Anyway, me and Ann waited and sipped wine and I smoked cigarettes until Squirrelhead and Billy got stinking drunk. Then I snuck off into the bushes to my LaPierre without them even seeing me leave. Once I was out of sight Ann jumped up and yelled "Gator, gator, gator. A gator's got her."

Those two idiots tried to follow where Ann told them the gator drug me using matches to see by. "Right here," she said, "see how the grass is all flat where he drug her. Oh that poor little girl. Oh, that poor little girl." But they was falling down drunk and I heard Squirrelhead say, "We better get back up on the porch before a gator gets us too."

After that, me and LaPierre just got in his boat and glided through the swamp to his cabin where we began a life of romantic bliss. Most every day we dined on chicken and fish and poke salad and had a fine time.

And that's what really happened and I don't care what my stupid brother said.

(May 12: Copy to Mr. Barker) Today it was my good fortune to be staying at the charming little boarding house run by Honey McDougal. Miss McDougal was the foster mother to Ann McBroom, the wife of the man whose sister was taken by the alligator that horrible evening. Miss McDougal came to my room late in the morning to inform me that Mrs. McBroom was in the parlor and had asked that I join the two them for tea.

Sheriff Taterhead has asked Mrs. McBroom to talk to me about her role in the tragedy.

# ANN'S LIFE SO FAR

Being a whore was the best thing that ever happened to me. Except for having a daddy that loved me.

When I was real little my mama ran off to the big city. She said she couldn't live in a mosquito-infested rat-hole anymore and she left.

And even though my mama didn't love me enough to keep me, she knew my daddy really did love me, so she gave me to him. I was his "Little Annie McFanny" and he took me everywhere he went. If he went to pick poke salad, Little Annie McFanny went too. If he tried to catch a catfish, Little Annie McFanny was there too. We were always together. Sometimes it seemed that I loved him almost as much as he loved me.

Daddy and I were miserable poor. We lived in a shack that weren't really more than some swamp brush with a couple pieces of corrugated tin as a roof. We slept on some old rags and except for poke salad, we didn't have much to eat. Once in while, with pomp and ceremony, one of the town ladies would give me a dress. "Oh, you poor little thing," she would say, looking around to make sure everybody was watching. "You can have one of my little girl's old dresses. She don't need it no more." She may have been a mean woman but Daddy and I still appreciated the dress.

We never had luxuries like shoes.

When I was thirteen years old Daddy got a cough. His cough just got worse and worse for a whole year. One day while Daddy and I were trying to catch a catfish Daddy said, "I have to die now pretty soon, Little Annie McFanny."

I told Daddy I just couldn't live without him. "Don't worry, my Little Annie McFanny. I talked to God about it and he promised to take good care of you. He said any creature that is loved as much as you are must be very special. Besides, Little Annie McFanny, you're smart and you're pretty. You'll do just fine in this big old world."

I was fourteen years old when my daddy died. I still miss him every minute.

The preacher was a big mean man with a loud voice and a job to do for God. So, a month or two after my daddy died he showed up at my shack and grabbed me by the hand and took me to the church. "I'm going to marry you off to someone who will take care of you and feed you," he said thrusting me in front of an old man.

Just then the door to that church flung open and in came the prettiest woman I ever seen. She was wearing clothes made of lace and carrying the prettiest parasol. "You're not turning that little girl into another baby factory," she shouted at the preacher man and dragged me out of the church.

That pretty lady told me that her name was Madame Butterfly and she was going to take me to her home that was down the road a piece. She said that Madame Butterfly was the name she used for business purposes and I should call her Honey. She said I was going to live with her in her mansion and have my own room and learn my letters and take a bath every day and have shoes to wear and nice clothes.

Then she took me to a beautiful room with lace curtains and a bed. "This bed and this room is all just for you," she said. "This is where you live now." Then Honey put me in a big tub of warm water and scrubbed me with a brush. Even my teeth!

(May 12: Copy to Mr. Barker) Mrs. McBroom was a woman with refined manners one might not expect in a small farming community. She was also beautiful. Mrs. McBroom explained to me that she had lost her mother while quite young. She had a loving father who devoted his life to raising her but he died when she was fourteen. After that, she was taken in by Miss McDougal, who saw to her education and made sure that she received the very best training in social etiquette.

Except for missing my daddy so much, life was wonderful. I had nice things and wore shoes when I was outside. The other girls there were "working girls" but most went to school too and they were nice to me and fun to be around.

"Everybody has to make a living." Honey told us. "We each use the talents we got. But not until we are fifteen." On my fifteenth birthday me and Honey dressed up in our best and went into town. "It pays to advertise," she said.

In town she introduced me to the men. She would say with a big smile, "Why hello there John. I'd like you to meet Miss Ann, who is our newest hostess at Madame Butterfly's." The men would lift their hats off their heads a little and say, "Why hello there Miss Ann." Then turning to Honey they would say, "She certainly is a beauty, Madame Butterfly. Where did you ever find a girl so beautiful?"

"Never you mind about that John," she would say. "Just be sure to stop by for a closer look soon."

John did stop by soon and so did many other men. Life was good and business was good and the men in town took off their hats and called me "Miss Ann" when I was out shopping. Of course the church ladies just said "humph" and turned their backs when I came by.

Once I told Honey that those church ladies should say, "Why hello Miss Ann. Thank you for doing those nice things for my husband. I could take care of it myself but you see, I've got this broomstick stuck way up my butt and it makes it hard to do anything except go to church."

Honey said I was being mean and I should not judge those church ladies. "That is up to God," she said.

Years went by and finally I was almost twenty-one years old. Just before my birthday, Honey came into my room. She said, "Ann, Sweetie, you're getting too old to be a whore anymore."

I said I didn't care. I just wanted to live in the mansion and have everything go on just as it was. But Honey insisted. "You've got to think of your future, Sweetie. The time has come."

As it turned out, Honey had found me a husband. His name was Jimmy McBroom and he owned a real nice house and some very fine farmland. "But here is the best part," she said. "He is a drunk who's probably going to die soon from drinking rot-gut moonshine. Once you marry him, you'll be set for life."

So I did what Honey told me to do and married Jimmy McBroom and that's how I ended up on the porch that night when me and Rosie pulled a fast one on Jimmy and Billy.

And just in case you might be thinking that my life so far is not what you would want, let me explain why my life is so good. If when you are a little girl, you've got a daddy that you know really, really loves you with all his heart, well then that's enough to keep you going for the rest of your life. Even if you get to be real old.

(May 13: Copy to Mr. Barker) Sheriff Tater may be one of the great lawmen of our time, maintaining order and civility with an even-handed justice. Truly a law enforcement officer respected by all of his constituency.

# SHERIFF TATERHEAD
# NEVER CARRIED NO GUN

## (Munchkin and LaPierre are captured)

My name is Ned and I came from a town about thirty miles away. Yes, it is the same town where Miss Ann was born.

We'd all heard how Sheriff Taterhead was the greatest sheriff in the South. And me, craving adventure, I went straight to him to ask for a job. Just for the summer of course, because I had to be back in the fall to help Pappy get the crops in. When I told him what an honor it would be just to watch him work, he right away pinned a badge on my chest. I was just an honorary deputy though. Room and board at the jail. No pay.

Sheriff Taterhead don't carry no gun. He always said that he wasn't going to take a chance on shooting nobody who might have voted for him. Of course, he also said, "If I found out that he voted for the other guy, that might be different."

According to legend, Sheriff Taterhead could spit tobacco through the gap in his front teeth hard enough to bring down a wild pig running at full gallop from twenty yards away. Not being one to brag, Sheriff Taterhead denied that this story was true.

When I worked for the Sheriff it was back in the days before the courts got all involved in our business. It was back in the days when matters were settled man to man and no one even thought of using a knife or a gun against his neighbor. Yes sir, the old ways was the best.

On Sunday, right after church, the widow lady O'Malley came into the sheriff's office to see Sheriff Taterhead. "Someone's been stealing my chickens," she said. "I've lost my best rooster and an old hen."

"It's probably just coons," suggested Sheriff Taterhead.

"No!" she said. "They left footprints. Little footprints. It was some kids."

Sheriff Taterhead promised he would look into the matter. So that very night me and the sheriff did a big-city type stake out by Mrs. O'Malley's chicken house.

For a long time, everything was quiet except for the sound of the crickets and an occasional howl of a coyote. Then about midnight the moon came out and it got real light. Right there sneaking along the fence by the chicken house was the funniest looking little man and what appeared to be a girl of about twelve.

Well we waited until they went into the chicken house and then we went in too. Sheriff Taterhead shined his light on them and said, "Halt right there. You're under arrest for chicken stealing."

What we thought was a girl turned out to be a little full-grown woman. I saw a little woman like her once when a carnival came to the local fair when I was a kid. The funny little man started to talk real fast with funny words I couldn't understand. Maybe he was some kind of foreigner. Then he ran out of chicken house and I ran after him yelling "Halt! Halt! You're under arrest for chicken stealing."

We ran around Mrs. O'Malley's house real fast but as we was coming past the chicken house again, there was Sheriff Taterhead. Sheriff Taterhead spit tobacco right in that little man's face. Then the man fell down and cried saying "My eyes! My eyes!" Also, he said some other words I did not understand.

Once the two criminals was captured and we washed the funny-looking little man's eyes with water from the hog trough, we all sat down to settle the matter. Sheriff Taterhead told the man and the little woman that they owed Mrs. O'Malley four dollars. "That's two dollars you owe for the rooster and one dollar you owe for the hen. And one other dollar you owe for the worry you caused Mrs. O'Malley."

The funny-looking little man said something in that funny language and then Sheriff Taterhead said, "Okay then. You can both work for two days for Mrs. O'Malley fixing her fences and mending up her house. Then don't steal her chickens no more." Everybody agreed and we all went home to get some sleep.

It was a great honor to watch Sheriff Taterhead work. Someday I will tell my grandchildren about how, when I was young, I was a deputy for the famous Sheriff Taterhead.

# WHAT REALLY, REALLY, HAPPENED

## (The part I'm not sending to my editor, Mr. Barker)

Sheriff Taterhead dropped by Jimmy's one evening and said he wanted to come over in a couple of days with some other people to talk about Munchkin. He asked that Billy and I be there too.

Ann baked a cake and made some sugar tea from cool spring water for the meeting.

Billy showed up first and accepted a glass of sugar tea from Ann. He seemed distraught. He put his elbow on his legs and sat staring at the floor.

Then came Sheriff Taterhead. He had a man and a boy with him. The boy was maybe seventeen. "Hello Sir," said the man, addressing Jimmy. My name is Ted Kutapopinski and this is my son Krzyszotop. I took my son to the doctor the other day because of what has happened to him and the doctor said we should talk to Sheriff Taterhead. Sheriff Taterhead has asked us to come tell what we know about your sister."

Sheriff Taterhead motioned toward the chairs and asked that everyone sit. "Where are you from Mr. Kutapopinski?" Jimmy asked.

"Poland. We come here two years ago. We learn English some before we come but is not too good sometimes."

"Krzyszotop, why don't you tell us who you are?"

More alert now and looking off to the horizon, Krzyszotop said, "I am The Frenchman. I am the Pirate of the High Seas. I am Feared or Loved by all who know my reputation."

"And what do you do, Frenchman the Pirate?" asked the Sheriff.

"I have adventures on the high seas. I rescue damsels in distress."

"You see," said Krzyszotop's father, "when our boy was young we gave book to read him. It was called The Adventures of the French Pirate of the High Seas. He loved that book. When he went out in our little flat bottom skiff to try to catch a fish for dinner, he never go fishing. He go after treasure and damsels in distress."

"The kind of things most kids do when they are playing," said Sheriff Taterhead.

"I was a pirate for a while myself," said Ann, "when I was about thirteen."

"Tell us about the damsel in distress, Krzyszotop," said Sheriff Taterhead.

"I learned of a damsel in distress, who was right here in this very fortress," said Krzyszotop, rising with a dramatic pause and a wave of his arm. "She was The Lady La Rosa."

"And did you rescue her?"

"I waited for her right over there," he said, pointing at a bush by the porch. "When she escaped the dungeon I took her away to my pirate's den."

"He has a fort he built close to the house. He goes there to play," his father said.

"And what did you and the Lady La Rosa do?" asked Sheriff Taterhead.

"We had many adventures on the high seas. We captured fine gold and silver coins. Upon each return from our adventures, there was great feasting."

Billy looked up. "You mean it was all just kids playing?"

"I'm afraid so," said Sheriff Taterhead. "Just two kids playing pirate games."

"Mr. Kutapopinski, will you please tell us about Fred?" asked Sheriff Taterhead.

"Certainly, Sheriff. The water is close to our house and we throw our food scraps in the water. There is a big gator that hangs around to get those scraps. We named him Fred, after my wife's uncle who help us come to America."

"The bad pirate Fred capsize my ship and take The Lady La Rosa to his dungeon," said Krzyszotop. "I search the dungeons everywhere, but I do not find The Lady La Rosa."

"It seems that the gator tried to surface but came up under the boat and knocked them both into the water. The girl just disappeared. My son dove over and over into the swamp looking among all the tree roots. He kept diving until it got dark. Now he is The Frenchman all of the time. He hardly sleeps and he eats very little. He starts searching for her as soon as it is light every day. You can see why I took him to the doctor."

Krzyszotop said, "I have to go look for The Lady La Rosa now," and he jogged down the driveway.

"Let him go. He has to go back to searching for his friend," said Mr. Kutapopinski. "The doctor said each of us has to grieve in his own way."

# THE REST OF ANN'S STORY

That newspaper fella ain't been around no more so me and Honey are going to tell you the rest of the story by ourselves.

After Sheriff Taterhead and the rest of them left, Jimmy just sat staring into the swamp. Then he started to cry. Not like other men cry. There was no sound. The tears came and he started to shake. He would shake like it was real cold, but it was really quite warm.

"I always knew Munchkin had just run off again. Billy knew too."

After a time, I put my hand on his shoulder. I had never touched him before. He didn't seem to mind. When he stopped shaking, he got up and took his jug of whiskey and poured it out on the ground and broke the jug with a rock.

When he came back he started to shake again. Cautiously, I put my arms around him and he didn't seem to mind that either. We sat for a long time not talking.

At last, Jimmy got up and went out and started plowing the field. I needed to do something too so I went into the house and started to clean things and fix things. I even fixed dinner.

My daddy loved me and took care of me. Honey loved me and took care of me. But never before had someone needed me to take care of him.

I can't tell you what it was like in the next few days but it was as if a sheet of clear ice that had covered my heart like a window pane shattered into a thousand pieces leaving me frightened and helplessly and hopelessly in love. Lost. Completely out of control.

That's all I have to say. I have to go back to work now. I have a husband to take care of, and there are things to do in case we have a child.

# MRS. TATERHEAD

## (But he just calls me Honey)

I have never heard the sheriff swear before. Maybe no one has.

I have never seen the sheriff mad before. Maybe no one has.

Right there in my foyer. Mad as a wet hen, he was, pointing an accusing finger at me. "You close down this damn whore house and marry me or I'll close it for you and put you in jail for whoring," he said. Then he turned around and stomped out.

What a way to propose to a girl. I used to dream that one day Sheriff Taterhead would get down on one knee and say, "Honey, I've always loved you and I want you to be my wife." Then he would slip his mama's ring on my finger and I would cry tears of joy. Kinda like in the movies.

Well life is not always like in the movies and if I let this opportunity pass, Sheriff Taterhead might never get up the courage to ask me to marry him again. I was not going to let him get out of it.

So right away I got my two fourteen-year-old girls adopted by a nice farm couple who had no children and were happy to have the girls.

My sixteen-year-old married the widower who owns the general store.

The last girl, Louise, went to work for the big city fellow who started his own newspaper here in our little town. She stayed on as the first boarder at Madame Butterfly's Boarding House until she married her boss. Of course we didn't charge her nothing.

And me? Well, once Sheriff Taterhead said right out loud that he wanted to marry me I clung to him like stink on a bug. And Sheriff Taterhead's friend Jimmy told him he was going to show up at the wedding with his shotgun to make sure the sheriff did not try to weasel out of marrying me.

So that is how I became Mrs. James Elroy Tater. But most people around her just call me Mrs. Taterhead, and I like that. You can call me Mrs. Taterhead too, if you like.

(Note to Mr. Barker: How would you like to be a Godfather?)

# JOHN N. BARKER

John N. Barker, a Washington native, has lived in Vancouver since 1974. Retirement in 1987 has afforded him many years to pursue several interests via FML courses. Good health has permitted him to participate in extensive travels with Elderhostel, affording once-in-a-lifetime adventures in Europe, the South Pacific, and the Americas. Writing short stories is a hobby that he enjoys as inspiration strikes.

# SPIDER

The first time I saw her, Spider was swinging on a thread anchored to the roof over my balcony. As I watched from my vantage point atop the picnic table, she attached the thread to the balcony rail, some six feet below. Then, with surprising speed, she ascended her anchored "cable" to the roof, where she attached another "cable" from the rail; then began the process of rigging laterals. As dusk descended I finished my glass of wine and went into the house, leaving Spider to her work.

Next evening I returned to my vantage point atop the picnic table to watch yet another gorgeous autumn sunset and sip another civilized glass of wine. Spider was nowhere to be seen. However, the fruits of her labor shone in the setting sun: a stunning gossamer web of the intricate symmetry only accomplished spiders can create. Spider had indeed been busy.

As I sat watching the changing cloud patterns bathed in the rich colors that sunsets can display in the fall of the year, a luckless gnat hit the web. It was then that Spider appeared. Running full tilt to the gnat she immobilized it in an instant, and took it up to the roof line, where both disappeared. The performance was repeated several times as after-glow turned to dusk. Spider was not only successful, she was shrewd enough to stash the evidence of her success where neither she nor her cache would be conspicuous to any passing predator.

The next few evenings Spider prospered. She grew bigger. She enlarged her web. The cache of her wealth, originally hidden, began to show at the edge of the roof where she had trussed up her surplus. Yet, as Spider prospered, she started getting careless. She began leaving the evidence of her wealth out in the web where it was caught. By week's end she was dining out on the web as well. It was this last evidence of prosperity that was her undoing. As I watched, a passing Sparrow stopped, hovered in front of her, and plucked Spider from her web without even disturbing the meal she was eating.

The web is still there, empty now, a silent reminder of the lessons Spider taught me. She had been ambitious (no other web spans the distance between roof and rail), industrious, persistent in attaining her goal, and...successful. While she had been shrewd enough to keep herself and the evidence of her success in low profile, she ultimately chose to display it, and herself, for all to see. Look at me! LOOK AT ME!

# BUFFALO EDDY

Eddy's beginnings are a bit murky. Born on a ditch bank in Southern Idaho, 'tis said, sometime after the turn of the 20th Century. A kind farmer found him still alive and took him to a local church. Nobody knows why they named him Eddy. His first name was for the farmer who found him. He grew up in orphanages and foster homes in southern Idaho and eastern Oregon. A tall, good-looking kid, he couldn't dance, but liked to sing. The girls thought he was Mr. Wonderful, even in a town as big as Lewiston, Idaho.

Eddy took to the rodeo circuit in his early teens. He had a natural ability for bulldogging steers. Instead of roping the steer and bringing him to a stop with the aid of his horse, Eddy favored leaping on a steer at a gallop, then bringing him to ground in a cloud of dust, amid the cheers of the onlookers.

"Damn fool crazy," snorted the men.

"Wonderful," sighed the women. "And he can sing, too."

As he matured, Eddy took to bulldogging Brahma bulls, in the same manner as he did the steers. Needless to say, he developed quite an ego. He would like to bulldog buffalo, he bragged; thus the nickname, "Buffalo Eddy."

One night he was drinking with some of his pals in a Pendleton, Oregon, bar when Eddy bragged again that Brahmas were getting too easy, and he would like go to bulldogging buffalo.

When everybody laughed, he got mad and said he could damn well do it. There were no buffalo anyplace around; otherwise he would prove he could do it right then and there.

It just so happened there was a trucker in the bar that night who was on his way to Portland with a load of three buffalo for the zoo. He'd just stopped for supper and to refresh himself. When he heard Eddy's brag, he announced himself to the gathering, and allowed that nobody had ever bulldogged a buffalo because nobody could. He backed his claim with a $100 bet; cash on the bar, and offered to let Eddy take his pick of his cargo.

They could go out to the rodeo grounds and he could bulldog a buffalo right then and there under the lights, the rest could watch from the grandstand. The gauntlet was down, and Eddy had no choice but to go for it or become the laughing stock of the entire rodeo circuit.

"Buffalo Eddy," they jeered. "Put up or shut up."

With his reputation at stake, Buffalo Eddy was just drunk enough to accept the dare. He stalked up to the bar and plunked down his I.O.U., since he hadn't seen $100 at one time in his entire life.

Word of a bulldogging exhibition traveled fast, especially in a rodeo town like Pendleton, so it was quite a parade out to the Round-up Grounds that night.

The field lights were turned on, Eddy got his horse out, and many hands guided the biggest, meanest bull buffalo into the chute. Speculation in the grandstand was rampant. Arguments, side bets, even a scuffle or two as audience members attempted to predict the outcome of the contest.

When all was ready, the gate was opened and the buff', confused and aggravated, galloped onto the field. Eddy's horse knew his job well and came alongside the buffalo at top speed. The story of what happened next in front of all those witnesses (few of whom were sober), depends on how many times the story has been embellished as it was told, and the veracity of the teller. It is said the events of the next few minutes, went roughly like this: Eddy didn't rope the buffalo, or even try to slow him down. He just dove for the buff's horns, and most agree that he grabbed them. The startled buff' jerked his head up and Eddy was flipped end-over-end, landing face down on the animal's rump. Sliding off, he grabbed for anything he could hold onto, which turned out to be the buff's tail. The startled animal continued to gallop, with Eddy bouncing along on the ground behind, hanging on to the tail for dear life.

Fate was with Buffalo Eddy that night. On one bounce his body rotated half a turn or so. The pain of his twisted tail caused the buffalo to miss a step. With a bellow he came down hard on a shoulder and slid headlong, crashing into the bleachers at the end of the field.

The impact knocked him momentarily senseless. Eddy, true to his training, crawled forward, hogtied the buff, raised his arms in the air, and collapsed, stupefied, on top of the prostrate animal.

A great cheer went up from the grandstand. Buffalo Eddy had made good his boast and become a legend in his own time. Some say they even named "Buffalo Eddy," a Native American site in the Snake River, after him.

Eddy never quite recovered from the damage his body took that night. He had a broken leg, four cracked ribs, herniated disks in his back, and some internal injuries.

After the doctors had stabilized him, Eddy was sent to a hospital at Hot Lake, Oregon to recuperate. His doctor told him that maybe he should learn to sing, 'cause he sure as hell was no good for rodeo anymore. He was, after all, still a young man. While he was in a rehabilitation facility there, fate stepped in again to rescue Eddy.

He was singing of love to one of the nurses when a talent scout, whose name was MacDonald, heard him singing and came to investigate.

"You sing pretty good, son," he said to Eddy. "I'm looking for a tall, good-looking baritone to team with my daughter Jeanette. What's your name?"

"Buffalo Eddy," he replied.

"You can't sing love songs with a name like that," said MacDonald, "what's your real name?"

Buffalo Eddy blushed. "The Sisters called me Nelson, Nelson Eddy."

# PRODUCERS

After so many years to come to this. My firm, so slow to build in those early years. Hard work. Diligence. Study. How to succeed. How to prosper. How to grow.

And grow we did. Interviewed and hired people smarter than I. Listened. Took risks. Learned from failure as well as success. Expanded some more. Worked later, made more decisions. Stress was just part of the process.

A heart attack? At MY age? Slow down? Delegate more? Help subordinates to grow? Step back and observe? Advise? Relax? But what will I DO? Must I reinvent myself again? Retire? At MY age? Preposterous.

# GRANT BIGELOW

Grant Bigelow. I have had a passion for writing since I was in high school. In the 1970s I began keeping a personal journal that contains highlights, dreams, feelings and achievements. In 2005 I wrote a 150-page book entitled "The Country Doctor," about my father and his ancestors. Last year I finished another book about my wild and fun-filled days as a bus operator in the Rose City. My wife Barbara and I have four children and twenty-one grandchildren.

# NEW CARISSA

In March of 1999, my family and I traveled to the Oregon Coast to see the New Carissa, a freighter from the Philippines that was carrying crude oil and ran aground near the mouth of Coos Bay. As the vessel lay mired in the sand, I was so intrigued by its predicament I wrote the following essay. A decade passed before the remains of the ship were finally hauled away.

This once mighty ocean-going ship was now like a beached whale–deserted, cast aside on a lonely, isolated beach. At one time alive with a hungry group of sailors and an important mission to perform, now lying abandoned, like so much debris or rubbish.

Six hundred and ninety-four feet of cold steel, now beaten and whipped by the angry waves of the Pacific Ocean.

It seemed strange that a ship so huge could be caught so tight by something so small as a sandbar. The jaws of the bar were clenched like a trap, and not even a powerful tug could pull the ship loose.

The curious on-lookers craned their necks, like small birds in a nest anticipating food, to see the poor thing trapped helplessly on a cold wind-swept piece of ground.

There seemed no hope for this vessel, and yet as we stood looking at it, for some strange reason it seemed to creep forward as if trying desperately to pull away from the trap. The anxious onlookers were confident that the New Carissa had not given up, that somewhere deep within its soul there was a desire to accomplish its purpose in life.

Someone yelled, "Wait, I think I saw it move!" Now all eyes were glued to the scene. We could not chance blinking an eye for fear of missing the ship's victory over the sandbar.

After waiting for what seemed like an eternity the crowd and our family finally decided to give up the struggle and leave the unfortunate carcass for another day. Some of us said good-bye while others just waved and hoped a stronger tug could pull it free tomorrow.

# MARJORIE CALLANAN

Marjorie L. Callanan is a native of Minnesota, but has lived most of her life in the Northwest. She met her future husband in Denver, Colorado, when they both served in the Air Force. Marjorie has four grown daughters, five grandchildren and two sons-in-law. She is widely traveled, having lived in England for two and a half years and having visited all fifty states.

# LIVING IN ENGLAND

High up in the clouds at 30,000 feet, I looked out of the plane window. The clouds looked like suds in a washing machine. It was August 1965, and my three daughters and I were on a commercial airliner with other military dependents. My oldest, Kathy, was four years old. Maureen was two and Sharon was seven months. We were to meet my husband, Bill, at Heathrow Airport in London.

Bill and I had been married for six years. He was a tall, dark-haired good-looking man of 26. Bill's Air Force job was repairing radios on military planes. In May 1965, he was assigned for three years to RAF Lakenheath in England, about 90 miles northwest of London. Bill left for England to start his job at the base and find a home for our family.

Earlier in the year, I had told Bill about my childhood English pen-pal, Jean Brown. Jean, her husband, Jim, and two daughters lived in Boston, England. Bill visited them and arranged for us to live with the Browns temporarily. I didn't like the idea of staying with strangers, but everything was finalized.

At Heathrow Airport we got a rental car and left for Boston. Jean and Jim greeted us—a couple in their middle twenties with two young daughters. The little girls had rosy red cheeks that reminded me of a popular song sung by Petula Clark: "England swings like a pendulum do / Bobbies on bicycles two by two / Westminster Abbey, the tower Big Ben / The rosy red cheeks of the little children."

Jean and Jim lived in a small square red-brick house with a thatched roof and a garden. In the United States we had yards; the English had gardens. There is a huge difference. Most yards back home consisted of a green lawn with a bush or two. Compare this to a small space packed with rose bushes, hollyhocks, petunias, and irises. A couple of trellises completed the garden.

Bill returned to RAF Lakenheath the following morning. The girls and I stayed with Jean and Jim for two weeks. Jim was a farmer and Jean was a housewife. Culture shock was in store for all of us. Meals were served four times a day–breakfast, dinner (the main meal of the day), tea at 4:00 p.m. (the children's dinner) and supper at 8:00 p.m. for the adults. Jean and I were busy all day making meals, washing dishes, washing clothes and watching children. There wasn't much time for relaxing.

Even though it was early August, the weather chilled me to the bone. Jean asked if I couldn't handle the summer weather what was I going to do in the winter. "Honestly, I don't know," I told her. The kitchen was closed off from the rest of the house. Kathy and Maureen left the doors open when they went out to play. This drove Jean crazy. She asked them, "Were you born in a barn?"

After the two weeks passed Bill called me to ask Jim if we could stay longer. I didn't think that they would agree to it but Bill insisted. Jim responded to my request with a flat "No." The next day, Bill came to pick the girls and me up. We left Boston for Mildenhall, where he had found an apartment.

The flat (apartment) Bill rented was above a bakery. The new part of the building was 300 years old and the old part was 400 years old. The living room was large with a fireplace that was only a foot wide. There was coal in the cellar for fires. A kerosene heater was the only other means of heating the apartment. Our landlord owned the bakery. He brought us cakes for birthdays and our anniversary.

Across the street from our apartment was the town market. Each Saturday vendors displayed fruits, vegetables, jewelry and clothing. To the south of our building were a cemetery and an Anglican Church. Farther down the street was a candy store–Kathy's favorite place.

The English started their children in school at age four. I thought it would be good for Kathy so I entered her in the nearby school. She adapted very well; soon she was talking and eating like a "bloke."

The base nursery was free on Wednesday, Friday and Saturday nights. Bill and I would go to the NCO Club on the weekends. Top entertainers came there from the United States. Two I remember were Little Jimmy Dickens and Eddie Arnold.

In May 1968, Bill's tour of duty was up. He was assigned to Mather Air Force Base in Sacramento, California. We left England for New York City, and visited family members on the East Coast. Then we set out on the long road trip to California. From one extreme to the other.

# A NEW MILLENNIUM–ALASKA
# JANUARY 1, 2000

My daughter Maureen and I had been looking forward to spending the millennium in Anchorage, Alaska; we were finally on our way. We planned to spend Christmas and New Year's Eve with my daughter Sharon and her partner, Malcolm. I had been to Anchorage twice before, but only in the summertime. This was Maureen's first visit to Anchorage.

Anchorage, South Central Alaska, is surrounded on three sides by the Chugach Mountains. The mountains protect Anchorage from severe winters. Anchorage faces the Cook Inlet leading to the Gulf of Alaska, which stretches to the Pacific Ocean. The Official Visitor's Guide to Anchorage states: "Anchorage municipal boundaries stretch more than 50 miles from Portage Glacier to Eklutna, encompassing 1,955 square miles–about the size of Delaware. Nearly 261,000 people make their home in Anchorage."

Our flight left Portland, Oregon, on December 23, 1999, at 9 p.m., and it was midnight when we landed at Ted Stevens Anchorage International Airport. Sharon and Malcolm were waiting for us. We got our baggage and went outside. The low hanging clouds and the sparkling snow cast off an orange glow. I looked at the streetlights and saw that they were orange. Vancouver has white streetlights.

We all had a good laugh when the TV newscaster said Anchorage was warmer than Vancouver that day: Anchorage was 44 degrees, while Vancouver was only 30 degrees. Anchorage's warm spell did not last long, though. During the next few days, the temperature fell to five degrees below zero, where it remained for the rest of our stay except for New Years Eve. That night the temperature dropped to 17 degrees below zero. I could only stand to be outside for five minutes. Even with a scarf over my face, I could feel the icy wind going deep into my lungs.

The morning of December 24 I awoke and went to the kitchen, where Sharon was preparing breakfast. Out the kitchen window the Chugach Mountains were so close I felt I could reach out and touch them. Maureen and I ate breakfast and prepared to go downtown.

We walked to the bus stop and took a bus to downtown Anchorage, where we went to the Log Cabin and Downtown Visitor Information Center to pick up brochures. The first place we visited was the Anchorage Museum of History and Art. We spent several hours looking at the exhibits. Then Sharon took us to Earthquake Park. "The 1964 Good Friday Earthquake was the most powerful tremor ever felt in North America, measuring 9.2 on the Richter scale. Anchorage and South-central Alaska were hit hard. Earthquake Park marks the site where huge tracts of land slid into the inlet, destroying 75 homes." (Official Visitors Guide to Anchorage, Alaska)

On New Year's Eve, Anchorage had an annual ice carvings exhibit downtown. Huge statues carved in ice sparkled under the streetlights. The Alaska Center for the Performing Arts (PAC) was open to the public. PAC consisted of several buildings; each held a different exhibit. After visiting two of the buildings we headed for the third building. We saw streams of people leaving; no one was entering the building. Soon policemen were telling everyone to leave the PAC and the town square immediately. The next day the Anchorage newspaper reported that someone had called in from a pay phone to say that a bomb was set to go off at the PAC. The police caught the prankster; he had stuck around to see the excitement.

The day we left Anchorage Sharon and Malcolm took us to the airport. Maureen and I took the red-eye leaving Anchorage at 1:32 a.m. I thought the airport would be deserted at that hour—was I in for a surprise. The place was mobbed with people going back to the lower 48. (Alaskans, with some disdain, call the continental United States the lower 48.) Huge crates of fish were everywhere.

Maureen and I said goodbye to Sharon and Malcolm at the gate. Then we boarded the plane. The only seat I could find was way at the back—a straight-back with no recliner, right up against the restroom. I had a long uncomfortable trip home. When we arrived in

Portland, the night seemed very dark. Anchorage was much lighter at night than Portland, with its light reflected off the low-lying clouds and its sparkling orange snow.

My daughter Kathy and her husband, George, met us at the airport. We had enjoyed our trip to Anchorage, but it was good to be back home again.

# A VISITOR FROM THE PAST

In January of this year, I received a phone call from my ex-husband, Bill. It had been forty years to the month since we were divorced. Our four daughters—Kathy, Maureen, Sharon and Laura—saw their father only three times in all those years. Bill was invited to Kathy's wedding in 1984 but did not attend. Bill did attend Laura's wedding in 1992. I thought that would be a good time for him to reunite with his grown children, but he did not stay in contact.

Bill married a second time and had a son. Laura, my dad, and I did get to meet Bill's wife, Jean, when Laura graduated from the Air Force Non-Commissioned Officers' School at Mather Air Force Base in Sacramento, California.

Now Kathy is married with three grown children. Maureen lives with me. Sharon lives in Anchorage, Alaska, and Laura, the youngest, is married with two small children. Eighteen years have elapsed since Bill attended Laura's wedding. There was little contact during that time and a lot of resentment. I nagged the girls to send him birthday cards, but he rarely acknowledged their birthdays. No cards or phone calls at Christmas or any other time. The girls grew up and made their own decisions about remembering his birthday. I tried to keep him abreast of the family, but finally grew tired of it. Although Bill and I exchanged pictures of our respective families, he remained a stranger to our daughters. They grew up without a father in their lives. Laura told me she accepted whatever she could get, but did not expect anything.

It was into this situation that last summer, out of the blue, Bill called my oldest daughter, Kathy. His son, Michael, was living in Eastern Oregon and wanted to relocate to the Portland-Vancouver area. Since Bill would be in the area to help Michael, he asked Kathy if he could visit the family here. She agreed. Shortly after that, I received a phone call from Bill asking if I would take Michael into my home until he could find a place to live. I agreed. Together Michael and I checked out apartments in the area. He found a suitable apartment and moved in shortly afterwards.

Last summer Laura's boy, Anthony, played baseball all of us went to his games. My daughters got reacquainted with their father. The grandchildren finally got to meet another grandfather. Bill got along great with the kids; they really took to him.

My son-in-law George invited Bill up for Christmas. The girls were wary and didn't think he would show up. I secretly groaned; I wished George had never asked Bill for another visit.

A few days before Christmas, Bill showed up. He planned to stay a month; Kathy and George agreed he could stay with them. Bill would also stay part time with Michael. At first, everyone was awkward, but gradually, we got to know one another and relaxed a little. Bill was talkative and charming as always. The grandchildren liked him a lot.

The day Bill left to return to California, George invited us all to dinner. Laura's two children, Anthony and Alyssa, were the centers of attention. Bill left early in the evening so as to miss the traffic on I-5.

Afterwards my daughters and I discussed how we felt. Kathy said she was glad her father had come to see them, but was looking forward to getting back into her routine. Maureen said only that it was a nice visit. Laura commented that her father kept bugging her about spending time with her. It was difficult to make the time. She has a full-time job besides a part-time job in the Air Force, two children and a household. She told Bill that he could not make up for those lost years, but it was good that he came up to visit.

I had told my daughters beforehand that I thought he realized he was getting older. If he didn't come now, he might never visit them. It was just as I had said. Bill stopped by my house for a visit and to look over old picture albums. Then he said he knew he was getting older and wanted to spend time with the family. I told him we could not get back those lost years, but we could move forward.

I felt his visit was worthwhile overall. The past cannot be forgotten, but forgiveness helps to heal old wounds.

# HELEN CARTALES

Helen Cartales. After 56 years of marriage and 21 moves throughout Oregon, Washington and California, my husband John and I retired in Vancouver. We wanted to be close to our families in Portland, but not too close. We have five children spread from coast to coast. Before his death in 2006, John encouraged me to pursue my love of writing. So I did.

# LIVE AND LEARN

## 1. Something for Me To Do

It was 1978. The last of my five children was in high school and I was beginning to have a little time to do something for myself. Then John, my husband, came home from work one night bursting with enthusiasm.

"I talked to a realtor today and there's an apartment building for sale in Northwest Portland. I think we should buy it. It'll give you something to do now that the kids are older and don't require so much of your time."

Like I needed something to do? For 28 years my role in life had been one of a wife and mom. With five children, that's a busy life. I was a Hail Mary, Our Father, church-going, strait-laced, naive, trusting wife and mom. An apartment building I did not need to keep me busy. But there was no stopping him.

"It's a real deal. It needs a little work, but we can do that. You painted all the houses we lived in—and I'll help." John worked 12-hour days and he was going to help?

We visited the building with the realtor. To say the building needed "a little work" is like saying Niagara Falls is just a little drip. But we bought it.

It didn't take me long to learn the building came with an alcoholic manager, two prostitutes, a pimp, a young man recovering from a nervous breakdown, an old man recovering from a heart attack, several drunks, a variety of liars and cheats, three very nice elderly people, a youngish Navajo and a well-educated gentleman with degrees in History and Library Science. What was he doing in this building?

Note the type of tenants I had. Now refer to the paragraph above where I describe the type of person I was. I was in for an unbelievable education.

After we had signed the final papers for the building, and discovered Don, the manager, kept the rents he had collected (and not yet spent) in the cardboard tube of a roll of paper towels, John and I decided I would take over managing the building immediately. My first weeks alone in the building, I vacillated between fright and bravado. I always locked the door when I worked in a unit. I tried not to go into any apartment when I collected rent. When a tenant insisted, I stepped in but stayed close to the door, ready to cut and run. I did not trust any of the tenants yet. My habit was to go straight to the bank with any money I collected. It didn't take me long to learn that if a tenant paid with a check I should get it to the bank the same day. Sometimes that wasn't soon enough.

My biggest fear was going to the basement. It was one big dark room, four small storage rooms and another room housing the boiler and water tank for the heating system. All the storage rooms were locked. There was a short, dark hallway to the outer basement door. The five garbage cans were kept in that hallway. One storage room housed tools, cleaning supplies and spare light bulbs. Anything the tenants could steal was kept under lock and key. Near the washer was a bench, where tenants could sit and guard their laundry while it was washing so no one could steal it. There was a small table near the dryer in case anyone wanted to stay in the basement to fold clothes.

Tenants were constantly stealing the light bulb at the top of the stairs. The fixture took a 50 watt bulb, barely enough light to shine down the first eight steps; the last two steps were in the dark. The only other light fixture in the basement was near the washer and dryer against the far outside wall. There were two small windows above the washer and dryer but too dirty to let any light in. Halfway between the stairs and the laundry equipment was a support post. It took only one time walking into the post and whacking my head to realize it was wise to navigate through the dark basement with my arms in front of me feeling the way, to turn the light on.

I made trips to the basement Mondays and Thursdays, garbage pickup days. The garbage man, no more tidy than the tenants, always left a mess for me to clean up after him.

I had been making these cleanup trips for about a month when one morning I noticed a horrible smell as I reached the foot of the stairs. The weather was starting to turn cold so my first thought was that an animal had snuck in and died. I carefully walked over and turned on the light by the far wall. I glanced around, but didn't notice anything unusual. I unlocked the storage rooms, turned on the lights, and walked around checking in corners looking for a dead animal. Nothing. I locked the rooms again and went to the room where I kept brooms and cleaning supplies. I picked up a broom to clean around the garbage cans and as I came out of the storage room, I noticed what appeared to be a body lying on the bench by the washer. My back had been to the bench when I turned the light on so I hadn't seen it before.

"Oh my God! Someone died down here," I whispered. "Worse yet, what if someone got killed down here? This is such a crazy neighborhood."

I didn't want to check. I was terrified. If it was a body, I had to call the police. I stood rooted to the floor. My feet didn't want to move. Thoughts of "Where is John when I need him?" ran through my mind. I cautiously took a step closer. The body rolled over and sat up. The action frightened me more than the thought of a body did.

"What in the hell are you doing down here?" I yelled.

"Sleeping," a man answered, as though it was common knowledge he slept there and had every right to do so.

"Get your stinking ass out of here and don't you ever sleep on that bench again."

Frightened and shaking, I watched him casually stand, brush and straighten his filthy clothes as though he wore a Brooks Brothers suit and was on his way to a Board meeting. Without so much as a "thank you" for the use of the bench, he walked out. The mess around the garbage cans didn't get cleaned up that day. I couldn't have held the broom steady if I tried.

On Thursday, the next garbage pickup day, I had to visit the basement again. I was halfway down the stairs and the stink was there again. At least I knew what it was. His bedroom of choice this time was the small space between two of the storage rooms, just wide enough for a person to lie on the floor. I turned on the light by the laundry equipment and looked around, but didn't see him. I followed the smell and found him in the cubby hole.

"I told you not to come in the building and sleep." He didn't frighten me this time.

"Yes, you did." He was so damn polite.

"I'm telling you again, stay out of this building!" What made me so fearless of him? His politeness or my stupidity? I wanted to take his arm and march him to the basement door but his smell and filthy clothes kept me from touching him. I walked behind him to the door, making sure he left.

After finding him in the cubby hole for the third time, I brought some boards and nailed them over the opening. That should keep him from sleeping in the basement. I was confident all his sleeping places had been eliminated.

One morning I was working on the second floor and went to the hall closet to get the vacuum cleaner. When I opened the door, the familiar stink of the man hit me. He was curled up asleep on the floor. I woke him and again told him to stay out of the building, walking him out the front door.

All my yelling wasn't effective with my nonpaying tenant. He was so polite, calm and nonthreatening each time I marched him out of the building I was having a hard time being forceful with him. I was reasonably sure if I did get him out of that closet he would find another place in the building to bed down for the night. I could see I was going to need help from John.

John had been letting me run the building in my own softhearted, blundering, inexperienced way. He had mentioned if I needed him, he would help me. I needed him. I told John about the bum sleeping in the building.

"Where is he sleeping?" John asked.

"First he was sleeping in the basement on a bench and I chased him out. Then he slept in a little cubby hole between two of the rooms down there so I boarded it up. Now he's sleeping upstairs in the storage closet."

"I'll stop by in the morning on my way to work and take care of it, but I'll need your help."

The next morning when we arrived at the building John said, "Go up and see if he's there sleeping but don't wake him. Come down and tell me."

He was in his closet bedroom and I reported to John.

"OK. Go back, wait five minutes, wake him, then chase him down the stairs and out the front door. Don't let him go in the basement."

I didn't know what John had planned. I went up and waited five minutes, then woke the man and chased him down the steps and out the front door.

When he cleared the front door, John was waiting. John doused the man with very cold water from a five gallon bucket and warned him never to come back again. That was the last time the man slept in my building.

I saw him a few times sleeping on a bench across the street from the building, still in his dirty smelly clothes. Then he disappeared from the neighborhood.

Months later I was sitting in the manager's office waiting to interview applicants for a manager. Again. A nice looking man, about 40, dressed in well-pressed khakis, walked in and sat down. I thought he was applying for the manager's job, but he just sat looking at me.

I smiled a "hello" at him.

"You don't know me, do you?" he asked.

"No, I don't believe I do. Should I?"

"I'm Carl."

"Hello, Carl." I didn't know anyone with that name and I couldn't remember seeing this man before. He seemed to know me.

"Remember that bum you caught sleeping in your basement and your husband doused him with cold water?"

"Do I ever."

"That was me."

It was hard to believe Carl and the bum were the same person. The bum always walked away with a slouch and the clothes he wore never fit him. In his days of being a bum, he always reminded me of a dog running away with his tail between his legs after he had been reprimanded. This was a different man. He was good-looking, clean, standing straight with a proud posture. He smelled good and his clothes fit his well-proportioned body. No slouch-of-a-bum Carl.

"Wow! What a great surprise. You look a little different now. I didn't recognize you. The first time I found you on the bench in the basement, I thought you had been dead a few days. You didn't smell very good. I never did get a good look at your face; it was always your back on your way out of the building. Your clothes were different too. I'll give you credit for one thing: you were always polite when I yelled at you to leave."

He laughed at that and said, "I stopped drinking and cleaned up. I was walking past and saw you sitting by the window and thought I'd stop and say hello."

"Congratulations, and thank you for stopping. It's good to see you've changed. Sorry about the cold water."

"Don't be. I deserved it."

As we sat visiting, I thought how good it would be having him as manager. He was sober and clean now and certainly a pleasant person. But, could he remain sober and was he honest? How good was he at bookkeeping and maintenance work? He didn't ask to apply for the job and I didn't ask him.

# 2. Business as Usual

It wouldn't be long before I would learn if I had hired Carl to manage the building he couldn't have been any worse than some of the managers I did have. So far I was batting zero on managers.

My score wasn't much higher on tenants.

My tenants were a gaggle of misfits, three nice elderly people and, I would later learn, an honest Navajo and Belinda. In 1978, the entire Northwest Neighborhood was made up of all the above and possibly another honest Navajo.

My first encounter with Belinda was the evening we went to inspect the building after our purchase. She was walking out as we walked in the building. Belinda was dressed in a T-shirt and cut-off shorts. She was accompanied by a strikingly dressed black man–fedora tipped to the side, a pin-striped suit and a graceful walk that was part dance, part walk, part roll. Quite a contrast between the two of them.

"I suppose you're the new owners of this shit hole and you're going to raise the rent," Belinda said in passing.

"Nice meeting you too honey," I thought as she walked out.

A few days later, I would have a face to face meeting with Belinda. She hadn't paid rent for two months. I had to find out why. I knocked on her door.

Belinda answered the door with a "what the hell do you want" look. I could see we weren't going to be best friends. She was slightly taller than me, a little chunky, cute in a rough and tumble sort of way with a "don't cross me" attitude. She wore the uniform of the neighborhood, a T-shirt and frayed cut-off jeans. Her vocabulary was quite descriptive. I learned that by her reference to my building as "a shit hole."

"Hi, I'm Helen, the new owner," I said, trying to be pleasant.

"I know that," Belinda said with a scowl.

"The rent record shows you haven't paid rent for two months."

"That's right and I ain't going to pay it."

"Is there a problem?"

"Yeah, there's a problem. I told that son of a bitch manager my toilet was broke and he hasn't fixed it yet," she said.

"I'm sorry. Won't it flush or does it keep running?" I tried to make Belinda think I knew something about plumbing.

"NO! I said the damn toilet was broke." She was shouting at me.

"May I see it?" I asked. I was still standing in the hall.

"Be my guest," she said as she waved me into her apartment.

The Venetian blinds were closed tight and the room was dark. All I could see was the outline of the Murphy bed by the wall. The bathroom was a few steps from the apartment door. She stepped in, turned on the light and said, "See–the toilet is broke."

She was correct. The water tank was sitting on the floor and the toilet had a big visible crack. I didn't go any closer than one step inside the door. I didn't want to ask what she had been using for a toilet and I sure didn't want to check.

"I'm really sorry. I didn't know about that. I'll have it taken care of as soon as I can get a  plumber here."

"I ain't paying no rent for the two months the damn thing was broke," Belinda said.

I thought it would be a good idea to change the subject. I wondered about the nice-looking black man who had walked out of the building with Belinda a few nights earlier. Was he a friend or did he live with her? They were so different in appearance. He was neat and nicely dressed, she was sloppy in her cut-off jeans and T-shirt.

"Does the young man you were with the other night live here too?" I asked.

"No." Belinda didn't offer an explanation of who he was.

The toilet was replaced with a new one, but still no rent was paid the next month.

I didn't see Belinda often but the black man went in and out of the apartment at all hours. It appeared he was more than a visitor. It was obvious Belinda wasn't going to give me any more information. I decided to ask one of the other tenants.

Ray, in apartment five, had mentioned if I needed to know anything about the building or tenants he could tell me. The next time I met him in the hall, I asked about Belinda's visitor. "I've noticed a nice-looking black man that seems to visit Belinda quite often. Do you know who he is?"

"He's not visiting. That's Albert, her pimp," Ray said.

Belinda still hadn't paid her rent and I didn't have a license to run a whorehouse. I gave her a notice to move. She had 30 days to find another place for her business.

One night, before Belinda moved, John was helping me paint a vacant apartment. We noticed two people going into Belinda's apartment. After my confrontation with her about the broken toilet and the eviction notice, I didn't want to face her again.

"John, would you mind going to Belinda's apartment and asking her to let you check and see how much work needs to be done in there?"

As John reached Belinda's apartment, Albert walked out. John assumed the apartment was empty. "Do you mind if I go in and see what needs to be done in there?" John asked.

"No, help yourself. Go right in."

The door wasn't locked. John walked in. The room was dark and he was trying to find the light switch when a man's voice came booming from the bed.

"What the hell are you doing in here? What do you want?"

"Oh, I'm sorry. I didn't know anyone was in here." John left and returned to the apartment where I was working. He had only been gone a few minutes.

"Wasn't there much to do in there?" I asked.

"Well, I wouldn't say that."

"Wouldn't Belinda let you look?"

"I'm not sure it was Belinda in there. The room was dark, but I don't think they wanted me looking."

"What do you mean Belinda wasn't there and 'they' didn't want you looking. What was going on in there?"

John looked at me with a big grin plastered across his face and said, "Business as usual."

# 3. Ben

I had been working in the building several weeks and had met all the tenants in my newly acquired apartment building, except Ben, the man the manager referred to as, "that damned Indian." Ben had a hasp and a padlock on his door and refused to give the manager a key to the lock. Hence, "that damned Indian." Having met the soon-to-be-fired alcoholic manager, my thought was three cheers for Ben.

There were days when I worked near Ben's apartment well into the evening but he came and left so quietly, I never heard him. One evening I noticed the padlock wasn't on the door. Ben was home. Finally, I was going to meet "that damned Indian."

I knocked. The door opened a crack.

"Yes?"

"Hello, I'm Helen, the new owner. The manager said you haven't paid your rent yet.

"He lies. I have my receipt. I'll get it for you." Ben gave me a look of complete distrust and closed the door in my face. He returned and without saying a word, handed me the receipt. He had paid his rent. Before I could say a word, Ben reached out and said, "I want it back."

I returned the receipt and apologized for the misunderstanding.

"I would like you to take the padlock off your door, please," I said.

"Is the manager gone?"

"Not yet. I told him he could have enough time to find another place to live."

"I'll take the padlock off when he leaves." Ben closed the door in my face again. There was no arguing with this man. Not only was he a man of few words he would be intimidated by no one.

Some of my original tenants had moved, which was fine with me. I had months of cleaning and painting ahead of me and another empty apartment wasn't going to bother me. This was my first meeting with Ben, but there was something about him that made me want him to stay.

I had seen many drunk Indians on the avenue. When the manager referred to Ben as "that damn Indian," that was what I expected to see when I knocked on his door – a drunk Indian. What I saw was a sober, scrubbed, youngish man, dressed in fresh clean clothes, standing tall, looking me straight in the eye. He was somewhere between mid 30s or early 40s, I couldn't tell. He did not look like the other Indians on the avenue. Yes, his skin was dark, his hair was black as were his eyes. His face was flat. He looked at me as if to say, you are not going to push me around. After meeting him, I knew if I was walking behind him on the street, I would recognize Ben. What was it about him? As I drove home from the building that night I wondered. Then I understood. Ben stood proud, straight and tall. Later Ben told me he was a Navajo and I could see he was proud of it.

There were many evenings when I worked in the building. Sometimes I met Ben in the hall when I was leaving. I always said hello to him. Sometimes he would answer, other times he would nod and if he didn't feel friendly, he would walk right past me looking down at the floor, not saying a word.

I knew Ben worked at a dirty job. His clothes were dirty and greasy when he came home. I also knew he didn't like being dirty because I could hear him walk through his door, take a few steps to the bathroom and turn the water on to fill the tub for a bath. This building did not have soundproof walls.

One night I was working late in the apartment across from Ben's. It was a hot day and I had the door and all the windows open. I had my back to the door. I could feel someone in the doorway. I had an uneasy feeling and thought, damn, I should have locked the door. I turned around slowly and Ben stood there.

"Hello, I'm Ben. I took the padlock off my door," he said. The manager hadn't left yet.

"Thank you. I'm Helen, the new owner." We shook hands.

After that meeting, Ben didn't come in quietly any more. He started to trust me. Often when I worked late, after he had cleaned up, Ben would come to where I was working and talk to me. I had the feeling he wanted to talk about something special, not just visit. Knowing how long it took him just to say hello, I didn't want to ask if he had something on his mind. Seeing how quickly he cleaned himself up when he came home from work, I thought he was working up the nerve to ask me to clean and paint his apartment.

One evening I was putting all my tools away and Ben came to the door. "Hi Ben." He didn't startle me this time, but just stood there. I waited for him to speak.

"Can I show you something in my apartment?" he asked. Here it comes, he wants his apartment painted.

"Let me put this stuff away first."

Ben waited  and we crossed the hall together. Wow! I was expecting a spotless, tidy apartment because he was so clean about himself. Mr. Clean his apartment was not. It had been a long time since the carpet had met up with a vacuum cleaner and there were cockroaches skittering around the floor and under the lonely picture hanging on one wall. The bathroom was clean, but I didn't want to chance looking in the kitchen.

As we entered the apartment, he glanced around and said, "Sorry about the mess. I don't keep house very good." He hesitated for a moment then walked around the unmade bed. He pulled a long cardboard box from under it, hesitated again then placed the box on the bed.

"I want you to look at these and tell me what you think." In the box was a stack of precise drawings.

"Ben, I don't know a thing about what I'm looking at, but you got an A+ on every one of these. What are they?"

"It's mechanical drawing. When I got out of the army I went to Community College and took classes in Mechanical Drawing." The drawings were neat and perfect. I couldn't detect an eraser mark on them.

"Are you still taking classes?"

"No, I'm working now. I have a job as a mechanic and I  hate it. My hands are dirty and greasy all the time and sometimes they crack." That would explain his first stop at the bathtub when he walked through the door after work.

"Why did you quit school?"

"When I was in Viet Nam I started drinking. I quit for a while when I was going to school, but I started drinking again and didn't go back." He was quick to add, "But I don't drink now."

I didn't know how long it had been since Ben had his last drink. As long as I had been working in the building, I never saw him drunk. Standing before me was a young man who would like to be more than an auto mechanic, a job he hated. I had only known Ben a few months but I instinctively knew if he continued on the job he had, it was a matter of time before he started drinking again. I wanted him to do more with his life than become another drunk Indian like the ones I saw in the neighborhood. My motherly instincts kicked in.

"Ben," I said. "Go back to school."

After I saw Ben's apartment, it must have inspired him to do a little house cleaning. One day Ben walked in the unit where I was working and startled me. He was so quiet this time, I didn't hear him come in.

"Can I paint my apartment?" he asked.

I was a little leery about him painting. I had hinted it might help his roach problem if he would clean his apartment, but I didn't mean paint it. I just wanted him to vacuum the carpet and sweep the kitchen floor and mop it. Maybe if I let him paint, he'd clean the kitchen too.

"Okay. You can paint, but you have to use the same paint I'm using in the other apartments. Tell me what you'll need and I'll get it for you. Nothing crazy in there. Agreed?"

"Okay, I just want to clean it up," he said.

The first thing Ben did was patch a hole the size of a fist in one of his doors. Knowing Ben had a temper, I had a good idea how the hole got there but decided not to ask. There wasn't as much as a dimple in the door where the hole had been when the patch was completed.

Ben started the job of painting by sanding the walls. He was a perfectionist. If he wanted his walls perfectly smooth before he started painting, that was fine with me. If Ben was in his apartment working, he wasn't out being tempted to drink.

Ben had been working a few days when the manager stopped me in the hall as I did a walk-through check of the building.

"I want to talk to you," she said in an angry voice.

Oh-oh, now what?

"You talk to that Indian in six," she said through clenched teeth.

"Are you talking about Ben?" I asked. "That's his name. Ben." I made a point of using his name.

"Yes, you'd better talk to him."

I wondered why she was so angry at Ben and whether he had started drinking again.

"The tenants are calling me at all hours complaining about all the noise he makes on his walls at two and three in the morning. You tell him he has to stop." She still wouldn't use Ben's name. This coming from the manager the tenants complained about because she vacuumed the halls all hours of the night after everyone had gone to bed.

"I'll speak to Ben as soon as he's home," I said, trying to hide a smile. Ben worked days so I knew he was painting in the evening. But I didn't understand how painting a wall could make enough noise to disturb the other tenants. How much noise could a paint roller or brush make?

I knocked on Ben's door after I was sure he had taken his bath. I learned early on, he would not answer his door until he had cleaned up from his job.

"Ben, what are you doing to your walls at two and three o'clock in the morning?" I asked.

"Sanding them with my sander."

"Why?"

"To make them smooth so I can paint."

"No. I know why you're sanding them – but why at two or three in the morning?"

"That's when I feel like it," he answered.

"When you feel like it? You can't do that. The other tenants are sleeping. They have to go to work. You're waking them up and they're calling the manager about all the noise you're making."

"Well, I go to work too, but I do the walls when I feel like it," he calmly explained. He cocked his head and looked at me as though I needed to have something explained to me. Then he told me about "Indian Time."

"Have you ever heard of Indian Time?" he asked.

"No. What's Indian Time?"

"That's when you do what you do when it feels right to you. If a father wants to take his son fishing and he is building a house, he stops building the house and he takes his son fishing because that is when he feels it is the right time. That's Indian Time."

"That's a wonderful concept, but this is a 9-to-5 world. You can't do that here. No more sanding at two or three in the morning. Okay?"

Ben didn't sand during the early morning hours any more. He finished painting and cleaned his apartment. The walls were without a flaw and smooth as a baby's butt. Then Ben went on a drinking spree.

Every time Ben came back to the building drunk and I caught him, I gave him a long lecture. When he was sober again, I repeated the lecture. He stayed away for days and sometimes weeks when he was drunk because he knew what would happen when he came home.

One day I heard loud thuds coming from his apartment. It sounded like something very heavy was being dropped on the floor. I knocked on his door to see what was going on. Not a bright thing for me to do if I thought he might be drunk and having a fight with someone. He had come home with bloody knuckles a few times.

Ben answered the door. Sober. Behind him in the room were five other Indian men – drunk.

"What are you doing?" I asked Ben.

"Cooking breakfast for these people." I could smell bacon cooking.

The men were trying to lift Ben's weights. They got the weights as far as their knees and dropped them. That was the thud I was hearing. It would have been comical if it wasn't so pathetic. They were all strong young men and if they had been sober, they could have lifted the weights easily. I knew eventually one of them was going to drop a weight on their foot and get hurt.

"Who are these men, Ben?"

"I don't know."

"You don't know them?"

"No."

"Why are they here and why are you cooking for them?"

"I met them on the street. They were hungry. I told them I would make breakfast for them." I followed Ben to the kitchen. He turned back to frying bacon and breaking eggs into the pan.

"Ben–" I started to say.

He sensed my frustration and said to me, "They are my brothers."

I looked at Ben and then at the other men. Ben was a Navajo. He did not resemble the other men. I opened my mouth to say something, but before I had a chance to make a fool of myself, Ben softly said, "They are Indians. They are my brothers." No other explanation was necessary. I already knew of Ben's kind heart.

A few days later, Ben disappeared. When he didn't come home at night, I knew he was drinking again. He must have gone out of the neighborhood to drink or he saw my car and was hiding from me. He knew he would get the usual lecture from me when I saw him drunk.

## 4. Not All Sweat, Swear, Tears and Fear

My routine after the purchase of the apartment was to get the kids off to school in the morning and go to work at the apartment. I worked until it was time for the kids to get home from school at 3:30. I still had to cook, clean and do laundry for my family. There were a few times when I had to stay at the building and work after 5:00, or there would be work that had to be done in the evening and I would go back after dinner. John would come and help me in the evening.

At times I was exhausted and felt I'd be happy if the building burned to the ground, but it was brick and that wasn't going to happen.

There were days I would be angry at the previous owner for letting the building get so rundown. My emotions would swing and I would be disgusted and angry at the tenants for allowing themselves to live in such a shit hole. That was what Linda called it, a shit hole. Then I would vow to make it a better place for the tenants to live. But why did they stay here? Every block in N.W. Portland had an apartment building. All were much nicer than mine; it had to be my low rent.

My emotions were on a roller coaster. Anger at the previous owner, feeling sorry for the tenants, anger at the tenants for living here, disgust with the tenants for living in such filth. There were days when I just wanted to junk the whole project and go home to my family and be a wife and full time mom again. Strangely enough, I was never angry at John for buying the apartment.

It wasn't always sweat, swear, tears and fear. As the work went on, I was proud of what was being accomplished in this building. There were times when it was fun being there. I no longer felt threatened by any of the tenants. Most of them drank and often were drunk. Except for once when Ray told me I had nice thighs and I'd be nice in bed, which he probably considered a compliment, the tenants were all polite and respectful with me. Ray died the night of his remark so he never became a problem.

There were times when I went home laughing with a funny story for my family.

One day Mr. Lee called to me as I passed his door. "Helen, would you come in here please." I stepped in his apartment and he continued, "Look at my pants and slippers. They are all wet."

Mr. Lee was quite elderly; I could understand that his pants might be wet and he not remember how they got that way. But I asked, "What happened Mr. Lee?"

"I don't know, every time I wash my hands at the bathroom sink, my pants and slippers get wet."

I looked at him and I could tell he wasn't wetting himself. His pants were wet below his knees. "Let me check your bathroom. Maybe something is leaking."

The previous tenant had done some creative decorating in the bathroom. Multicolored strips of carpet were glued to the outside of the tub. The floor was covered with carpet. When I stood checking the sink, I could feel the carpet was soggy and something was making my jeans wet.

I got down on my knees to check the supply lines under the sink and was greeted with a tiny stream of cold water in my face. There was a pin hole in one of the supply lines. It wasn't something that had happened that day; the carpet was saturated. Mr. Lee's pants had been getting wet for several days. I stood up with my wet knees and face and explained the problem to Mr. Lee and assured him it would be fixed as soon as possible. The supply line was fixed and he was happily back in his rocking chair.

Ben's water problem was a mystery. After arriving home from work early one day, he came storming into the apartment where I was working. "Come and look at my apartment. It's all wet."

This was the first time I had seen Ben angry. I knew something was drastically wrong, because Ben was still in his work clothes. He never left his apartment wearing his dirty work clothes or before taking a bath .

I cautiously walked into his apartment, not knowing what to expect. I could see water pooling in the kitchen doorway. The carpet in the living room was serving as a sponge, soaking up the water from the kitchen. As we stood there, I could see the wet spot spreading further in the room. I walked to the kitchen door and looked in. The floor had almost an inch of water and floating in the water were dozens of dead roaches. Ben's water faucet was not turned on but the kitchen sink was overflowing.

"What happened?" Ben yelled. His black eyes were blazing. I had a hard time keeping a straight face. I had often teased Ben about his pet roaches and seeing so many dead ones floating struck me as funny. Not so Ben.

"Ben, I don't know."

I stood quietly and could hear water running. The sound came from the apartment above Ben's. "It sounds like the guy above you left his water running. I'll go up and turn it off," I said.

I ran up and turned the water off. There was no damage in that apartment. The water was going down the drain. The building was old and water from the second floor drained down through the first floor pipes then to the sewer drain in the basement. Something in Ben's drain pipe was keeping it from continuing to the sewer drain.

"Is there something in your drain or covering your drain that's stopping the water from going down?" I asked when I returned to Ben's apartment. Ben often had dirty dishes piled in his sink.

"I don't know, I'm not a plumber. I don't have anything in the sink." He was still angry.

"I'll help you clean this up. Nothing seems to be damaged. The carpet's wet, but it will dry."

We worked together sopping up the water on the counter and the floor. By the time we finished, Ben wasn't quite as angry. He wasn't happy either. I had been through enough of Ben's drunk and sober days with him to know I could tease him about his messy apartment and the roaches. I thought I'd try a little humor.

"I'm really sorry about all your pet roaches drowning, Ben. Too bad they couldn't swim."

"You're not funny."

"Look at the bright side. How long have I been asking you to clean your apartment? Look at the counter, spotless, and the kitchen floor, it shines. It's never been so clean. Even that little bit of wet carpet by the kitchen door is clean. You might want to clean the rest of the carpet now."

When he looked at me, his eyes were no longer blazing; he was almost smiling.

"Maybe you'd like to do that for me," he said.

I ignored him and went on, "Nothing of yours was damaged. We did clean your kitchen. I'm sorry about the loss of your pet roaches, but I'm sure there are more around you can train. I saw some skittering under that picture on the wall in the living room."

Now he was smiling. The anger was gone. As I stepped out in the hall and closed the door behind me, I heard the water running in Ben's bathtub. I smiled to myself. Ben was back to normal.

Roto Rooter checked the drains from the apartment above Ben down through Ben's apartment and to the sewer. There was no blockage anywhere. Maybe it was just The Great Spirit's way of helping me get Ben to clean his apartment. It worked.

# 5. Scary Scary Night

I had cleaned and was painting one of the upstairs units. Ben walked so quietly, I didn't hear him come in. His "Hi" startled me.

"Ben! Not working today?"

"No, I quit my job."

"Are you going back to school?" I still had hopes for him.

"I don't know yet. Maybe. Can I help you paint this apartment?"

I really didn't like getting on the top rung of the ladder to paint the ceiling so I was happy to have his help. "Can you paint the ceiling for me?"

"Sure, I can do that."

Ben got up on the ladder and scraped the loose paint off the ceiling. He started sanding. "Ben, this is NOT Buckingham Palace. You don't have to sand it."

He ignored me and kept sanding until the ceiling was smooth and perfect. He started painting and finished half the ceiling. The next day he disappeared.

Three days later I heard noise in Ben's apartment and went down to check. He'd had some drunk Indian visitors one day. I wanted to make sure they hadn't returned.

Ben was back–physically.

He was standing in his kitchen trying to make a sandwich. He had all the ingredients. Two slices of bread, sandwich meat laid out on the counter and a knife in his hand with a dab of mayonnaise on it. I watched Ben as he tried to spread the tiny bit of mayonnaise on the tip of the knife onto the bread. He completely missed the bread and tried again.

Ben didn't realize I was next to him watching. I took the knife from his hand and, taking his arm, led him into the living room to a chair.

"Sit down Ben, I'll make the sandwich for you."

I walked back to the kitchen and returned with the sandwich. He was standing where I had left him, but appeared to be asleep.

I took his arm again and said, "Sit down Ben. I made a sandwich for you." I placed the sandwich in his hand. He just held it as though he didn't know what to do with it.

"Take a bite of your sandwich Ben." I spoke to him as I would a small child. He took one bite.

I made coffee and poured him a cup. Hot and black. When I took the coffee to him, he was holding the sandwich but had not taken another bite. He appeared to be asleep again. I put the mayonnaise and meat back in the refrigerator, trying to kill time. I didn't want to leave him until he started eating.

Back in the living room Ben sat as I had left him, the sandwich in his hand, one bite gone. I stood looking at him thinking, he's not asleep. His body would be more relaxed and slouched and his head would be hanging down but he's sitting there straight as an arrow with his head up. I talked to him.

"Ben, can you hear me?" He nodded his head, "yes."

"I made some coffee for you and I want you to drink it. Understand?"

He nodded "yes" again. I took the sandwich from his hand and gave him the coffee.

"Drink some coffee , Ben. Be careful. It's hot." He took one sip and sat holding the cup with both hands.

"I want you to eat something, will you do that?"

He nodded "yes" again. I took the coffee and put the sandwich back in his hand.

"Take a bite." Ben took another bite. "Will you eat all of the sandwich, please?"

He nodded "yes" again.

"Ben, I put a cup of coffee on the floor by the chair, will you drink it?"

"Yes." Ben spoke to me, that was good.

I looked at Ben. He was in a stupor. He couldn't be just drunk. He didn't walk like he was drunk. He was fairly steady on his feet. Ben just didn't seem aware of what was going on around him and he kept closing his eyes. I had been around plenty of drunks since acquiring the building but I had never had experience with anyone under the influence of drugs or alcohol and drugs. I didn't know what to do for Ben.

I went back upstairs to work for two more hours. If Ben fell off his chair I would hear him. After I finished working for the day I checked on him. Ben was still upright in the chair, coffee on the floor, sandwich in his hand with two bites gone. His eyes were closed.

I thought about waking him and trying to get him to his bed but I didn't want to take the chance of him becoming violent when awakened. He had always been kind and respectful towards me. I wasn't sure how he would react in this condition. I had seen him with bloody knuckles after a drunk and I didn't want to take a chance.

I left him in the chair and went home, but I couldn't stop worrying. I called William Temple House and spoke to one of the counselors and explained what was going on with Ben.

"Could you please send someone over to check on him? He's in the apartment building across the street. The address is 2066. He's in apartment 6. I'm really worried about him."

"Yes, I will go over and do that myself," the counselor answered.

The next day I was painting in the apartment above Ben's. This time I heard Ben when he walked in. He looked a wreck.

"Did you send someone from William Temple House to check on me last night?" Ben asked.

"Yes, I did."

"Thank you, thank you very much."

Ben's eyes told me he was grateful but he was still that proud Navajo and thank you was all he could say.

By the end of the week he was back to being the normal Ben again. I don't know what mixture of drugs and alcohol he had ingested but he scared the hell out of me that night. I was afraid Ben was going to die.

# 6. Ben's Good-bye

As the owner of an apartment building, I was learning to do things I never dreamed of trying before. The building was at N.W. Glisan and 20th Avenue and it was the late 1970s. The area was home to prostitutes, pimps, drunks, druggies and a variety of counter culture groups. All new to me, a stay-at-home mom before we purchased the building.

Along with cleaning and painting, I learned to be assertive. With my original tenants, I learned to stand toe to toe with them, yell, swear like my tenants, and demand they pay rent if they wanted to live in my building. I had gone through four managers and was looking to hire another. I gave the present manager, who was on the dishonest side, the choice of being fired or quitting. His choice was to quit.

Again, I was in need of a manager. Finally I had a building occupied by honest, rent-paying tenants. All my original tenants had moved out to harass and not pay rent to another apartment building owner. All except one, Ben.

Ben had been on one of his drunks and didn't know the manager had moved. He wasn't expecting to see me working in the manager's apartment when he bravely came weaving through the front door. When he reached the apartment where I was working, I called out, "Ben!" and startled him. He tried to hurry past but I didn't let him get far.

"Get in here." Ben knew he was in for a drinking lecture from me. It was standard policy every time I caught him drunk.

There were no chairs in the room so I made him sit on the floor opposite me while I delivered my lecture.

"Have you eaten anything today?" I asked after the lecture.

"No, not yet. I was going to make something when I got to my apartment."

I knew that wasn't likely and gave him half of my sandwich and a cup of coffee. I don't know if it was the food or the fact that I had startled him, but he was starting to sober up. Maybe I could talk some sense into him now. After my routine drinking lecture, I said, "Ben, I want you to promise me something."

"What?"

"I want you to promise you'll stop drinking."

He looked at me shaking his head. "I can't do that."

"Yes you can. Go over to William Temple House. Remember the night I called them when you were in a drunken stupor and asked if they would send someone to check on you?" He nodded a yes. "He was a drug and alcohol counselor. He'll help you. That's one of the services they have."

"I'll try."

"No Ben. I don't want an 'I'll try.' I want an 'I will' from you. You go for months without drinking. You can do it. Don't you want to quit and stay sober?"

He nodded yes. He got up from the floor and stood with his head bowed. Although he stood above me I felt like a mother reprimanding a small child. This is not a good time to get soft with him, I thought. I stood up, waiting for an answer.

"Okay, I will." He started to walk out, then came back in. "Thank you for the sandwich and coffee." He walked with a steadier step down the hall to his apartment.

Ben stayed sober for several months. I had hopes for him. Then he disappeared again for two months.

One evening John asked if I'd heard from Ben.

"No, but he'll be back. He always comes back and pays all his rent." Wishful thinking on my part.

"Has Ben been gone this long before?"

"No," softly.

"You know how he is when he gets his check. Every Indian in the neighborhood is his brother. Sometimes he gets in fights. Remember the bloody knuckles? Something might have happened to him."

I didn't want to think of that possibility. "Okay, I'll go over tomorrow and start cleaning his apartment."

I had been checking Ben's apartment every time I visited the building. Each time I checked there were things missing. He had sold all his mechanic tools. His weights and TV were gone. The first day I started cleaning, only the Murphy Bed, a broken-down couch and a few boxes of odds and ends were scattered around the room. Even the chair Ben had been sitting in the night I thought he was going to die was gone.

It was my second day of sorting what to pack, to keep for Ben, and what to throw away. I was sitting on the floor with my back to the door. I didn't hear anyone come in, but I felt someone in the room. I turned to look. It was Ben.

"Hello Hell-n." This was the first time he had ever called me by my given name, not quite correct, but close. Ben was sober.

"Ben! Hello!" I was so happy to see him.

"You're packing my stuff."

"Yes, I didn't think you were coming back. You've never been gone this long before. You haven't paid rent for two months."

"I know. I'm sorry. I don't have any money for my rent. It's not fair to you. I came back to tell you to take anything you want and throw the rest away. I'll move."

"Thank you, but there isn't anything here I can use. I'll pack it and store everything for you in the basement. When you have a place to live, you can come and get it." He stood there saying nothing. "What have you been doing the past two months?"

"Nothing. Just drinking. I knew if I came back you'd yell at me."

"You've got that right. Do you think you'll go back to school?" I couldn't give up on him.

"I don't know. I don't think so."

I was still sitting on the floor looking up at him while we spoke. I stood up wanting to look Ben in the eye.

"What are you going to do with your life Ben? You're still a young man. Are you going to just drink yourself to death?" I was the mother reprimanding the small child again.

"I don't know. Maybe I'll go back to the reservation."

I knew it was a matter of seconds before I would start to cry. I looked at Ben and saw tears well up in his eyes. I didn't want to embarrass him by letting him know I saw the tears. He was still trying to be that proud Navajo. I took a step forward to hug him but before I could, his arms were around me like a vise. With a sob deep in his throat he whispered to me, "You're the only person who has ever been any kind of mother to me." With that, he turned and hurried out of the room. I heard his running footsteps thunder down the hall and out the front door.

I knew when Ben ran out the door I would never see him again.

I sat on the floor and cried.

## 7. Hello . . . Good-bye . . . Again

Ordinarily a telephone ring was a "stop and rest" signal. Today it was a fingernail down the blackboard irritant. I was in a mood. I didn't want to talk to anyone.

"Damn, why didn't I turn the answering machine on?" I said to no one. I hesitated a moment, looked at the clock and thought maybe it was one of my children calling. We had five children, now scattered from coast to coast.

I picked up the phone. "Hello."

"Helen?"

"Yes."

It was Sallie, the lady I had hired to manage my apartment building when we were transferred to Spokane. It was all I could do to keep from groaning when I heard her voice. Sallie was a talker. She often called with a minor problem then spent forty-five long-distance minutes chit-chatting about nothing. I was in no mood to talk to Sallie about a problem she could figure out herself.

"Ah—there's someone here who wants to talk to you." I could hear mumbling and the phone being transferred.

"Hell-n?" There was only one person I knew who said Helen like that. I hadn't heard his voice since the day he hugged me and with a catch in his voice told me I was the only person who was anything like a mother to him.

"Ben?" I whispered, then shouted "Ben!" In my mind's eye I could see his black eyes crinkle and his hand holding the phone jerk away from his ear. One thing Ben had was excellent hearing. A million questions ran through my mind. Where are you living? What are you doing? Are you staying sober? Are you off drugs? But all I could say was, "How are you?"

"Well," his answer was coming slowly, "I'm okay now. I hurt my legs and I have to use a cane for a while, but I'm okay."

"How did you hurt your legs, Ben?" I wasn't sure I wanted to know. "Were you in an accident?"

"No, I'm embarrassed to tell you." His voice was almost a whisper into the phone. "I was doing drugs and I stepped out of a second floor window."

A chill ran through me. He heard my sharp intake of breath and quickly said, "Hell-n, I'm okay now. That was a year ago. I don't drink or do drugs since then."

He had answered some of my questions but not all of them. "Where are you living now? What are you doing?" I asked.

"I live in Seattle, but I came here because I want to go back to school. I need to find a job and I want to pay the money I owe you."

I smiled. I had heard that song before.

"Hell-n, I just wanted you to know I'm okay now. I want to get a job here and go back to school; learn about computers and pay you back. I'm going back to Seattle today, but I'll come to Portland again."

"We're moving back to Portland. Call me when you come back Ben. Sallie will help you get in touch. We'll meet for lunch. You can tell me what you've been doing for the last five years."

He never called. I never heard from Ben again.

Nineteen years later, I had lunch at the Gypsy in Northwest Portland.

Something was missing. No one was sitting at the bar. Wayne, Sallie's husband, should have been there. Ben too. And maybe Dick and Ray and even Don, my original tenants and manager.

The bartender didn't say, "What's a nice lady like you doing in a place like this?" when I walked through the door.

I had no fear this time. Not like the first time.

The Gypsy is a nice restaurant and bar now. Nice ladies have lunch here.

A nice-looking clean-cut young man ushered me to a booth to await my lunch friend. The young man and I visited while I waited.

"Some big company bought the Gypsy. They're going to tear it down," he said.

My heart fell. Where will the ghosts of Wayne, Ben, Dick, Ray and Don go for a drink?

Ben—where are you?

# GEORGE COFFER

George Coffer was born in Pittsburgh, PA in 1946, graduated from high school in Adelaide, Australia, and always wanted to write. He has a master's degree in English from the University of Denver. He owned a used bookstore in Boulder, Colorado, and currently is a mental health counselor in Vancouver, Washington. He looks forward to retiring to fish, write, and row a small boat. He has a daughter, Dot, a wife, Pam, and a cat named Tabby.

# LOOKING FOR LYDIA

The woods were filled with red oak and yellow big leaf maple leaves. Red-winged blackbirds were singing their territorial mating calls. Silver trunked Oregon oak trees appeared by the side of the road. This was wonderful country–God's country some would say. Kevin walked west on Interstate 14 toward Beacon Rock. It was fall 2008, and Kevin was about as happy as he had been in the last eight years. He had taken the Gorge bus, only a dollar, from Camas along the Columbia River to White Salmon, then hiked west. He was thinking about what had happened on that drunken, disastrous night in Portland eight years ago.

It had started out as a good day. Harry, an Army buddy from the Gulf War, had suggested they go bar hopping in Portland. So they left his 13-year-old daughter, Lydia, and her mom in Vancouver and drove across the old green steel I-5 bridge to Portland. They stopped in North Portland at a topless bar, The Dancing Bare, by the Paul Bunyan statue. Then they decided they were a little drunk and should go downtown to eat at Jake's Grill.

The atmosphere was old world, with lots of bar brass and dark wood tables. The food and the prices were good. He must have still been feeling the effect of the six or eight drinks they had earlier because everything at Jake's seemed to glisten and the colors ran into each other. The waitress was attractive and it went further than the low- cut blouse and the come hither look in her green eyes. He loved his wife and yet the waitress looked as good as any girl he could remember.

After the dessert, a kind of double chocolate torte, he told Harry that he thought they should leave before he made a total fool of himself with the waitress. Harry said sure, he understood. He wouldn't mind asking her out either–and his wife was back in Springfield, Missouri.

Kevin said, "Why don't we go to the bar across the street?" If there was anything that Kevin could change in his life it would be his decision to go to that bar. He should have guessed by the pink exterior wall that this was not a good place for drunk Army buddies.

They walked in and went to the bar. Harry took one look at the bartender and shouted to Kevin, "He's a fucking queer." At this point four patrons rose and one particularly big one said, "Hey, asshole, we are all fucking queer. So what are you going to do about it?" Harry picked up a beer bottle and broke it over the guy's head.

Kevin did not want to get involved but three guys started beating on Harry with fists and bottles. Even today Kevin cannot remember much of what happened–except the blood running down his face from a cut over his left eye and four guys lying on the floor around him. Harry was getting to his feet but two of the guys on the floor looked green and one seemed to have trouble breathing.

The police came and charged Harry and Kevin with disorderly conduct and first degree assault. Harry spent three months in jail and had two years' probation. Kevin was not so lucky. One of the guys on the floor died. Another went to the hospital with a detached trachea. Kevin had hit him in the neck. Kevin got eight years in jail for manslaughter and first degree assault. He got out in seven years three months for good behavior. His wife divorced him while he was in jail. He wrote to his daughter, Lydia, but she never wrote back, and he lost track of her. There was no Lydia Babcock in any of the telephone directories.

So now, eight years later, as he walked through the trees, those beautiful yellow, red, and orange leaves of autumn, he thought about what might have been if not for that one night in Portland, and his crazy friend Harry's starting a fight in a gay bar on Stark Street. He passed Beacon Rock Park and walked around the corner a mile or so to the Skamania Grocery. He bought a ham and cheese sandwich and a soft drink from the girl there, who looked about seventeen. She would be younger than Lydia now by four years. He stared at her and she looked at him and smiled. He saw how young she was: first bloom of youth, nice figure, no makeup, and country-air complexion. He felt a tear roll down his face and then another.

"You okay, sir?" she said.

"Oh, I'm sorry. I was just thinking of my own daughter and how much I miss her. I'm sorry I stared at you."

"Oh, that's okay. I see now. You weren't staring at me; you were missing your daughter."

"Yeah," he said. He felt old and foolish. He was forty-five years old and he was sniveling.

"I'll just have another Coke and sit out there on your porch."

He had just started to feel like his old self again when a black panel truck pulled up and a young guy with spikey hair ran into the store.

"This is a stick-up. Give me all your money, now!" Kevin heard the guy say. "I said, give it to me now, bitch." Then Kevin heard a firearm discharge twice.

Something clicked. Kevin felt rage well up inside him. The next thing he knew he was inside the store and had grabbed the guy's gun arm, disarmed him and broken two of his fingers. He had the guy in a choke hold two feet off the floor when he heard a voice say, "It's okay, Mister. Don't kill him. I've got his gun and I know how to use it. Let him go."

Kevin dropped the young man, who must have weighed 140 pounds to his 220. He put his knee on the kid's back. The kid screamed, "You broke my fingers, man. You tried to kill me. You can't do that. I was only robbing the store."

Then Kevin heard a man say, "This man try to rob you?"

"Yes, Hank," said the girl.

Kevin turned his head, still pinning the boy to the floor, and saw a young patrolman behind him. He felt foolish. The girl was okay. The young man was either a really bad shot or just trying to scare her. Kevin should not have grabbed him and broken his fingers. Kevin could see the bars slowly circle around him, feel the loneliness of being in a cell. Here we go again, he thought.

The officer cuffed the young man Kevin was holding. He looked at Kevin and said, "Thank you, sir. You're a real hero. You disarmed this shitbird. We've been trying to catch him for weeks. I'd like to tell you how happy I am to meet you." He reached out his hand. "What is your name, sir?"

"My name is Kevin Babcock," he said, relieved, and shook the officer's hand.

"Really, now, isn't that a coincidence. Babcock is my wife's maiden name."

"What is her first name?" Kevin asked.

"Well, sir, her first name is Lydia. Now, isn't that a pretty name?"

"Yes, it is, son, yes, it is." Kevin smiled. He felt truly happy again.

# ODE TO A GUINEA PIG

A creature small whose love was sage–
After he ran laps outside his cage
I'd set him down upon my chest,
Then pet his head and let him rest.
Black velvet coat, eight inches long,
On my chest he'd chirp his song.

His little paws and great big heart
Both held me from the very start.
Did Blackie know love puts things right?
Extracts the sadness, hatred, pain
From deep inside the human brain,
Pulls emotions into the light
To writhe a while, then lose their fight
And drift away like geese in flight?

Crisp parsley, green and curled, I bought;
Spinach of freshest hue I sought
For my wee black-eyed velvet beast
So he could come and have a feast.

Four years he held me in his paws
And taught me to accept my flaws.
But now that time has come and gone,
I miss my friend, eight inches long.

# JENNI GAINSBOROUGH

Jenni Gainsborough moved to the US from London, England, 30 years ago. After living in Los Angeles and Washington DC, she and her husband settled in Vancouver in 2008. Jenni has been a failed school teacher, a technical editor and a researcher and advocate for criminal justice reform. Now her days are filled with grandchildren and creative writing classes.

# GROWING OLD GRACEFULLY

I am not in denial about growing old. I know it is inevitable; after all I see it happening all around me. My spouse, my friends and my siblings are all aging gradually but obviously from day to day. I know that it will happen to me eventually and, when it does, I will accept it gracefully.

Sometimes other people behave inexplicably though. I was on the bus to work one morning. I had taken an unusual amount of care in dressing as I was going to a large meeting. I felt quite elegant in my black dress pants and stylish jacket. I was wearing smart black boots instead of my usual granny walkers. I had even blow-dried my hair and applied some minimal make up. The black leather back pack was the final detail that proclaimed my youth and hipness. I was feeling sharp.

As I stood on the crowded bus, a young woman seated on the aisle caught my eye and smiled. I smiled back to show her that we were equals–two strong women making their independent way in the world. Then she stood up and offered me her seat. There must be some mistake! Perhaps there was some old person standing next to me. I turned to see an athletic-looking young man listening to his iPod. It seemed unlikely that he was the one deemed in need. The young woman touched me on the arm and pointed to her seat. "Please do sit down," she insisted. Refusing to sit would only draw more attention to my embarrassing situation so I sat. And she stood there looking so smug and self-satisfied, her fresh young face glowing with the good deed she had done, her long sun-kissed blonde hair blowing in the breeze from the window, the hem of her cute little skirt occasionally brushing against my black pants. I thought evil thoughts all the way downtown.

Another incident occurred one summer weekend. To deal with the typical oppressively humid Washington DC heat, I was dressed in cotton capri pants (the better to cover my swollen arthritic knees–an affliction that hit me at a surprisingly young age) and a short-sleeved tee shirt that fitted quite snugly across my chest. Two young men rounded the corner and walked toward me. As is so often the case with young (and not so young) men, they approached with their eyes focused on my chest, not my face. As they drew closer, however, both looked up and froze in horror. I could read their minds through the looks of terror on their faces as they tried to avoid eye contact with me and with each other. They had been lustfully eyeing the secondary sexual characteristics of a woman who could be their mother (aggh!) or even their grandmother (yuck!!). It was probably enough to put them off sex for life. And I did not feel the least bit sorry for them. I just hope one of them is dating the young woman from the bus.

# SANDRA GOODWIN

Sandra Goodwin. My business is sold, and it is great to be retired. Finally free to pay attention to my life-long companion—a noisy, vivid imagination. I intend to follow where it leads. Robert Frost's poem "The Road Not Taken" has always had special meaning for me. Through all the twists and turns in life's experiences, I am drawn to follow unexplored paths and "that has made all the difference." For me creative writing is the beginning of another road not yet taken.

# SECRETS HIDING
# IN A LIVING PORTRAIT

"Every character has regrets. Every character has secrets.
Every character has a public self and a private self and
a self that he doesn't even know about. Every character
has a history, a formative past. No character exists in a
vacuum."

John Dufresne, *The Lie that Tells a Truth*

In my school days I was a tall, skinny girl wishing for curves.
When the curves finally came they arrived in increasing proportion
and caused me to yearn for the skinny physique I used to have.

At this time in my life, my reflection in the mirror shows a
variety of shapes and bulges. My sharp features are softened by loose,
wavy hair frequently colored to keep the gray at bay. My grin and laugh
manage to keep my facial muscles from slipping into a gloomy or a
pensive expression. Clothing choices, perfume, even shoes are part of
my efforts to try to present an image that satisfies my ego.

Sometimes I want to ask friends and family: "What do you see?
Do you truly know who I am after all these years?" My personality,
deeds, mistakes, and adventures blend with my appearance as everyone
takes me in through the lens of their own making. Nevertheless, I
wonder if they see the secrets I hide.

In my varied career choices my former employees—and once
upon a time students—had no clue that my manipulation of them with
carrot rewards and cheers for their successes was as much about me as
about them. "Look what I got them to accomplish!" is the secret, pride
I felt and still feel.

I hear, "Oh, you are such a good cook. What a lovely dinner
party." Luckily my guests can't see how badly I cook my personal

meals. At this stage in my life I hate being tied to the kitchen. No one realizes that each time I cook for friends and family I am competing with myself to present an even more sumptuous meal than the time before. It is my secret game.

"Should I be like my glamorous friend?" She won't allow anyone to see her unless she has showered, molded her face, and dressed in brilliant color. I have to make a calculated effort to put on my best rainbow and paint a glow on my countenance when I plan an evening out. It is always a relief to wash from my face the decorative camouflage and slip into sloppy clothes to become comfortable me. I long ago concluded that glamour is hard work and I am too lazy to fully embrace it.

"You are tired," another friend says to me with concern. "You try to do too much." She does not realize I am a day dreamer who loves to envision imagined adventures and accomplishments when working hard to make things happen. While painting my deck in the hot sun, digging in the flower beds, or wall papering, I dream secret desires and wishes too far away to grasp. Will I get to Paris, write a good book or run for public office?

My children and grandchildren are independent, accomplished, and full of life. What a relief! "Don't worry me with your doubts and struggles," I say silently to them. "Handle your own problems. I do not want that burden." What type of mother would think such thoughts? Would my four grown kids be puzzled about this internal reaction to their potential needs as outwardly I continue to give unsolicited advice and support and coo over their accomplishments?

They probably would be surprised that I have a secret distant perspective on them now that they are on their own. My control of their future is over. Now it is up to them to make their way.

All those around me who enrich my life might be hurt if they knew they don't always fill me with satisfaction. Would they be amazed that sometimes I want more from them and that I wish they were different in some way? It is exhausting trying to exhibit the best in me to everyone while balancing my life-long earned doubts, anger, nasty thoughts and selfish motives. It is equally unrealistic for friends and family to be expected to live up to my expectations of perfection. Probably no one really wants to know everything I think and feel as they are busy cultivating their own inner turmoil. For all of us the big dilemma is understanding who we are.

The joke could be on me–those from whom I think I am keeping small secrets may know more about me than I realize. If truth be known, I really want my lofty, wicked, frivolous, and rebellious secrets to remain private. After all, they are mine!

Today I have important things to do. I am planning to teach a granddaughter how to create the perfect pie. Then I look forward to assembling my attire and façade to enjoy an evening at the theater. If my plans for today seem to contradict my inner musing, perhaps the difference between my secret thoughts and outward actions merely means that I am complicated.

# INDULGING MY IMAGINATION

As I look through my living room window, I see that the wind has slapped you on the back, tipping you over to land with your pink bottom in the air and your arms resting on the ground. You look like a person on his hands and knees. I have been meaning to lift you to an upright position, but the rain and wind have deterred my good intentions.

I admit I can't decide what to do with you. I think you know that your behavior annoys me—the way your peeling paint lets your original pink color show through. You have deliberately thwarted my efforts to relieve you of that inappropriate color. I only wanted you to blend in with the rest of my patio furniture.

When I selected you from a pile of discarded things left by someone two years ago, I recognized, little chair, that your shape with the tilt of your fluted back and the height of the seat were guarantees that you would be comfortable to sit on. Comfort was your appeal, but your color was crazy.

I washed your smooth, unblemished surface in preparation to paint you a refreshing white. During that first summer we were together, you began to shed that white coat of Rustoleum fail-proof paint. Perhaps I did not prepare your pink surface well enough for the new paint to adhere. The next spring I repeated the process but with better care. You shed your new coat of paint with even more vigor. All summer long curling strips of the white floated loose exposing your pink skin once again.

I have occasionally wondered where you came from. Who chose to clothe you in a bright piggy-bank pink? Are you trying to tell me something about yourself as you seem to defiantly shed the image I attempt to give you?

As I look at you now in this undignified position, I am reminded of what it is like to be asked to conform to an image or behavior set by someone else. I have lived long enough to know I like who I am at my core. Perhaps, little chair, you are showing your true self in that baked-on pink skin you wear that seems so determined to shine through. Granted, your color sets you apart from others who look just like you. Maybe we are not so different from one another. The older I get, the more I appreciate and celebrate my uniqueness. Am I usurping your chance to be one of a kind?

Okay, you have reminded me how important it is to be true to oneself under all the trappings that get piled on through the wear and tear of life. You have convinced me to quit trying to change your image.

Yes, little chair, I am coming to pick you up and place you on the deck under the eaves of the house to shelter from the winter weather. I pledge that I will remove the remainder of the flaking white paint off your contours. I see how solid and smooth your pink skin is and I will celebrate it. For your seat and back I promise to make a cushion and pillow with a vibrant pink and orange material that will be the envy of every chair in the garden. You have earned the right to be the flashy star on my deck.

# DOUG HICKS

Doug Hicks is a reluctant technologist, now retired and consulting. He's a math graduate of Ohio State, from a time when computers filled entire rooms, and is owned by one cat, Molly. He lives happily with his new wife in Portland but would live in Tuscany in a heartbeat, with his new wife. Currently he is learning to like eggplant and develop compelling characters. Both are a struggle.

# MY LAST FIFTY YEARS

Each of the last fifty summers, I've spent at the lake. I grew up on a lake. It's where I wrote my books, where I found the little bit of peace that is mine to find. The Adirondacks surround us there; loons call and frogs thrum in the night. From the big window in the main camp, we watch storms roll in from the northwest while a fire warms the room.

Changing weather can make for great sailing. But when the wind swirls, trapped against the pine-covered mountains that surround the lake, sailing is all tacking and short reaches. I complain but I delight in it too. Time is hardly noticed with a tiller in hand. If it's true that "God does not count against a man's allotted time those hours he spends sailing," I should live close to forever.

This apparently will not be so. Within the past three years, I have become a prisoner to this body. I sailed, I walked, I danced–oh, how I danced with beautiful Anna Lee–and lived on my own. Now I'm just worn out. I still get along pretty well but it's a struggle to do a lot of things–write legibly, button my shirt, do my taxes, cut my food.

At 92, I'm still able to think. Or so I think. Ha! Is this the sly deceit of memory loss? I'm told I talk constantly. That part of me still works. But most everything else is sore and weak and weary. I grimace and frown now. Wait until everything hurts. You'll understand.

I was good at writing textbooks. It was tedious, leaving little to the imagination, a perfect fit for my singular focus. It was a solitary endeavor and I liked it. I was accountable only to my co-author, my publisher, and myself. I wrote for hours in my study, a Chesterfield burning nearby, punching out the endless instructional materials, first on a manual typewriter, then on the first IBM electrics.

The typewriters are long gone since I moved from the house into a condo, but I never forget their whispering whir and the striking of each letter on the platen. The black Royal had small, shiny black keys on the keyboard, many of the white letters almost rubbed away, and a chrome lever that moved the carriage back to a new line. Does anyone nowadays remember "carriage return" like I do?

I pored over the long galley sheets, writing my changes in the margins. My daughter sometimes slept on the desk near me. I never made anything of that, didn't ever think it was my attention she wanted. It was sweet to have her near, but then I had to write and so she fell asleep. She conceded to my muse, I guess, as did I.

Textbooks put the kids through school and paid for the camp at the lake. And at the camp, I discovered my delight in building things. How I loved the early September days, the chill of New England fall already in the air, when my son and I built the deck out front. Night after night for so many summers thereafter, I sipped a Manhattan while watching the sun set over the west mountain ridge, content until the mosquitoes and no-see-ums chased me inside. The view from above and down the lake is glorious beyond words.

My wife suggested I write a book using sailing as a metaphor for my life. I never much cared about feelings though, never really looked inside. I suspect I made her life lonelier as a result. But in truth she had her demons; we all do. After the war, I earned my PhD and she accepted the cultural expectation of full-time housewife. Alcohol soothed and then ravaged her. Our third child was an attempt to give meaning to her meaning-lost life. I sailed through it all, ignoring the signs of her disease. Yes, I see how the metaphor eludes me in my telling.

Can you tell I'm still alive in here somewhere? How odd to live so long and want to live still longer. Is it selfish not to give up even when the wheels creak so?

And yet what remains to do? There is comfort in the patterns of my life. That is enough most days. I sleep; I eat; I take my meds—I take them exactly when I'm supposed to. My children worry about my certainty about these things. Is it true that I have taken my meds, eaten what I should, done my 300 steps around the living room and kitchen?

And is it true I can still drive? This is where my children and I most disagree.

It's like I am sixteen, pleading to be given the car. The heady freedom it calls forth—now as then—is ultimate indicator of grown-up responsibility. I tell my children, I can get in and out and manage the walker; I can see and respond—all the requisites. I admit, only to myself, to a faltering confidence that I'm always in control and attentive. This is their concern, a reasonable one it is, but not one I will acknowledge. I rely on bluster and emotional persuasion. And rank. How could you, I intimate. I'm your father!

I wish I could be amused by all this. The aches and pains draw my mouth into a tight-lipped smile. I'm not comfortable with my body anymore. I shuffle here and there, my feet uninterested in moving too much. I'm afraid of the next fall, the one that will be my last. Death isn't welcome, but the uncertain, slow decline isn't much better.

Still, I know if I slow down, whatever it is will catch up with me faster. So I keep moving, keep trying to do all the things I've done before.

It was the slightest edge of a throw rug that caught my toe. My walker offered no help when I began to fall. My legs and arms didn't respond. As I looked up from the floor, I went into mild shock, aware I was probably not going to be okay this time. They brought me to this place a month ago.

You get used to being handled, undressed, toileted. Dignity is hardly possible. So I go along with the regimen, less willingly as I get better. When I think enough of my strength has returned, I get cranky about going back home. Can't they see I'm unhappy here? Can't they see I'm ready to leave?

I've been so tired lately; everything is such a chore. It feels good to just lie here. "You can go," my family said last night. "We'll be fine." I feel good about that, that they'll be okay. I'd like to sail again but there's no more wind. So I wait for my time to go.

# A PROGRAMMER'S MEDITATION

I smile and type the quirky codes
That bring to life a virtual realm
To simplify, uncomplicate
A hurried world that overwhelms.

As master of this universe
I choose its colors and terrain
The placements and the look and feel,
The rules defining this domain.

A certain hubris visits me.
I think the world is mine to change.
Through technologic certainty
And sciences beyond arcane.

Before my ones to zeros turn,
I'll come perhaps to see the truth:
A minor god is all I am,
A vessel only, for God's use.

# CONNIE ICENOGLE

Connie Icenogle. I was born in Seattle, Washington, during WWII; my family lived in Billings, Montana, until 1956, when we moved back to Seattle. I became interested in writing in junior high, and was on the student staff of the student newspaper at Ballard High in Seattle. I raised two sons and worked various jobs while the boys were growing up, though being home with them was my priority. When the youngest graduated from high school, I decided to expand my skills, took a semester of business classes at Clark College and eventually became Personnel Director for field employees of Realvest Corporation. After retirement, I was pleased to see there was opportunity to register for the Creative Writing class for seniors at Clark College and I am now in my second year with the class.

# THE LITTLE BROWN HOUSE

The little brown house sits abandoned on a corner lot at a busy intersection. Forgotten and ignored by many, yet in plain view of hundreds of drivers and passengers, bike riders and pedestrians. How could its existence be so vague? What history could it tell if only it could talk? Where are the builders who constructed it? Where are the people whose lives it sheltered during the harsh autumn, winter and early spring storms?

A metal stove pipe rises straight and steady from the roof top. Did it keep its people warm? Offer a place to cook hot meals and have clean, wet clothes hanging nearby to dry? The scratches on the door jamb—could they have been made by a family dog? The marks on an inside door frame—could they have been markers of a child's growth?

There is a porch at the side of the house, a boot and shoe scraper embedded in the concrete step. Could it have scraped the mud from the boots of a hard-working man? The man, glad to be welcomed home to the warmth of the three-room house, greeted by his wife and child, the top of the wood stove holding a pot of beef stew. Fresh vegetables from the garden, grown in the hardscrabble earth surrounding the little brown house, simmering in the pot.

The garden was tended by his wife and child. Planted with seeds carefully placed; buckets of precious water were carried from a long-forgotten well by the woman and child, careful not to spill a drop for it was needed to irrigate the plants that will rise from the carefully tilled and tended soil into a harvest of fruits and vegetables, to be consumed by the family year round after careful preserving.

Who remembers the love that poured forth from the little brown house? Where are the people who lived here? Does anyone care that the stone foundation that once held the house level now sags at one corner making it tilt to one side a little? Who shuttered the doors and windows so intruders can't get in?

Will anyone care if a homeless family takes refuge in the little brown house on the corner? What if they remove the wood that covers the doors and windows, clean up the stove pipe and start a warm fire in the stove to cook their meals, and sleep nearby. Will anyone care if they stay and shore up the foundation? Will anyone notice that they cleaned the windows to let the sunshine in? Will it be all right if they plant a small vegetable garden near the back door and some flowers by the front steps? Will anyone care if the little brown house comes alive with a family lovingly living in it again? Will you notice the love and care the little brown house is offering to a family? Will you care?

# MY MOTHER'S HANDS

A memory stands out in my mind: my mother's hands. Mom has beautiful hands. I have always thought so.

She worked hard with her hands. Her hands were in hot water, cold water, bleach water and cleaning water, bread dough, pie dough, cookie dough and Play-Doh. You could find her washing diapers, hanging wash, and preparing food for her family, her hands were always busy.

Mom played hard with her hands, too. She taught us to play jacks and marbles, she helped us comb our doll's hair and dress our dolls, with those tiny little buttons, snaps and ribbons. Her hands could handle any challenge with ease.

Mom took time for herself by manicuring her fingernails. She would file, trim and polish. Her fingers are long and narrow. She has pretty "moons" and she assured me that as I grew older I too would have pretty moons. I'm still waiting, at the age of 65, to be old enough to have them. Mom polished her nails daily. The most opportune time for her to do her nails was while she was talking on the phone. To this day she keeps her nail supplies in a drawer by the telephone, within convenient reach.

When I was a child and sick with a fever, nothing felt better than Mom's cool hand on my forehead, assuring me that I would be okay. She could bring assurance to my hesitations with her steady hand in mine. Oh, she could bring me into line when I was naughty too, with her hand placed firmly on my bottom!

What a thrill it is, when we share a quiet moment together, to reach out and touch those hands that always brought great comfort my way. Mother's hands are not as strong now. She can't wring out a heavy wet sweater that has just been washed and this bothers her. Her hands feel fragile in mine. Arthritis has brought bends to them where they were straight before. She has had surgery on some of her fingers to straighten them and relieve the pain arthritis has plagued her with.

She doesn't like the look or feel of her hands any more, but she still keeps them manicured and lotioned. They have been a comfort to her for many years, as well as to my siblings and me. Mother's hands bring peace to my mind as I touch them, think of them, and see them. I consider my mother's hands two of my best friends.

# JANE JACKSON

Jane Jackson. I have a BA degree in art, a Masters in Library Science and a second Masters in Education. My first real jobs were as a case worker in the inner city of Detroit, Michigan, and later as a permanent substitute. I became fascinated with how people solve life's challenges, a quest that has taken me to live in New England, the deep South, and now the Columbia Gorge. Today I have a dual career as a park ranger at a national park, and as a librarian, most recently in Louisiana. The work I love most is as a costumed storyteller.

# SHE TOLD ME . . .

A gray October day,
My mind dull with busy routine,
My complacency was disrupted.
She told me a tale of horror, shock and disbelief:

"One day as I worked at the hotel,
A huge wave approached.
I ran upstairs.
The wave crept after me.
I ran outside and up a hill.
To my dismay, the wave reached me.
I grabbed a tree and clung.

"As the water receded, I saw the road ahead.
In fright, I realized that the other people
Who had been in the water were dead.
I climbed up to the road past them.
A rescue truck came.
I squeezed aboard.

"When I returned to the hotel, I saw I was listed as dead.

"I became a refugee in California and then in Portland .
I like Portland, have friends, and a good job.
I learned to drive and bought a car."

Abruptly, she paused.
Then detailed her parents' deaths.
Wondered why she told me she was a Sri Lankan tsunami
survivor.
Confided her brother was pressuring her to return to Sri Lanka.

She said no more.
She, her brother and friends
Drove off in her late-model American car.

# DAVID

David, David I miss you!
The email subject line read
"Bonneville employee passes."
I wondered if I knew the employee.
Then with horror, I read your name.

Lying peacefully in your bed
Closed your eyes and never woke.
Sickness came years before.
Heart medicine prescribed in vain.
You left us distraught.

We depended on you too much.
You captured all audiences' hearts
With your charismatic descriptions
Of natural and managed environments
You inspired each of us.

David, David you showed us how
To tell a complex story.
To explain how electrons
Can dance from copper atom to copper atom
To illustrate how electricity can gush from water's flow.

David, David I miss you!
You inspired each of us.
Children were mesmerized.
All of us were fascinated.

Postscript:
In the months since you left us,
The work you did with sensitivity,
We divided between us.
Your programs evolve.

Others speak your puppet-show lines.
Silence replaces your laugh.
No more frequent teasing,
Tenseness permeates our cave-like office.
The reality of your death
Cuts sharp as we look at your desk:
Bulletin board vacant
Computer off.

Phone soundless.
Death is final.

Closure:
David!  A majestic Noble Fir,
Planted one Sunday evening,
Honors and symbolizes your accomplishments.

# HEALING

Skin regenerates and heals.
Scars witness life's adventures.
Which is more important?
Experience?  Or facial flaws?

Perhaps this child grows up
To understand that fate
Can bring opportunities
For deeper vision and insight.

Who has more wisdom?
The person who has faced life's challenges
Or the one who has lived a sheltered life?

# CROSSING THE CONTINENTAL DIVIDE

After months of worry, paperwork, preparation,
Pick-up tuned up, new tires, route mapped,
Food, water, blankets, uniforms, and extra clothing packed.

I arrived at my long anticipated challenge,
The Continental Divide!
Sign said, "8391 feet elevation."
I had never been this high except in an airplane.

Sun shone on snow peaked mountains, grassy hills, and meadows.
My gas-pedal foot touched the floor.
My speed was below the speed limit, 45 miles per hour,
Cars whizzed by, honked.

I had the insecurity of starting something new –
I felt like I was about to start high school, college, or graduate school.
Would I succeed? Would I finish? Would I like the Northwest?

Eastern Oregon mountains worse, I recall.
Finally I reached the Pacific Northwest.
I found my new job the next morning.
I discovered that people were as curious to meet me as I them.

# COMPETITIVE SIBLINGS

"Jane! Why don't you visit?"
"Jeff! Will you be home this weekend?"
Drove from New Hampshire to Georgia.
Reminisced about our competitive childhood.

I pointed to his cowlicks,
"You have horns on your head."
Would people still ask, "Who is older?"
"I am," I would brag.
When I entered high school,
I boasted, "I am older,
AND I weigh more, 93 pounds,
And am taller, five feet three inches."

At our reunion in Georgia,
I noticed his cowlicks were gone
Everyone had gray hair.

Would anyone still ask
"Who is older?"
The question came up!
He said, "I'm older, I'm the fossil."
Then confessed that as a child,
He dreamed to be older, taller, and heavier.
We looked at each other–these contests no long matter.

# WINTER FISH LADDER

Gently, back and forth, the steelhead sways.
Its greenish streamlined body bedecked with black spots.
A rose-colored band flows across the body and highlights the head.
Blunt, square shaped tail acts like a paddle.
As if waltzing, swim constantly to keep up with the water flow,
Then dart quick when startled by humans.
The bullet-like head pierces the water.
They have swum thousands of miles in the ocean.
While they return to their natal home, they eat no more.

They bear the scars of their travels, escapes, and age:
Scales scraped off and infections inflate their flesh;
Did a fisherman release and accidentally injure a fish?
Is a fish hook, line, or bobber still attached to tell an escape story?
These fish are survivors determined to produce the next generation.

In fall, their primordial companions are the sturgeon.
Can they live more than 100 years and weigh 1,500 pounds?
Primitive black and white bony plates, scutes, march from head to tail.
They appear and disappear between fish ladder structures.
A park visitor stares and declares that this one would be good smoked.
Another says baked would be best.
In winter, only steelhead can be seen swaying rhythmically.
They wait for spring to depart.

As the spring water temperature rises, Spring Chinook appear.
Fishermen crowd the Columbia River shore and salivate.
Next come Sockeye and fishermen drool.

Shad come in great numbers, but picky Western taste buds do not bother.

So few survive to return and spawn.
Who should eat these fish?
The fishermen? The eagles? The osprey? The seals and sea lions?
Who knows?
Cartoons will be created.
Editorials will be written.
Laws will be enacted.

# BECKY LEVENTIS

Becky Leventis. I was raised on a farm in the foothills of the Blue Mountains of Eastern Washington. My background includes Whitman College, living in Hawaii and on the East Coast, and moving with my family to Vancouver in the 1970s. For 20 years I sold skylights and for a time designed and built houses. I've always loved art and currently teach watercolor painting.

# PINK CARNATIONS IN A BLACK & WHITE WORLD

On the same day each year, I would wake up to a world of white outside my window. Icicles dripped from beneath our eaves and as far as I could see a deep blanket of white covered everything. A beautiful stillness had come to this normally noisy world. The only thing I could hear was the soft sound of the river in the distance. Even our black Labrador would be huddled inside her heated doghouse. To walk around in this cold world was delightful, with each step making a crunching noise as the crust gave way beneath my boots.

Inside our home, Mom was always busy in the kitchen, preparing. Preparing for this special day.

Slowly up our driveway, in this world of white, came a large black Buick. Out stepped the older woman dressed in black coat and black boots. As our black Lab rushed to greet her, out came a bouquet of beautiful bright pink carnations. I never knew which was pinker, her cheeks rosy from the cold, or those beautiful fragrant flowers—so precious in the dead of winter.

These memories are as sharp as if they happened yesterday. For you see, this day in this special world of contrasts was my day, the day I had been born.

# VOICES FROM ANOTHER WORLD

Every summer night when we went to bed, Dad would open the bedroom windows. Slowly the sounds of the quiet evenings would drift in—the crickets, the nearby river, the occasional roaming barn cat, the horses snorting down in their corral. The warm summer breezes would enter gently through the windows, fluttering the curtains ever so slightly. The black velvet of the night would envelope the room. Other people and other worlds seemed a million miles away as I lay there in my bed.

Many nights I used to lie there and wonder what my life would be like when I grew up. Where would I live? Who would I marry? Would I always live in the country? What were other teenagers doing in other areas of the country?

One summer my grandparents gave me something new for the nightstand by my bed. It was a shiny radio with a face that glowed green in the darkness. The newfangled lever would shut itself off at a designated time. RCA had done itself proud. As I quickly discovered, the sounds of the night life, the big time, THE city—San Francisco—came in clearly on the strongest station on the West Coast, KGO. That summer and summers after that I would quietly turn on KGO to listen to what that other part of the world was doing. Was there a girl like me in San Francisco who listened to the radio before SHE went to sleep? What was her life like, hundreds of miles away in the city.

Years later, as a grown woman, I was in San Francisco on a warm summer night. I remembered all the evenings I had listened to the city. Was there a little farm girl out there still listening?

# THREE ANGELS

What is your idea of an angel? A human form with wings that comes down from heaven to help us out? Or is your idea completely different? Mine is.

When I walk down the street and look at other people, I wonder–are you the one? Or you? Or you? Are you large or small, black or white, young and timid, old and bold?

I will never know you, nor you me, but I will never forget you. The thought of you will live inside my brain for as long as I live, in my heart for as long as it beats. You were my salvation, you kept me alive when all else failed. A part of you is a part of me. Forever will be. Your blood courses with mine through my being. For you were my donor, along with two other souls, who saved me from death.

I WILL remember you with each living breath.

# CHARLOTTE LEWIS

Charlotte Lewis, a retired accountant, lives and works in Vancouver, Washington. Besides writing, Charlotte enjoys reading, knitting and spending time with friends and family. She is active in her church and community. When her grandson Jerry returned from Iraq he built a website for her. Please visit Charlotte at charlotttelewisonline.com.

# ATONEMENT

Carl Naden has been my doctor for more than forty years. But he knows little about my past beyond the forty years. At the moment, he believes I am dying. My husband and I were in an auto accident–a real doozie. I didn't recognize the car I'd owned for four years even after the paramedic pointed it out to me. Of course the fire department had pried me from its grasp and I am sure the car is some the worse for that. I was angered at first with the driver that hit us. He was driving drunk, for pete's sake. He totaled his truck and our car. Mark, my husband, had the car serviced the day before the accident. It had been a beautiful car. Now it isn't good for much–probably not even parts. In my younger days I would have been really upset; $200 for service, the car was paid for and now it's in the junk yard. I heard one of the EMTs say the driver died. What a total shame–makes the loss of the car a minimal situation.

As I have aged, I have mellowed. And what I once was is long gone. I have tried to be a good citizen, to do what is right, to protect the environment. I can be grumpy at times, especially when the arthritis makes my joints cry out in pain. I try to be even tempered; be the good guy.

But now Carl thinks I should be making peace with my Maker. He is sure I am going to die. In forty years he's suggested white wine over red, more exercise and less pastry but never to make peace with anyone let alone my Maker.

Dr. Naden is in the hallway now talking with my children. I saw them come in, one by one, half an hour ago. I can just barely hear the drone of his voice–a calm dulcet tone. Carl is one of those old-fashioned family doctors that are gradually disappearing. He's in his late 70s, snow white hair, wicked wit, good friend. His office is two blocks from our home. Mark told him if he ever wanted to stop by after office hours for a dip in the pool or a drink, he'd be welcome anytime. Over the years, especially after his wife died, his visits were almost weekly. Yes, he's a good friend as well as our doctor.

I am sure he's saying they'll keep me comfortable until the end. He told me the damaged spleen was the least of my worries. He removed it but said everything else inside me was mangled more than a bit. I asked about my husband, Mark, but Carl just continued to harp on my imminent demise. "It is inevitable," he said. "Make your peace, Margaret, make your peace."

He must know I haven't always been a miserable old woman. What reason does he have to believe I need to make peace with anyone?

Make peace with God? God and I have had an understanding for years. I won't trouble Him with my petty concerns and He won't require me to make any last minute death bed prayers for salvation or redemption, or whatever. Make peace? Have I hurt anyone, other than myself, so badly that I need to make peace with Him now. I hope not.

Damn, here comes that nurse. I want to see my family, not that starched white pillar of humanity. What's that she's saying? Her mouth seems to be in slow motion. "Your granddaughter brought you a CD she burned especially for you. She says she remembers most of this music from her growing up at your house." The nurse slipped the CD into a small portable unit I hadn't noticed before.

I'm not sure she is waiting for an answer but I'll just wiggle my fingers a bit. Good, there she goes.

Nursie didn't say which granddaughter. I have four. Well, if it's something I'm supposed to like it's probably from Jennifer. She's the only one not into rap, hip hop or heavy metal. And she's the only one who might know what I like. She did live with us for a spell while she was in high school. Did I play a lot of music when she was there? I don't recall.

What's that music? An overture! Dum dum de dum—good Lord, it's the overture from Poet and Peasant. I haven't heard that in a very long time. In fact, when did I hear it last?

That long, eh, Margaret? Remember George Andres–that little mustached bartender from Canada? He was so hung up on me I nearly had to give up drinking, or change bars. George was so ardent. He wanted to marry me and was convinced the Poet and Peasant Overture would be the perfect music for the wedding. My God! I guess I was rather brutal there at the end. George Andres. What memories. I can't believe how long this overture is. Hurry up–be done with it. I don't want to remember George. I left him standing at the altar. Never looked back, until now. Maybe I do have some atoning to do. But be reasonable, I was only twenty-two. I have no idea where George might be. I think he went back to Montreal.

Slaughter on Tenth Avenue–how I love this piece. Don't recall hearing it for a while. Years, in fact. No one plays it anymore. There was a piano man at a bar who played it–I was so young I had to ask the title. Oh cripes, Jerry Pell. I met him at that bar, the Velvet Turtle. What a dancer he was. He used to tell everyone he was five feet 18 inches tall. He towered more than a foot over me. That man chased me for years. He didn't want to give up. I should have Jennifer go through my cedar chest and throw out all of his love letters before her mother finds them. Oh, what the hell! I'll be dead and gone. What difference will it make if my daughter finds love letters from men other than her father? I was young once. Her Dad will laugh and say something witty–"Your Mom always had a way with the guys." Or something like that. I believe my daughter Beth has always regarded me as a drab old woman. Let her be surprised. Still, maybe I do have some atoning to do. I wasn't cruel to Jerry–I just shut him down. We kept in touch for several years. A few Christmases ago my card was returned marked "deceased." I called his son, Chuck, and he said Jerry had died in a VA Hospital that October.

Rhapsody in Blue–a favorite of mine and of Jim's. Jim Clark, service writer at the dealership where I bought my first new car. How long ago was that? Fifty years? Jim was not only handsome but a bit frisky under the covers. I was surprised to learn he was married. He never mentioned it and I never asked. I saw no ring. As I recall, his wife left him when she learned about me. He should have told me he was married or at least worn his wedding band. I heard through the grapevine that it was an ugly divorce and he blamed me. Hey, Buddy, it takes two to tango. But maybe I do have some atoning to do. Why is my face wet? I can't see the tissues and I don't want to ring for the nurse. My heavens, why am I crying? For loves lost or for the terrible way I cut them loose? Damn. Is dying supposed to be this emotional? I wish someone would come in and shut off that CD. How can one little disk have so many reminders? Memories?

An aria from Madam Butterfly. Sam Davis had never been to an opera. He was a world-class chef but had no taste outside his kitchen. His beautiful red hair had caught my attention. I don't recall who moved on who first. We had some good times together. He loved the horses and we spent two or three afternoons every week at the racetrack before he headed to the restaurant for his evening shift. Months into the relationship, I asked him to accompany me to the opera. My, my, how handsome he was all dressed up! It was great fun while it lasted. Sam's friends told me I was wasting my time. He wasn't the marrying kind. I told them that neither was I. I wasn't ready, then, to settle down. Turned out, he was the marrying kind. It broke my heart but I walked away from him. He hounded me–sent tickets to other operas, concerts; I had to quit going to the racetrack. He seemed to be everywhere I went. Once he proposed it was all over as far as I was concerned. I reminded him we had an agreement: this was fun and games–no seriousness allowed. He begged me to reconsider. I did–it wouldn't work.

Everyone blamed me when his car, with him inside, took a header off Mulholland Drive one summer night. I had nothing to do with that. He was a grown man.

Maybe I do have some atoning to do.

Chopin something or other in C sharp minor. I can never remember the name of this piece but I love it when it gets to the part that sounds like "I'm always chasing rainbows." Henry Wolf gave me an album or two, or was it three, of Chopin. We used to sit at his club close to the piano sipping very dry martinis and munching crab cakes. Henry paid the pianist to learn this piece. I don't mean tipped him to play it; I mean actually paid him to buy the sheet music and learn it. Henry was sure hung up on Chopin. I remember how upset he was when he stopped by my apartment one evening unannounced and found Simon and Garfunkel blaring from my stereo. The ensuing argument was totally ridiculous but, once he started it, I was determined to finish it. I wonder whatever happened to Henry? I know he was at the Betty Ford Clinic for a while. Was that my fault? No, of course not, he was a drinker long before I met him.

But maybe I do have some atoning to do.

Oh! What a Beautiful Morning from Oklahoma. Finally something I can listen to with fond memories. Mark and I saw the stage play *Oklahoma* and then *Fiddler on the Roof* at the Dorothy Chandler. And then he asked me to marry him. I have never loved one person so deeply in all my life. I have no atoning to do here. I have been a good and faithful wife to Mark for over forty years. We go to concerts and plays and we still dance. The knees and the backs protest sometimes, but we dance anyway. Life has been good to me.

So why are the tears still flowing?

Because I realize I am not ready to die. I have another song to hear; another tune to dance to. I wish they'd let Mark come to visit. I figured as we are married, we could share the same hospital room. An auto accident shouldn't keep us apart. Maybe he's not as badly injured so doesn't need to be hospitalized. I wonder where he is? He was taken from the accident scene in a separate ambulance. Watch—the two bills will be outrageous. We could have at least shared an ambulance.

Here comes that damn nurse again. Ah! She's giving the CD to Jennifer. Good, I've done all the remembering I care to do. What is she doing now? Unhooking the IVs? Why is she unhooking the IVs? Here come my children. They will tell me what's going on. I should thank Jennifer the CD, even if it did make me cry.

"What happened? Didn't she want to hear the CD?"

"She did wiggle a finger. I believe she understood me. But the portable wouldn't play the CD."

"She looks so peaceful. How could she just slip away like that?"

"It happens sometimes. The heart just quits."

"Why are there tears on her face? Was she in pain?"

"No. I'm sure she wasn't. Tears are a natural phenomenon at death sometimes."

"Do you think she knows Daddy was killed instantly?"

"I don't think so. She asked for him constantly while she could still talk."

"Margaret, what took you so long? I've been waiting for you."

"Mark? Oh, my love, you should have come for me sooner."

# DAWN TO DUSK

The time from dawn to dusk is short. Not quite a twinkling of the eye but close. Time slips away.

Dawn arrived more than 90 years ago. Is that a twinkling of the eye? Not hardly. But, at the same time, it is not so long ago. The dawn of my years went quickly. From infant, knowing nothing, to teen knowing all. It was a glorious time, as I recall.

Learning to read was such a thrill! Before I began school I was reading backs of boxes in mother's cupboard. Dick and Jane–rather exciting at first but boring before I was out of first grade. My fourth grade teacher had been in the Army!

Winning the fifth grade spelling bee and beating out Mary Louise Dyer was one of my finest moments. Auditioning for the seventh grade choir and actually reading the words was a triumph. The audition piece was "I've Been Working on the Railroad." Everyone knows the words, right? But they are different on paper than in most people's memories. Yes, that was a triumph.

Climbing a rope swing with two of my brothers was exciting. I was eleven; they were younger. The rope swing belonged to the big kids of the neighborhood. It was too dangerous for us. I shinnied up the tree to the Y where the knot of the swing was kept. I soared almost as high as the tree tops and could see for miles. I didn't break anything when I fell. Yes, it was a definite triumph. Keeping the secret from my parents for nearly forty years was another triumph.

Graduating top of my senior class–such memories. My Aunt Della gave me yellow roses as a graduation gift. How grown up can you get? The girls wore white robes; the boys wore blue. Pomp & Circumstance still brings tears to my eyes.

Mid-morning of my life came to me in college. I met a fascinating man there. After we both had graduated, we married. Mid-morning was a difficult time, often. Keeping house, cooking two meals a day, plus the laundry–well, I hadn't trained well enough at home to do these tasks easily. Although I always had chores at home, I never had been totally responsible. Learning to juggle tasks was more difficult than earning my degree. It took a while. And then I was delivered of my first child. Everything else seemed simple in comparison. But we all survived. I shudder now to think what a poor excuse I was as a mother. My baby frequently didn't wear shoes. His face wasn't always clean. But he was well fed. And he grew.

The second child was no easier. She was born with several medical problems. Children numbers three and four were delights. By the time they arrived, I had a handle on the motherhood idea. They didn't wear shoes all the time either.

It was about noon in my life when my children graduated from high school and went off to college. I decided it was time to use my college education for more than deciphering recipes and found a job outside the house. With only my husband and me at home, life was easy. The chores I had found so hard just two decades prior were done almost without thinking. I had developed into a good cook–not just a passable cook but a good cook. Life was great. We enjoyed weekend trips and long vacations. We traveled and saw a great portion of the world. We renewed our passports several times as we never lost our wanderlust.

Mid-afternoon hit with the first grandchild. How could I have grandchildren when I was so young? It made no sense to me. Grandparents are supposed to be old, wrinkled, gray-haired. I was none of those.

I did enjoy being a grandmother, however, and even took up knitting. I knitted for each grandchild as he came into the world and then knitted sweaters for Christmas and birthdays. When the grandchildren came to visit, we baked cookies. I acted the grandmother part even though I didn't look it. I enjoyed it. The best part was being able to return the child and sit down to rest. As they grew, my grandchildren shared their adventures with me. High school, college, marriage. "What was it like in your day, Grams?" It was fun to remember and share.

Late afternoon of my life arrived when my spouse of sixty-plus years died. How he had the audacity to do that to me I'll never know. He gave no warning. He died one afternoon on the golf course. The 13th hole. I was in a fog for several days. While he had thought ahead and made plans, I was still in shock that he would die first. For some reason, I was sure I'd be the first to go. I vaguely remember going through all the rituals of death. After the fog cleared, I sat myself down and revised my own end-of-life instructions. I rewrote my will and made major changes in my financial plans. I was then ready to go on with my life, get back into the groove of living.

I was surprised to find things are different when you are single, widowed. People treat you differently. It's as if your sudden marital change is a deadly disease. I slogged through late afternoon for many years. I needed things to do and began volunteering my time. First at church, then at the church school, then wherever it was apparent an old woman could be useful. I developed a routine. But it has become a rut. I want out. I'm tired.

I realize that now I am in the dusk, the twilight of my life. Things have slowed down. Several chores are difficult, again. I no longer cook for the joy of cooking. I don't feel adventurous—some days just getting to the mailbox is a major achievement.

As the sun sets on my life, I know I am one of the fortunate. I've had a long, full life. While things often could have been worse, they could never have been better.

Dawn to dusk—my life has been good.

# A POEM FOR AUTUMN

Annually there is a race
In the autumn of the year
When Mother Nature shows her face
And Father Time his rear.

The days are shortened, tick by tick.
The winds blow strong and cold.
The trees are then quite quick
To change from green to red and gold.

It's hard to tell when autumn ends,
Though the calendar gives a date.
As Mother Nature oft pretends
And makes winter lie in wait.

The cold, brisk days of autumn clearly
Make us love the sun more dearly.

# HUGH LEWIS

Hugh Lewis. I have spent many years on the veterinary faculties of the University of Pennsylvania and Purdue University, eventually retiring as Dean of The School of Veterinary Medicine and Professor of Veterinary Pathology at Purdue in 1996. For the last 12 years I have been part of the leadership team that developed Banfield, The Pet Hospital, a national veterinary practice with hospitals in almost every state in the US, as well as in Mexico City. Mair, my wife of 45 years, is also Welsh, and we have two sons. Although in retirement, I am still busy with veterinary projects and I have started to write a medical mystery novel that has been in my head for many years. The stories for Elderberry Wine were written as homework for the creative writing course I attended at Clark College, my most recent Alma Mater.

# I BELIEVE IN FATE

As a youngster in Grammar School I was large for my age and an all-around athlete. I was on the swim team, the rugby team, the cricket team, the athletic team (sprinter, long distance walker, javelin thrower), and even the chess team. I stopped growing when I was fourteen, but all my contemporaries didn't. I had always been the one to beat–and beaten I was. By senior year I was only on the chess and debating teams.

During my heyday I had to train fiercely: one mile of swimming plus various sprints before 6 am, 5 days a week; intense circuit training at lunchtime; weight training and specific team training after class. I built up an impressive muscle mass I was fit, I mean really fit. However, by senior year I had developed an intense hatred of exercise.

After Grammar School, and in the absence of organized or mandated exercise programs, my vast amount of muscle gradually turned into a vast amount of fat. I tried various diets rich in either fruits or vegetables to help me lose the fat. But, I loved fruit and ate a lot of it, maybe too much because I didn't lose weight. I also liked veggies but had to back off when I started to chew the cud and had to have an operation for an impacted displaced abomasum. So, there was nothing left but to bite the bullet and start an exercise program.

I joined a racquet-ball and exercise club and took up golf and skiing. Several years later I had scars on my knees from three operations, chronic backache, sciatica, tendinitis in both hands, bursitis in my right shoulder–and a big belly. I tried to claim that the belly was due to a space-occupying lesion rather than fat–until I was diagnosed with large tumors on both kidneys. They were excised but the belly didn't go down. I had to face it, I was obese!

The tendinitis in my hands was caused by lifting weights and particularly affected the small finger on my left hand, and the center two fingers on my right hand. When the inflammation was active, these fingers would lock in the bent position, but would occasionally and suddenly pop up unbidden. While recovering from one such bout I attended an auction of used exercise equipment with my wife. (I'm a glutton for punishment!) As always, I rested my arm along the back of my wife's chair as it eased my bursitis.

And then an interesting piece of equipment came up for bid: it was a vibration platform which apparently had been used by the Dallas Cowboys to speed up muscle healing following injury. They found that it was also effective for shedding excess fat. One just stood on it and enjoyed the vibration for ten minutes a day for maximal benefit. My ears pricked up when I heard this. I've long been interested in any concept that involved passive exercise. One of my fingers must have popped up at the critical moment and sealed the winning bid, because suddenly the platform was mine. My wife was aghast and wanted me to explain to the auctioneer what had happened, and refuse delivery of the platform, which was huge. But I believe in fate.

# A JOLLY GOOD SHOW

Several universities in the UK have Royal Air Force programs on campus. The University Air Squadrons are essentially a recruitment mechanism for future RAF leaders. Students selected for membership (it is highly competitive) are trained as pilot officers, receive a stipend, and are obligated to attend regular lectures, flight training sessions, and summer assignments at RAF facilities around the world. The program is similar to the American ROTC programs.

My paternal uncle had taught me to fly when I was 16 (he was a Spitfire ace in WWII) so I was attracted to the idea of joining the Air Squadron–particularly when I learned that they paid you to fly and the Squadron HQ had a reputation as the numero uno party place on campus. I was lucky to be chosen for the squadron and my social life improved immediately.

That first summer (1961) the squadron spent a month at an airbase in Norfolk England. It had been a bomber base during WWII, but now was used mostly for flight training on English Electric P1's (a jet fighter plane known as the "Lightning" with a similar performance profile to the F-15, only predating it by 18 years). We were flying the much slower and less formidable DeHavilland Chipmunks, and it was initially unnerving to be on the approach leg only to have a P1 screaming in overhead and landing before you.

It was traditional before the end of the summer to pull a prank so the RAF brass would remember your squadron. The previous year, another university squadron had caused havoc by redirecting all the signposts in a 20-mile radius of the base, but we thought that was sophomoric (a term I learnt after coming to the USA). During the summer we had visited the RAF Fighter Command HQ, only about 15 miles from our base. Outside the main HQ building two missiles stood guard. They were about 11 feet tall and bolted upright to posts either side of the entrance. They were presumably not armed with warheads, but merely emblematic of the mission of Fighter Command. A few of us suggested that we relocate one of them to our base, suspend it below a Chipmunk and take a group photo. The idea became our squadron prank.

Late one evening during our last week at the base, the "acquisition team" drove in convoy to Fighter Command. There were eight of us in three cars. Mine was an Austin-Healy Sprite, the only open car in the squadron, and we planned to use it to transport the missile, wrapped in a blanket, back to our base. We drove around the perimeter of the base and parked at the far end, away from most of the buildings. We fanned out to reconnoitre, agreeing to meet up at the car in two hours.

We discovered two perimeter fences topped with barbed wire, approximately 30 yards apart. There were two gates, both manned, and guards with Alsatian dogs patrolled the space between them each hour. We divided into three groups: two of us would help the others scale the outer fence and then stay behind with the vehicles; two more would stay inside the inner fence to monitor the patrols; the remaining four would proceed to HQ, unbolt the missile and carry it back.

Everything went like clockwork and we made it back to the cars in less than two hours. I'll never forget the sight of the missile sticking out of my car, its tail fins glinting in the moonlight as we drove along the back roads of Norfolk. The return was uneventful and we took the missile straight to the hangar and strapped it under the fuselage of a Chipmunk.

Early next morning we were gathered around the missile taking photographs when three large black cars screeched to a halt just outside of the hangar. A dozen or so men in identical long black leather coats (honest!) jumped out and confronted us. We were herded into the canteen and interviewed one at a time. The outcome was that all eight of us were taken back to Fighter Command, along with the missile. Later that morning, in the office of the Air Chief Marshall in charge of Fighter Command, we were told to stand to attention and wait for him.

He kept us waiting for 20 minutes and then strode into the room with a face like thunder. His eyes flashed, his lips curled, and his handlebar mustache twitched with anger. He stood before us and gave each of us a withering glare.

"Have you idiots any idea what you've done?" he snarled. "You broke into one of this country's most closely guarded bases and removed a missile, for God's sake! This is a huge embarrassment for us. This is my Command's HQ. If this gets into the newspapers it will cause a huge fuss—questions will be raised in the Commons, the Russians will sneer, and we'll all probably lose rank, or worse. As pilot officers in Her Majesty's Royal Air Force, what on earth were you thinking? You will all spend the rest of the day on this base and be dealt with as appropriate!

"Dismissed!"

As we filed out of his office feeling small and contrite, several of us thought we heard him say under his breath, "Jolly good show chaps!"

This was confirmed, I believe, because we each got to sit in and examine a Lightning later that day, and to spend time in the P1 simulator before being driven back to our base. No news leaked out and no further action was taken.

Unfortunately, none of the other squadrons ever got to marvel at our prank—you are the first to know!

# THE DINNER GUEST

Several months after arriving in America to take up a Residency position in the University of Pennsylvania's School of Veterinary Medicine, I had a remarkable piece of luck. The owner of one of the horses I was caring for told me of a farmhouse on his estate that needed a tenant: would I be interested? At the time we were happily renting an apartment in the town close to the Large Animal Center, but we went along to look at it anyway.

The owner turned out to be married to a DuPont heiress, and the estate was part of an 80-square-mile game preserve flanking the south side of the Brandywine River and extending from Chadds Ford in Pennsylvania, down to Centerville in Delaware. The farmhouse for rent was on a rise overlooking the Brandywine and girded by beautiful pastureland. The scene was idyllic. The rental part turned out to be the crossbar of a T-shaped mansion; the old couple who had farmed the land for the previous 40 years lived in the stem. "Our" part was three stories high, had a large lounge, a library, three bedrooms plus a full cellar. The kitchen and dining area was originally the ballroom, with a large chandelier and windows on three sides. The two largest windows were plate glass, extended from ceiling to floor and could be raised up into the walls creating a step-through onto the covered porch that surrounded the house. The farm itself was about 360 acres and used mainly for raising Guernsey heifers for the home farm, as well as pheasants for release on the Preserve. Best of all, the rent was only $80 per month. We said we would have it and moved in that weekend. We lived there for eleven years.

Over the years we accumulated an assortment of animals: Buck, our Lab-Malamute cross; Roger, our male Nubian goat; Rickety, a thoroughbred stallion; Dodi, our miniature Doberman; Alfie, our three-legged Afghan hound; several cats and chickens; and Bonaparte, our one-legged gamecock. This story concerns Alfie and Bonaparte.

Alfie came to us because his owner refused to take him back after we had amputated a front leg that was severely damaged in a car accident. He did look awkward when walking but had no problem running. Alfie's coat was typically Afghan-fluffy and always covered with burrs, so we kept it clipped short, except around his head. His single front limb was transposed by use to the middle of his chest. He used to sit in the driveway waiting for me to come home, looking like a huge sunflower.

Bonaparte was a French gamecock who had been savaged by a dog, and had lost one of his legs. He was always seeking warmth and liked to snuggle up to one of the dogs, or to stand very close to the potbelly stove when the weather was cold.

One November night we had a dinner party for a dozen international friends from the university. There were couples from France, Switzerland, Australia, England, Ethiopia, and Japan. Alfie was a notorious moocher so we put him into the screened-in porch. Bonaparte had leaned too close to the potbelly stove earlier in the day, producing a ghastly smell of burning feathers. We didn't want a repeat of this during the dinner so we put him into the space behind an old hot-water radiator spanning one of the bay windows.

At dinner the conversation and wine flowed freely and we were having a great time. Suddenly one of the women seated facing the window let out a shriek and pointed. We all turned to look and saw this enormous sunflower pressing against the window and looking so mournful. Everyone burst out laughing, especially the lady from Australia. She had a high-pitched cackle that went on and on, evoking even more laughter. Eventually we realized that not all the cackling was coming from the Australian lady. Some of it was coming from behind the radiator! Soon, a cackling contest was in full swing with everyone trying to out-cackle Bonaparte. It was no contest, the Aussie lady won hands down.

It was one of our best dinner parties.

# ON THE NATURE OF HUMOR

Have you noticed that the other side of the humor coin is often embarrassment? I have been wracking my brain trying to recall humorous events in my life and all that come to mind are embarrassing moments! Most embarrassing moments are, of course, not planned. Some of mine reflect misunderstanding, mishearing, unquenched thinking aloud, and ignorance. I specialize in unintended thinking aloud.

Years ago I was Events Coordinator for our local zoo when we planned a Spring Brew-Fest in June. Most of the local micro-brew companies had agreed to participate. Anheuser-Busch and its team of Clydesdales would be there. The Brew-Fest was our major fundraising event of the year.

One of our volunteers was a "large-boned" woman (actually mostly soft tissue) called Marge, who handled the logistics for the event. I was in my office the day before the event putting some finishing touches to the arrangements when Marge called and said she wanted to see me. I told her to come right in and a few minutes later there was a knock on the door.

"Come in," I yelled. Marge whooshed in like a train entering a station. Loose papers on my desk were sent fluttering to the floor as she descended into the chair in front of my desk, and gushed towards me, her bosom reaching almost halfway. I recoiled reflexively as a lavender tsunami overwhelmed my senses, and I was mesmerized by the sight of the enormous black suspension apparatus beneath the almost sheer blouse spreading across my desk. In my confusion I blurted out,

"All ready for the Bra-Fest I see!"

She didn't laugh. I didn't laugh. There was a strained silence as I turned beet red.

# MORNING

I look forward to my coffee every morn,
A quiet time to read the news is dawn.
I'm at peace when I start the local pages,
But always I find news that enrages;

The sports section—a constant tale of woe
Of local teams that failed to show.
The business section makes me weep
The recession sinks ever deep.

The international news is dire,
All the continents are on fire;
But worst of all is that I see
The crossword is too hard for me—
It must be Friday!

# PATRICIA McCULLOUGH

Patricia McCullough. I was born 72 years ago in Canada and raised in what we call The Kootenays. I moved to the United States in 1968 and have been here ever since. My interests are many and varied–from skiing, tai chi and golf to drawing, painting and writing. I have children, grandchildren and great-grandchildren, all living in this area, who keep me well involved in life. Because of the wide variety of "things to do" in my life, I am a sporadic writer–not as dedicated as some, but as completely committed to any piece I write as any other.

# SMALL THINGS

I remember this day as though it was yesterday. My mother tied the bow on the back of my dress and sent me into the yard to wait while she finished dressing.

"Now be careful!" she said. "We're going downtown in a few minutes and I want you to stay clean."

I skipped out the side door, down the short sidewalk and into the back yard. Our house on Topping Street faced a ten-foot cement wall and a set of a dozen stairs led to the street above. The house front was not much to look at, but the backyard was something else. Topping Street, as the name suggests, is high on the side of mountain. From the backyard you could look out over the entire city, down over the rows of rooftops on the houses in the streets below and across the river to the neighborhoods on the east side of the city. Those neighborhoods were backed by the mountains that marked the other side of the valley in which my home was located.

I was three years old. Standing on top of the rock stairway that led to the street below, I could see for miles. I felt like I was nine feet tall—very tall for a three year old. I sat on the top step, carefully spread my skirt around me and surveyed the panoramic view in front. Then I turned my attention to the Band-Aid on my knee. It was perfect.

I had been dressed for town once earlier on this morning. Then, while outside waiting for mom and skipping along the sidewalk, I tripped and scraped my knee. The fall sent me crying into the house. My mother took a look at my knee and immediately reached for the washcloth and cleaned the tear in my skin. There wasn't much blood after the dirt had been washed away, not even much of a scrape really, but I did need a change of clothes. So my mother took out another dress and once again got me ready for town. This time she added a special touch—she firmly placed a Band-Aid on my knee and smiled.

"There. That should do it," she said.

I didn't like scraping my knee, but I have to admit I really did like the Band-Aid. It would be visible because my dress was above my knee. Everyone we passed on the trip to town would see it! I could see the smiles and hear the comments even before we left the house. Such wonderful attention it would bring.

I don't remember whether people smiled and commented on my Band-Aid or not. I don't remember whether I got any special attention because of my skinned knee. I fact, I don't remember anything else about that day. But I do know that this is my first true memory and it is still clear 60 plus years later. A sunny day. A magnificent view. A Band-Aid! As I sat on the rock step I knew, as I have come to know many times over, small things satisfy.

# HAIR

When I was about nine years old, my mother decided to try to put some style into my perfectly straight hair cowlicks by giving me a home permanent. I was pretty excited about that and looked forward to the soft curly locks I imagined I would sport following the procedure.

My hair responded well enough. So well, in fact, that I could get neither comb nor brush through it for several days. Days that seemed as long as months. In place of soft curly locks I had a kind of spring-wired twist to each strand of hair. During those days of ultimate curl I wore a head scarf to school and endured the most embarrassing week of my life.

Many years later, when I was in college (an older student returning), I decided to do something about the fact that my hair had been dyed so many times each strand had grown in diameter and it seemed time to start over. Being a great do-it-yourself devotee, I chose not to go to the beauty shop but bought a home kit to tackle the problem myself. That leap of confidence would cost me another miserable time at school.

Instead of coming out basic beige that would allow me to put on a new color, my hair turned bright orange. To make matters worse the label on the box, when I finally read it, indicated that I would have to wait at least 24 hours before applying a new color. Seventy-two hours would be better still. Apparently this product was intended for platinum blondes only; I was a brunette. It was a very long 24 hours, eight of which were spent at school wearing the familiar head scarf and contemplating the virtue of reading instructions. This time I managed the humiliation without tears.

Now that I am much older, when things of this nature happen, I can't get too excited. I have been known to wear the left shoe from one pair and the right shoe from another to work on more than one occasion. Once it was one black shoe and one navy shoe. And if I memory serves, there was one time when I left my doctor's office with the back zipper of my dress completely unzipped.

As you might guess, these things do not go entirely unnoticed. One afternoon around 4:30 p.m. a coworker said: "I have to ask. Is your shirt on inside out?"

I looked down at the shoulder seams and sure enough, the inside seam stood out in high relief.

"Yes," I said.

"Are you going to change it to right side out?" he asked.

"No," I said. That late in the day there didn't seem to be any need to correct the problem. I'd be going home in a few mintues.

As for hair—well, a bad hair day these days is just that—a bad hair day. As I grow older each day has special meaning for the mere fact that I am alive and well. And I am happy to have my hair included.

# JEAN HEDENGREN MOULTRIE

Jean Hedengren Moultrie, a nurse and freelance writer, enjoys cookiebaking with grandchildren, plant collecting, photography, jaunts in the forests and "Adventure Travel." Jean is currently working on a memoir.

# DON'T SIT IN
# GRANDPA'S CHAIR

The Turnstile family civil war began with a squabble between Ralphie and Rodney during a holiday dinner. These six-year-old cousins kicked each other under the card table, sending up a squall from five-year-old Bethany, whose legs hung in the battlefield.

Admonitions from further up the dining room table to "Stop it!" and "Don't tattle!" satisfied neither the aggrieved nor the aggressors.

Despite the affluence of the host, the holiday dining table doesn't expand enough to include the younger family members–hence the card table wedged in at the end.

Cousin Will brought his new bride, Lavinia, to the holiday celebration held in middle America. One of the family cooks took a look at her and declared her an "upstart from out West."

When the boys continued to leg pummel each other, Lavinia whispered to Will, "Why doesn't someone separate them–move one up by us?"

Great Grandpa, hearing her, snorted, "You'd disrupt the natural order of life–we sit wrinkled to freckled."

The others grunted in agreement. This year, Great-Uncle Barnard, worried he'd lose his chair position, returned home from the hospital four hours post-appendectomy. While Grandma passed the next course, his nurse changed his IV bag.

Progress up the dining table chain is slow, and the order is so absolute in this long-lived Turnstile family that Uncle Rupert (unmarried and no children) was still at the card table when he started to collect his Social Security check. It was generally thought he wasn't damaged by this.

"He's a respected Civil Engineer," bragged Grandma.

"But how many adults," asked Cousin Daphne, "write a thesis about mashed potato dams and the hydraulics of pan-browned gravy?"

Everyone turned to stare at Uncle Rupert.

"Dig deeper!" he roared to a tot. "If you don't construct the mashed potato sides high enough, the inner lake bed won't hold the gravy. Leakage. One dribble…a leak…then a torrent of gravy drowning the town of turkey and green bean bake."

To save him embarrassment, the family turned away as he dribbled cranberry sauce down his bib.

Some households advance family members up the dining room chair chain faster than a bullet train. This happened to the neighbor, Sven Svorgen. A few of his family seniors head off to a sun-and-golf-saturated life in the fall and don't return home until the ground warms. This practice, along with an influx of babies, zoomed Sven up the chairs at the holiday table so rapidly he was held a prisoner of indecision not knowing which fork to use. Too paralyzed to eat, he turned gaunt and wasted. He graduated from jelly glasses and a camp stool to high society demands so fast he never had a childhood. It's rumored that this lack of time at the card table during his formative years led him in adulthood to throw away a thriving law practice to spend his days in the town park playing Parcheesi.

No worries of that in the Turnstile household.

Lavinia voiced a proposal: "Mix the whole family together—go multi-generational.

Hearing that, Great-Uncle Barnard sputtered so hard he couldn't catch his breath and had to be transported back to the hospital for oxygen therapy.

Great-Aunt Tillie went catatonic—stiff as a lamp post—and had to be carried up to her bed on her ironing board.

Some relished the prospect of an early move. Bethany hoped she'd land next to adults who prattle on about family doings she wasn't usually privy to.

Others listened to the proposal with horror. They'd served hard time at the card table and now might be sentenced back to card table boot camp with no chance of appeal or parole.

Great Grandma hyperventilated contemplating Ralphie and Rodney with her crystal goblets from the Old Country and had to be revived by breathing into a paper bag–the only one handy held onions and garlic. She survived but experienced blurry vision the rest of the day.

One of the uncles retorted that he didn't want to be moved about all higgledy, piggledy. Instead of conversation with peers, he feared he'd be sucked into discussions of invertebrate mobility as it relates to SpongeBob SquarePants.

By the end of the meal, no one was speaking to anyone else–except Ralphie and Rodney, who banded together after conspiring to slip gummy worms into Bethany's banana cream pie.

The debate turned so bitter they had to hire a mediator and schedule further family proceedings to be held in Switzerland.

Uncle Weston nudged Grandma, pointed towards Cousin Will and Lavinia and said, "This is what you get when a person from a red state marries a person from a blue state."

# THE PATIENT

"Broken neck--paralyzed. Won't speak. Flown in from the reservation. In his late teens."

The nurse finished the report before leaving to pass her medications.

"Oh, one more thing. He watches the TV reruns of The Beverly Hillbillies."

As a student nurse, I reviewed the patient's chart, gathered towels, wash basin and linens, then entered his room. His bed sat in the far corner of a three-bed ward. Walls formed the boundaries on two sides and his pulled curtains enclosed him on the other two sides.

"Hello. I'm Miss Hedengren. I'll be your nurse this morning."

No response.

The swimming accident had not paralyzed his vocal cords—only his hands and arms that now spastically curled at his sides, the fingers splayed above the flat palms, then bent claw-like at the tips.

After his bath, I reached to pull open the curtains. He protested with a frown and a mutter. He made himself clear. Keep the curtains closed.

Over several days of care he remained silent. When I finished caring for him, I'd flick on his television. He watched with uninterested eyes, never smiling or commenting.

From social worker notes, I learned that his passions had been racing horses across the prairie, hunting deer and game birds, fishing and swimming. Was it an unusually dry season that left the pool of water where he dove and swam more shallow than usual? Had a late, wet snow and a Chinook rain sent swollen streams tumbling with rotted logs from forested hills down the creek in spring—logs that tumbled against boulders, and then settled in the creek pool? Was it a leap from horseback, an overhanging tree or perhaps a railroad trestle that changed his life as neatly as a hunting knife peeling off a jackrabbit hide?

Anchored to his room for weeks, and no longer in critical condition, he required months of rehab therapy. I could not begin to feel his sense of imprisonment.

I had a childhood of fields thick with clover, lupine and the call of cock pheasants. In his childhood, he roamed on a pony through pine, juniper and sagebrush. My bicycle took me to Douglas-fir forests thick with salal and sword ferns. He tracked coyotes and mule deer. In blistering heat, he found shelter beneath cottonwoods along creek bottoms. In my world of rain, my younger brothers and I would rise on Saturdays before sunrise to tromp outside in the hush of the day, the drizzle dampening our rain slickers, black galoshes and red rubber boots. Some regain health at hearth and home–others receive healing from the hills.

Stifling.

The hospital ward was stifling. Air circulated–reportedly clean, but lacking the crisp snap of winter.

Knowing I had to be outside on a regular basis made me think about what I could do for my mute-by-choice patient.

"You want to get outside–even for a few minutes?" I asked.

His eyes flicked open.

"Being cooped up is terrible–how would you like to go out for fresh air?"

No response. His eyes followed me as I massaged his hands with oil.

"Are you outside a lot back home?"

"Yeah." His voice faint above the noise of neighboring television and radio sets, he turned to face me.

"Horses?" I asked. "You like horses?"

"Yeah, have my own. Used to ride all over."

Fishing tales, hunting stories, descriptions of ponies–he spoke in brief phrases with long pauses. He concluded, "I can get out–for a little while?"

I explained I could put him on a gurney–a stretcher-like cart with oversized wheels–and wheel him boldly down the hall, onto the elevator, down to the lobby, then out to the front sidewalk slick with slush and streets banked with plowed snow.

"But they'll catch us," I concluded. He smiled at the anticipated spectacle of him lashed to the gurney, me pushing in my blue student nurse's uniform and white cap and weaving through a forest of visitors while a posse of nurses and doctors stampeded after us.

Not sure if I heard an occasional chuckle or throat clearing as we discussed options.

Down and out. Would never work, we concluded. Too much congestion. Too many questions. Too much red tape.

He lapsed into silence. I went out to cruise the halls looking for other avenues, then returned.

I jostled his shoulder, knowing he wasn't asleep. "Not down. Up. Instead, we're going up and out. Perfect spot–up on the roof."

No response, then, "We'll never get out."

"Sure we will." I finished tucking in the sheets. "The secret is to spring it on them suddenly–not a lot of time for people to think of reasons not to go out. We'll try it tomorrow."

The next day with little conversation, I finished the care quicker than usual.

"Okay, here goes." I left the room and marched to the nurses' station.

The harried charge nurse gave scant attention, until I mentioned The Roof.

"I'm not so sure—is it safe?"

"There is a view point on the walkway that connects the two buildings. Medical personnel cut across when the elevator is full. Another student nurse will help transfer him onto the gurney."

"I don't know . . ."

"We won't be out long—just a chance to be outside—he needs . . ."

Another nurse interrupted the supervisor. "Mr. Simpson is back from surgery . . . requesting pain medication . . . dress has 8 cm of dark . . ."

"Please," I pleaded. "Just a few minutes—I've checked the area. Easy access on and off—we'll use the service elevator. I'll have help getting him up there."

The other nurse reached for the keys to the narcotic cupboard.

The charge nurse turned to me. "Not long, you understand. Perhaps I should ask the . . ."

I was already down the hall. I hooked the arm of a conspiring student nurse and slipped into the patient's room. Confident of the outcome, I'd stashed a gurney nearby.

We transferred the patient onto the gurney with the help of turn sheets and a third student.

Bundled up with blankets he grinned as we cruised down the hall and around the corner to the elevator. My classmate and I wheeled him onto the elevator and rose to the roof level. She helped me pull him onto the roof walkway and wheel him to a spot where the hills were visible beyond the city skyline. Then she returned to the elevator and shut the door. We heard the elevator grind as it descended to the floors below.

Silence.

Even in the city, the snow-packed streets and hospital height muffled the sounds of commerce below.

We breathed deeply. The air, fresh with winter tang, nipped my nose. Was I imagining it or could I smell sagebrush and pine resin, sheep flocks and pony corrals?

The hills, studded with brush strokes of timber, turned a dazzling green in the sun that slipped past gray clouds in a thin, blue sky.

I bent into a clump of snow, packed a chunk of powdery fluff and tossed the missile at the gurney. The snowball exploded and sent cotton puffs of snow across his blanket. He laughed and recalled snow-filled nights at the reservation as I brushed the snow from his covers.

I picked up another clump–leaving it soft and fluffy.

"Do you want to feel it?"

He nodded yes.

I laid the snow next to his chin, rubbed it gently along his cheek and then dried off the wet with a corner of his blanket.

I thought he might cry.

I started to chatter–the over-enthusiastic chattering of a person not quite sure what to say or do next.

Then silence. Both of us sucked in deep breaths as a breeze blew clouds across the sun and sparse snowflakes floated down.

I shivered. "It's getting colder. Better get back inside."

He nodded in agreement.

I navigated him onto the elevator. "I'm going home," he whispered, as the door shut.

I knew he did not mean the bed in the three-bed ward room with the corner wall and the pulled curtains.

# RON RIFE

Ron Rife. I was born in Salem, Oregon, and educated in West Los Angeles, Bakersfield, Fresno, Hawaii and San Jose. I'm retired both from federal service and from the California Department of Corrections. I returned to the Northwest in 2003.

# FIREBASE CORCORAN STORIES

## I. THE FIREBASE

A California State Prison is so much more than concrete, rebar, and pain.

The fear that permeates the area within the concertina wire is palpable. The inmate population consists of predators and victims. Murderers intimidate the enforcers who intimidate the armed robbers who intimidate the thieves who intimidate the forgers and everybody intimidates the child molesters.

The strict code of the prison food chain rules.

The California State Prison at Corcoran (CSP-Corcoran) is a Level IV or maximum-security institution located in the Central Valley of California. Three yards are GP (General Population) areas where inmates have privileges. When you seriously infract in prison, you graduate from a GP yard to the next level of incarceration, AdSeg (Administrative Segregation). Here an inmate is single-celled for an amount of time determined by a staff panel. In AdSeg, the inmate has no privileges. Each GP yard has one or two buildings designated as AdSeg Units. These are for short stays (less than 90 days). Inmates living in these units have no canteen, visitors, or yard time, and can leave their cells for only four hours once a week for exercise.

SHU (Security Housing Units) are for infractions that involve violence at some level. The two SHU Yards have five housing blocks each. Each of these housing units contains three separate sections–A, B, and C–with 20 cells per section. This is designed for security; if unit A "jumps off" (riots), B and C units can be contained. SHU sentences can run into years. Civilians are more familiar with the term "solitary," whereas prisoners and staff know it as "the hole."

One of these SHU blocks includes PHU (Protective Housing Unit); Charles Manson, Sirhan Sirhan and 35 other high-profile criminals live here. It is the only PHU in the United States. The correctional officers on this unit are trained to deal with inmates who require special protection. This is a major problem when you have a prison that that houses 5000 LWOP (Life Without Possibility of Parole) inmates who have nothing to lose by "tagging" one of these high-profile convicts. Reaching out and touching a PHU inmate will guarantee the tagger's reputation for the length of his sentence.

The same SHU block contains a PCU (Protective Custody Unit), for inmates who have "PC'd up"–they have Protective Custody status because they are snitches who have rolled over on someone with enough juice to have them killed. They also have not been involved in violent offenses since incarceration. Inmates' ratting out each other is one reason prisons maintain Gang Squad Intelligence. Informants allow the squad to identify and track prison gang leaders and lieutenants along with their replacements when the shot callers and assistants have been "rolled up" on the GP yards and sent to AdSeg or SHU. Gangs that run gambling, drugs, and prostitution in the housing units are identified by other inmates who want more privileges and protection from the bad guys. If you snort $1000 worth of heroin and cannot pay for it, it is time to PC up, give up the source for the drugs, and hope the Custody staff can move you to PCU before you are killed.

Respect is the fuel that stabilizes whatever sanity exists on the yards and in the housing units. The biggest problem every prison has had to deal with for the past two decades is incoming inmates who are younger, harder, and dumber. Prisons have always had prison gangs and each one is led by a "shot caller." Custody staff talking to shot callers solve most problems on the yard. Compromises are reached, tensions reduced, and stasis returns. That is how it used to be until the late 1980's. Since then, the Payback Crips, various "13" bangers, and other mustang prison gangs have no recognized leadership. Chaos and whimsy rule their daily lives. These inmates don't care if their actions result in the entire yard being down for an indefinite period. They act without thinking and take great pride in how much punishment they can give out and take.

When a serious incident happens–there has been a stabbing, suicide, rumor of an impending gang fight, the discovery of a cache of drugs or weapons, etc.–the yard is "slammed" aka locked down. All inmates and cells are searched for contraband–especially weapons. Each inmate is kept in his cell. After seven days, he is allowed out of his cell one day for exercise and a shower. The yard may be slammed for days, months or years, depending upon the seriousness of the infraction and the length of investigation. The procedure for opening up the yard is to let different gangs out in small groups; Blacks, Whites, Mexicans and Others are the categories used by the Department of Corrections. Everything that happens inside the wire relates in some way to gang or race involvement. Some prison gangs are the Tips (Crips and Bloods), the BGF (Black Gorilla Family), NLR (Nazi Low Riders), Nortenos (Northern Structure) and Surenos, Border Brothers, and "unaffiliated." It takes a certain kind of inmate (a masochist, mentally challenged or very very tough) not to be affiliated with a prison gang. Gangs provide protection and family. The inmate who walks alone is usually vulnerable to all gangs for many different reasons and will "pay rent" in one way or another. Gay inmates are always affiliated.

Inmates are under observation 24/7; classrooms, bathrooms, hospital rooms all have walls made of security glass from waist level high to the ceiling. An inmate who needs toilet paper must request it from staff when outside his housing unit. This is a not-so-subtle example of staff power over inmates.

One constant in prison is the smell roiling off the inmates–a mixture of urine, sweat, tobacco, Clorox and testosterone. The stench permeates the housing units, classrooms, and administrative areas on the yard. Inmates wash their state-issue blues (two pants, two shirts) in the toilets of their cells, and personal hygiene consists of one shower every three days. During lockdown, inmates shower once every seven days. The housing unit becomes very ripe, very fast during these periods. Imagine a housing unit in the summer time when temperatures can be 115 degrees outside the housing unit and 125 degrees inside. The inmate smell is distinctive and permeates every state-blue uniform on a prisoner. Most staff splash on an extra measure of cologne before coming to work.

The single most important area in penology is discipline. If you do not have discipline, you do not have a prison, you simply have a very rough neighborhood. The first level of discipline is to withhold privileges from inmates. Inmates can receive four packages a year from outside the wire; these contain approved articles paid for by friends or family of the incarcerated–provided the inmate has not been involved in any drama on the yard or in his housing unit. Every time an inmate infracts, the number of packages he can receive is reduced. This rule is a powerful incentive for keeping inmates in line.

Canteen is a privilege enjoyed by inmates who have money "on the books." (Money from home sent through prison channels ends up in a prisoner's "on the books" account.) Candy, coffee, ice cream, chips, soft drinks and tobacco are treats that, if the inmate has behaved himself, he will have access to once a week. Non-gang (unaffiliated) inmates who have canteen give up their canteen privileges to any number of predators. For example, giving a "celly" (cell-mate) your canteen privileges might keep him from assaulting you for a period of time. Gambling debts, drugs, alliances, friendships, and "dues" for not getting beaten down are threads held together with canteen.

Prison, like most societies, is a complex social mix broken down to its simplest common denominator–survival. Survival usually depends upon gangs. Race, cause, and the level of violence they are committed to performing define gangs. All of these things are represented by the tattoos an inmate wears. The purpose of tatts is "so people don't have to get close to you to know who you are and where you're from," explains a Border Brother.

Prison is more than concrete, wire and custody staff; it is a population morphing through yet another layer of fear every day.

# II. THE BISHOP

Harry Bishop was a man born with a need to lead, but without any talent to do so. He was devoid of common sense, so it was natural that he would end up in prison. Sadly, it was not as an inmate but as an educational staff member. He had the sensitivity of linoleum. He couldn't help himself. Messing up was his life's mission, and as a result he wandered from one catastrophe to another.

Bishop had been a principal at three different schools and had never lasted beyond 12 weeks at any of them. His last job had been at a small elementary school in the country, where he took it upon himself to spray an entire playing field with insecticide the day of the school district soccer playoffs. He did it because the custodian refused, stating that it wasn't safe for the children to play with toxic chemicals on the grass. During the soccer matches, 37 children were sent to the hospital for respiratory problems or skin rashes.

At his hearing he stated that the lawn was healthy now and looked great. And the sick children? "All parents know that there is a risk their child could be hurt playing soccer. What difference does it make if they have a broken arm or a little reaction to chemical spray on the field?" Much ado about nothing, he thought.

Another time, at a different elementary school, he again proved that he was a sideways-thinker. On the opening day of the hunting season, he walked onto the school grounds with his rifle to tighten up his scope mounts. All around him were children playing. Rather than go all the way back to his house he went to the school custodian shed to use a screwdriver. He waded through the children on his way. At the shed, the custodian asked him if the rifle was loaded and Bishop replied, "A rifle is useless without being loaded. When it is unloaded, what you have is an expensive club. I don't carry clubs."

He was fired from his principal job. Again.

Will Rogers once said of education: most folks learn about electric fences by reading, some learn by listening, but there are always a few who just have to piss on the wire. Bishop was one of these. He was incapable of taking orders or instruction. He knew he was smarter than everyone else. Employers would repeat instructions several times to make sure that he understood.

Through some major oversight, he was allowed to teach in a maximum security prison.

He managed to subdue his instinctive behavior until two days after his 60-day probation had been completed. It was then that he was caught bringing a four-inch folding knife onto the prison grounds. He had to be told over and over that bringing weapons into a maximum security prison was wrong. He was caught doing the same thing three days later. Repeating instructions over and over became known as "the Bishop Syndrome."

Every day, Bishop acted in bizarre ways that could—no, should—have ended his life. When one of these events tanked, he blithely went on his way to repeat the same offense on a different prison yard. Some staff members would forget and only give Bishop instructions once or twice. And they would pay for the oversight.

Once he came to work and parked his truck in the prison employees' parking lot. Unfortunately, his loaded hunting rifle was in the rack of his unlocked truck; two violations right there. The Correction Officers' Union tried to have him fired as a security threat to the institution. The charge failed because no incident had occurred as a result of Bishop's behavior. Shortly thereafter, he became the Local 314 Union President for non-custody prison staff, which undoubtedly kept him from being fired on several future occasions.

He had been threatened often—sometimes by inmates. The trick for the Correctional Education Supervisor was to transfer Bishop where he could offend the least number of people for the longest period of time without being assaulted. When he did get a new assignment, with the inevitability of a falling rock, Harry Bishop would find a new way to upset everybody with whom he came in contact.

His last job was as a substitute teacher. The thinking of the Education Supervisor was that by the time Harry had offended someone, he would be substituting on another yard. There were 18 classrooms. If he could stay in each classroom for a week, he might make it through a year. Wishful thinking at best. Bishop had already failed as a full-time classroom teacher, regular librarian, part-time librarian, office phone clerk, supply person, and Xerox operator for the Education Department.

Correctional officers would sneer as he passed.

One crisp January morning he was directed to his first substitute teaching job: the GED class on B yard. The day before, the regular teacher, Tony Zamerelli, had carefully gone over the lesson plans with Harry. Mr. Zamerelli was 6'5" and a serious weight lifter. People listened to Tony.

"It is very important," Zamerelli said, looking into Bishop's eyes for emphasis, "that you do exactly what I have directed in these lesson plans. I know you have a problem staying on task, but these inmates will take their GED test next week and we have worked hard for ten months to get to where we are right now. Do not vary from my lesson plans! My clerk, Rabbit, will answer any questions you might have. He is up on everything thing we've done to date. Look at me, Harry. Do not alter from my lesson plans. Do you understand?"

Harry looked like a whipped puppy. "Sure, Tony. No need to speak to me as though I were a dunce. I understand completely. Any questions and I can ask Rabbit. I get it."

Rabbit was the inmate clerk. His duties consisted of taking roll and filling out reports; he was the unofficial enforcer in the classroom. He respected Tony Zamerelli and consequently, so did the class.

Remembering the Bishop Syndrome Tony added, "I'm serious, Harry. Look these over and let me know if you have any questions."

Bishop read the very detailed instructions page by page and handed them back to Zamerelli. "Simple enough. Just standard language and essay review. I can do it. Nothing to worry about, Tony, I'll take care of it without any deviation of your plan. Promise." He crossed his heart.

"You understand, Bishop, that I will personally kick your ass across B Yard if you don't follow the lesson plan? I will beat you down until the cops come and put me in 5-point restraints."

"Don't be silly, Tony, I've got it under control. No problem."

The next morning, Bishop showed up on the yard in time to escort his inmates to the class room. Once they were seated,

Rabbit collected ID cards, took roll, and prepared the paperwork on attendance.

As Rabbit worked, Harry's eyes fell on a videocassette sitting on the corner of Zamerelli's desk. It was titled "Beautiful Tibet." A National Geographic film! A wave of excitement coursed through Bishop's body. He had never seen this video before. Videos in prison that are less than six years old are considered new. Yeah, Tony said that he shouldn't deviate from the program, but Bishop really wanted to see this film. Who knows, maybe there will be a Tibet question on the GED test.

"O.K. gentlemen," he said facing the class, "today we are going to watch a film on Tibet."

The class erupted.

"Yo, Bishop, we've worked on this for months and we get tested out next week," yelled the shot-caller for the Mexican Mafia. "We need to review, pendajo."

"This is bullshit, Bishop," said a Nazi Low Rider. "We're supposed to drill today. Don't do this man, please. I gotta pass this test and get it in my jacket before my annual comes up."

And so it went. "Pathetic, gentlemen, just pathetic." Bishop looked around the room with disdain. "Maybe one of you geniuses could tell me the population of Tibet? No? Well, let's all learn something."

He looked over to Rabbit, who stared back at him with intense eyes. The eyes of a contract killer–which Rabbit had been for thirty years.

Harry told him to set up the video unit so they could watch the film.

Rabbit didn't move.

"I have instructed you to set up the VCR, Rabbit–now do it." Bishop attempted to put some steel in his voice, but fell short.

Rabbit remained seated with pain forming behind his eyes, but continued a level gaze at Bishop. The class went silent.

"You know I'll write you up if you refuse my order, right?" Rabbit didn't acknowledge having heard Bishop. He just stared.

When Bishop realized he had been "fronted off" by Rabbit he announced he would be putting in paperwork to remove Rabbit from his clerk's job. Rabbit had been the clerk of this class for 17 years, but Harry was on a roll now. Rabbit remained frozen in his chair.

With the posturing of a third-world dictator, Bishop snorted and set up the VCR himself. He ignored the shouts and threats from the class. Feeling a tingle of triumph, he pushed the Play button on the machine. He was immediately pelted with wadded balls of paper. Yelling continued for another minute, before Bishop, with a great flourish, stopped the VCR. The class quieted down.

"If you don't like it, you may leave," he said with a smirk and a dismissive wave of his hand. He knew these felons weren't going anywhere without a staff escort. He was feeling pretty smug when he returned to the machine. He pushed Play and heard the clatter of chairs being moved and the shuffle of inmates behind him.

He turned to see inmates streaming out of the classroom. The volume on the TV blared, "…this quiet kingdom, this mountain paradise…" It took a moment for reality to register in his brain. They're leaving! He punched the red button on his personal alarm excitedly. The klaxon-alarm went off and filled the hallway with a cacophony denoting that something was seriously amiss.

When a personal alarm goes off, several things happen at once. All inmates get down on their stomachs and all correction officers not directly guarding inmates respond to the alarm. Non-custody staff's only job is to keep out of the way of custody, because when the cops come through the door, they are going to deal with whatever situation they find quickly and harshly.

By the time Harry came out of shock, the new corrections officer, Mona Garcia, was rounding the corner in the hallway. She saw a large number unescorted inmates rushing out of a classroom and heading towards her while the alarm filled her ears. Mona thought she also heard the faint sound of Tibetan bells and flutes. The inmates looked upset and were heading right at her. She could see through the windowed walls into the other classrooms where students were reacting to the alarm correctly by assuming the belly position on the floor.

C/O Garcia went immediately for her pepper spray canister while shouting, "Down, down, everybody down on your stomachs," pointing to the floor, as if these inmates had never done it before, while she liberally sprayed the gas towards them.

Under normal conditions, the inmates would immediately get on their stomachs. But the thirty-inmate class was still streaming out of the classroom into the hallway and the prisoners in the hallway were being pushed towards the now panicking Officer Garcia.

When the cops breached the building's front door, the hallway was filled with stinging gas. Tears ran down C/O Garcia's cheeks as she went for her second canister of spray. Bishop's inmates were fighting to get back into the gas-free classroom while Garcia was still yelling and coughing, "Down, down," in the increasing toxic mist.

It took about ten seconds for the duty sergeant, Terrell, to see what was happening. He ordered the coughing and tearing inmates from Harry's classroom escorted to the outside yard where the other students had been taken. Then he ordered that doors on either end of the building be opened to clear the gas. The all-clear signal was announced 20 minutes later and inmates on the yard got to their feet. Five hundred inmates were patted down and escorted off the yard and back to their housing units in small knots of 10 to 15 men.

Education inmates were checked out by the Medical Technician Assistant on the yard and escorted to their quarters with instructions to flush out their eyes with water.

Sergeant Terrell found Harry Bishop under his desk. Terrell had written up Bishop too many times to forget him. The last time he and Harry had been on the same yard, the sergeant had told him that the next time they met under adverse circumstances and there were no witnesses, the sergeant would beat Harry down with his baton, skin and stuff him and have Harry's head mounted on his wall by nightfall. Wise men feared Sergeant Terrell. Even Bishop.

After-action reports were taken and the building was cleared. Classes were cancelled for the next five weeks while the pepper gas was cleared from the building. Inmate crews would scrub every square inch of the hallways and five classrooms. The cancellation of classes affected every program on the yard, custody cops scheduling to feeding and exercising inmates. Duty slots would change for custody and teachers would probably be reassigned to scrubbing pots in the kitchen or to ripping up old text books in a cold, dusty warehouse. Yes, Harry Bishop had struck again.

After the hearing, it was found that the inmates were responsible. Harry was still confused about why the inmates reacted as they did. The GED test was put off for another year. Bishop stayed home for the next few weeks. He had heard that Tony Zamerelli was looking for him.

Bishop had finally reached the point when he was no longer safe anywhere in the prison. He exhausted every union procedure to stay on staff but without success.

He is currently working in the mail room at another prison in the Central Valley.

# III. SUPER SPADE VS. THE SYSTEM

Rashad Godbolt, B-334481, was doing triple-life for the murder of one Tyrone "Titty" Tiddell and two of his bodyguards. Rashad was known as Super Spade on the streets and in the joint. He had run the Black Gorilla Family (BGF) in Compton, and only his residential status changed when he was sent to Corcoran State Prison. He was in General Population for his first 11 years, and 4A Security Housing Unit (aka the hole) for the last four years, eight months, and 17 days. Only 55 more years until his Earliest Possible Release Date. Rashad's eyes hardened when he thought of his EPRD. Like Manson and Sirhan across the yard, his annual review was a dog-and-pony show that always resulted in a press release to the local newspapers saying his parole was denied, showing the civilians how criminals were handled by the State of California Department of Corrections.

But it wasn't all bad. He was still the head of the BGF and as the shot-caller for the baddest black gang behind the wire he had multiple perks. His Canteen supply was always filled; his cup literally ran over with candy, coffee, canned meats, and Top Ramen soups. The dope he supplied to other inmates gave him monetary and political power, and additional perks that could only be supplied by correctional officers. He was always able to find a bent cop. And now it was Corrections Officer Sarah Carvalho. Every Tuesday evening for the last few months, during Second Watch, he'd meet her for 15 minutes in the darkened and deserted gym. She also supplied him with weed, smack and crank, provided by Super Spade's mother. Yeah, he was doing very well compared to anybody else in the joint.

C/O Carvalho had been a cop on the yard for nine years. She had two beautiful children and one lazy-ass husband who was talking about getting a divorce and taking the children with him. Her children. Whenever she asked him to get a job, he countered with extortion threats. Her long duty tours, especially when pulling double shifts, taxed family time and provided fodder for his threats. Also, her husband didn't care for work. Any kind of work. She loved her kids above all else.

When she decided it was time to dump the lump, she selected Rashad Godbolt to do the dumping. He was the shot-caller over a prison gang with disciplined soldiers inside and—more importantly—outside the prison. He was housed in the SHU where she worked. He had no problem knowing everything that happened in Compton and on all the yards at Corcoran State Prison.

Sarah had him pulled from his cell and escorted him to the gym one evening in January. She opened up the unused gym, had him sit down in the dim light and explained their new relationship. Fifteen minutes later they left the building; Rashad with a slight smile on his face, and Sarah wiping her mouth on the sleeve of her olive drab uniform jacket in the cold night.

Rashad's mom–Jynx–met Sarah every two weeks in a bowling alley in Bakersfield, California. She would give Sarah a brown sack of contraband for Rashad. The bag contained a wide selection; weed, crank, tar – just your basic prison yard menu. Sarah's nerves started zinging the moment she left Jynx. She didn't know if the name was ironic or defined the arrangement.

When she drove home after scoring from Jynx, she was a bundle of energy ready to pop. Seeing her kids didn't help the high anxiety tight rope she was walking. The next morning entering the prison through the checkpoint, an officer asked if she was okay.

Sarah's nerves were slowly disintegrating. She was losing weight, her eyes looked hollow, and her temper was spinning out of control. Planning a hit on her husband, smuggling contraband into prison, lying to her fellow officers daily while maintaining a semblance of a family life was something she was not cut out to do without a heavy downside.

And so she began sampling the products in the sacks Jynx passed on to her. She found that heroin leveled her out just fine. An important upside of her deal now was that she had an endless supply of smack from just chipping away a little at Super Spade's stash. When she asked him how long until her husband was not a problem Godbolt told her that he was still making arrangements with his Compton homies for her husband's death, but it would take a little longer. It was always a little longer.

Rashad enjoyed routine; he exercised in his cell one hour in the morning and one hour in the evening. He showered once every four days, but washed in his house daily by soaking his shirt in the toilet. He spent his time reading books supplied by the library on the yard, and by law he was given two hours a week in the prison library to work on his appeal. He had been keeping this schedule from the third week after he was assigned to SHU for killing his cell mate in general population.

Those two hours in the library allowed him to secrete "kites," or messages, in the spines of certain law books for others to retrieve later and pass on. It was the underground communications system. He also distributed drugs through fellow BGF members who were library clerks or clean-up inmates from GP yards. They took drugs and kites back to their housing units on other yards to distribute. Godbolt was able to find out things happening back home on the streets from newly arrived BGF members. For important information from outside the wire, a BGF member would violate some rule on GP yards just to be sent to SHU so that he could communicate the news to Godbolt directly. Life was good for Super Spade. Until last week.

Sarah had escorted him to the gym and then before giving him the contraband from his mom, asked again when her old man was going to get whacked. Sarah was tired of being strung along and scared that she was going to get busted carrying his shit into the joint. She wanted her husband dead. Now. As always, he smiled and asked for his stuff. He added with emphasis, "Now, Bitch." He knew that he had the power in this relationship. She tried to put up a strong front, but it crumbled when she realized the position she had placed herself in these past few months. She had miscalculated badly.

They left the gym and ran into two C/Os escorting an inmate across the cold empty yard. Both C/Os were startled when the door swung open.

One of the cops, Gomez, asked what was going on. After a split second too long, Sarah responded that Godbolt had to go the can and she didn't feel like walking him back to the housing unit. "How'd he unzip while he was cuffed up from behind, Carvalho?" asked Tyrell, the other C/O. Tension crackled in the air now. She mumbled something about cuffing Rashad to the urinal, but she knew that not only was this a lame excuse, it was against regulations, for which she could be "walked off the yard." Fired. The inmate Gomez and Tyrell were escorting smirked in the darkness, while Rashad looked impassively out over the yard unfazed by the biting wind. Sarah grabbed his arm roughly and started back to his housing unit. Gomez and Tyrell continued their escort in the opposite direction.

Four days later, Godbolt heard his name called by the cop in the Control booth, to make ready for escort. Sarah must be back, he smiled. The elation lasted two corners of a heart beat when he came off his rack and saw two members of "the squad" waiting for him downstairs under the glass Control booth.

The Gang Squad is a special unit of seasoned uber Correctional Officers who got there with a track record of outsmarting inmates, getting confessions, finding hidden contraband, and never getting caught bending the rules. "This can't be good," thought Super Spade. He was right.

They interrogated him for an hour and he gave up Sarah and information about their relationship. He left out his mother and the drugs. He figured there was nothing else they could do to him, so he bartered for a few perks and then gave the goon squad all they wanted.

Two days later, C/O Sarah Carvalho, going through the check-in entrance to start her watch, was waved off to the three squad members waiting just inside the door. She felt numbness wash from her chest down to her boots.

The Squad members escorted her to a nearby office where a female officer did a cavity search on her, while the other squad members went through her soft-sided thermo bag, large enough to carry food for two shifts. Sarah's insulated bag contained three sandwiches, a quart of iced tea, a pound of weed, eight dime-bags of black tar heroin, and ten shrink-bags of meth.

At trial, Sarah received nine years in the women's prison in Chowchilla. Her lazy-ass husband got the kids, the house, the cars, the boat and her pension.

Nothing much changed for Rashad Godbolt, B-334481, housed in Building 2, 4B AdSeg Yard. Excluding the lack of sex for the moment, life improved for him overall. He negotiated to testify against Sarah in court and received a few more perks.

He already had an idea about who would replace Sarah as his "mule." The new correctional officer on the tier, Ortiz, had been running his mouth to another officer about needing a part-time job for more money to pay his alimony. Rashad overheard the comment and smiled. All in all, he had little complaint against the California Department of Corrections.

# ROBERT ROY

Robert Roy.   In his memoir, "As Always," Robert portrays the home of his childhood in small town in the North Woods of Wisconsin. His growing-up years set the stage for his continuing love of the outdoors. His writing also explores his committed, often humorous, relationship with his wife, Christine, in their efforts to navigate the ups and downs of pet ownership. He has a Masters in Social Work and has lived and worked in the Pacific Northwest for most of his adult life.

# AS ALWAYS, ROBERT

## CHAPTER ONE – HOME 1938-1948

The first ten years of my life I lived in a two-story framed house in a small town in Wisconsin. It sat on a plot of land of two or more acres. I'm not sure how old it was, but my guess is it was built in the early nineteenth century. The wooden siding was never painted or if it was the paint had long ago faded away. It was gray like the color of wood as it ages.

To the right of the front porch sat a barrel to collect rainwater from a roof drain spout. The water was used to wash clothes, water indoor plants and the summer vegetable garden. The porch was half the width of the house. It was used by all of us in the summer months to enjoy a cool evening breeze and watch fireflies light up the darkness. I vividly remember how, glass jar and lid in hand, I ran around the yard in pursuit of tiny winged flashes of light. Sometimes our evening respites were cut short by mosquitoes.

Alongside the barrel was a lightning rod attached to a wire that ran up the side of the house to a metal rooster weather vane on the peak of the roof. Severe summer thunderstorms were common occurrences and everyone took precautions to prevent lighting strikes.

I will never forget running back and forth, wall-to-wall, in the living room preoccupied with a tag-like game. Once when I touched the wall by the window lighting struck the house and knocked me backward. I lay on the floor stunned. My father picked me up; I gasped for air and started crying hysterically. Fortunately I was unhurt. Another time I remember standing in the middle of the living room with my mother's arms wrapped around me. I looked up. I saw fear in her eyes as thunderclaps shook the walls and jagged streaks of light illuminated the night.

The front porch and door faced west. A vacant lot separated us from the north-south railroad. My father warned me never to place a coin on the track in front of a train. He said a coin could cause the train to derail. I didn't believe it and decided to put a penny on the track to see what would happen. The next day, penny in hand, I walked down the track out of sight to wait for the train to come by. My ear firmly placed on the track let me hear the rhythmic sound of the oncoming train. I placed the penny and hid in a nearby wooded area. The train appeared and swiftly passed by. I walked to the track, looked for the penny and found it smashed flat. I looked up and down the track and wondered what my father was talking about. Penny in pocket I slowly walked home. It became part of a collection of boyhood memorabilia kept in a small wooden box for years to come.

The train depot, a long yellow structure, stood on the west side of the tracks. In back of the depot and across the street on the left stood the town water tower, a columnar structure with a large round dome. The tower was at least 100 feet high with a metal ladder leading to the top. The shiny silver dome could be seen for miles. I stood at the base of the tower, looked up and saw myself on top of the dome and decided to climb. I started up the ladder only to stop halfway, paralyzed with fear as I gazed down at the earth below. Then I slowly climbed down. With my feet safely on the ground I vowed never to try to climb it again.

In front of the tower was a rectangular two-foot deep depression the size of a football field. In the winter as temperatures dropped below freezing the area was filled with water. It quickly froze solid and became the community ice skating rink. I learned to skate on its smooth icy surface. On weekends and evenings during the week the rink was filled with skaters young and old. There were always bonfires scattered along the shoreline to sit around and warm body and soul.

The back porch of our house was enclosed and included a box for wood for the kitchen stove, an electric rotating tub washing machine with a hand-turned wringer and a metal scrub board, a sleeping area for the dog and storage for brooms, mops and other household items.

As you stood on the steps, to the left was our home water source, a well with a four-foot pump and handle. During the day water was pumped from the well into a large metal bucket and placed on a counter in the kitchen. A tin cup hung from the handle for drinking and cooking, and to fill a cast iron teakettle on the woodstove. The heated water was used for washing dishes or hands and face in a round white red-rimmed enamelware pan.

The image of the well pump with my tongue solidly frozen to the long handle is forever emblazoned in my mind along with the pain as I pulled it free from its frosty surface. I recall stories mom and dad told about other children doing the same thing. The warning not to do the same was given with a twinkle in the eye. I have shared this story and have been struck by the frequent nod of the head. Now I wonder what is so alluring about a frozen pump handle.

When it was time to wash clothes a copper double boiler was placed on the stove, filled with water and heated. Hot water was removed from the boiler with a metal bucket and poured into the tub of the washing machine. The water was also used for weekly baths. Standing knee deep in a round metal tub, soap and washcloth in hand to wash and rinse your entire body required skill and patience. Once a week was more than enough! Whatever water was left over was used to water houseplants or the garden—or if too grimy simply thrown out the back door.

From the back porch steps, two wood planks laid side by side made a path to the family outhouse, some 100 feet away, sometimes referred to as the "crapper." To the right of the path were the outdoor clotheslines, a woodshed/hen house and a wood shop. Behind the woodshed/hen house was a compost pit, called the slop pile. I was never sure what exactly was discarded into the pit. The chamber pot in my parent's bedroom along with leftover throwaway foodstuff come to mind. I do know that its rich decomposed mixture produced large night crawlers for summer fishing excursions.

Throughout the year the outdoor clothesline was used to hang freshly washed clothes. Several lines were strung between two wooden posts. The image of mom hanging or taking down clothes and dropping them into a metal tub to carry into the house is still with me. Seeing clothes frozen solid on the line, especially long john underwear, still makes me smile. The aroma of freshly washed clothes would permeate the house. To this day I can bring forth that scent.

The woodshed/hen house stands out vividly in my mind. There was always a rooster that roamed freely in the yard in front of the entrance. He had a propensity to attack anyone who tried to enter. One of my responsibilities was to fill the wood box on the back porch and gather eggs from the hen's living quarters. I would stand on the back steps and look out over the yard for the rooster. When he was nowhere to be seen I would run out to to collect wood or freshly laid eggs. I could often be seen running toward the back porch with an armload of wood or a bowl of eggs and the rooster on my heels.

The family outhouse is a story in and of itself. During the first ten years of my life in Wisconsin and the following decade in Oregon the outhouse was a constant family feature. I remember using it in cold weather, old Sears Roebuck catalogs as toilet paper, and worries about what might lurk in the large round hole upon which you placed your bare bottom.

In Hawkins, as in many other small towns throughout America, the outhouse became associated with Halloween. Tipping outhouses over and placing them on the town's main-street was widespread. I heard that an alternative to a tipped-over outhouse was to move it backward off the foundation to expose the deep hole filled with excrement.

In anticipation of this annual event my father would prepare, shotgun in hand loaded with rock salt, for a nightlong guard of the family privy. A shotgun blast of rock salt in the rear end was thought to be a preventive. I don't recall our outhouse ever being tipped or carted away and found the next morning down town—nor do I recall hearing a shotgun blast from the back yard.

I was too young to participate in this annual tradition, but I suspect my older brother did. I always got up early the next morning and ran down town to see what was strung up and down Main Street. Many outhouses were visible along with hay bailers, trailers and other large moveable items. Adult town folk stood around talking, and I listened to many stories of their attempts to guard their outhouses and other property, and how they were going to get them out of the street and back home.

Strangely, I never heard of anyone being caught or punished for these pranks. They were an accepted tradition.

North on the property that adjoined ours stood an old four-story brick hotel. I believe it was a home for permanent residents, although I don't recall seeing much of them. It's one notable feature was an ice cream parlor, which I visited frequently with a nickel to buy a double scoop chocolate ice cream cone.

On the edge of the hotel property was a faded gray wooden shed. I don't know what it was used for, but when I looked in its only window all I could see was an assortment of broken furniture and discarded household items.

One windy day I was outside with my mother's umbrella. The sensation of being lifted up whenever the wind caught the umbrella fascinated me. I imagined myself, umbrella in hand, floating through the air. I wondered what would happen if I jumped from the roof of a building—would I float slowly to the ground below?

I stared at the shed beside the hotel and decided to climb on its roof and jump off with the unfurled umbrella. I used my dad's ladder to climb to the roof, then eased my way down to the edge and opened the umbrella. I hesitated and stared at the ground below. I jumped. I dropped like a rock! Seconds later I lay on the ground below in a crumpled heap trying to catch my breath. I slowly got up; other than waves of pain throughout my body I was unhurt. I looked at the crumpled umbrella and wondered what I was going to tell my mother. I glanced up at the roof of the shed and muttered, "I'm not going to tell her I jumped off the roof. I will put it back and say nothing."

A well-worn dirt path entered our property from Main Street and ended at the front steps of the house. Alongside the path was a rutted road that ran up to the house, along the north side past the hotel and curved back out to the Street.

Adjacent to the path, about halfway between the house and Main Street, was an area where I fulfilled a boyhood fantasy. During one of Wisconsin's cold winters I came up with the idea of building an igloo, like the ones I had seen in books where Eskimos lived in the far north. I asked my friend Ronnie if he would like to help. He was eager to do so.

It was a cold winter. The foot or two of snow that covered the field was dry snow—no moisture to make it stick together for a snowball or snowman. With our shovels we piled a mound several feet high. Periodically, as the mound grew in size, we would pour buckets of water over its round surface. The snowy mass became compact with moisture.

Overnight it froze solid. The next day, with a shovel and a hoe in hand, we chiseled our way into the snowy mound. The finished product was a carved-out igloo. The front entrance was large enough for us to crawl into. We couldn't stand but could sit comfortably on cleared frozen ground out of the cold wind and falling snow. On several occasions over the next few days, my mother would make a thermos of hot chocolate. We would crawl into our igloo, sit with our backs against the icy walls and sip a cup of hot sweet chocolate.

The rutted road adjacent to the path was frequented throughout the year by a truck driven by the iceman to deliver blocks of ice for the family ice chest. The chest was wood with insulation and a metal liner inside. A block of ice was placed in a compartment at the top.

Periodically a truck loaded with coal slowly crept through muddy ruts to deposit a load down the chute into the basement storage area. Coal was used to heat the house in a potbelly stove in the living room. During the winter my dad would make sure that the stove was constantly stoked to insure livable temperatures throughout the house. Many times I would get up, gather my clothes, scamper down the stairs and stand around the warm black potbelly to dress for the day.

The road also provided frequent access to our home by a vehicle called a crummy driven by my father. The crummy provided transportation to and from a logging camp on the shores of the Flambeau River, where my father was foreman. The camp was ten plus miles from home. The crummy was used to pick up loggers for their weekly stay at the camp and to return them home for the weekend.

Over time, through use in all kinds of weather, the road became rutted and changed in appearance as the seasons passed.

On the south side of the house was the family garden, on a plot approximately 100 feet by 40 feet. Every year mom and dad planted rows of vegetables and berries for family meals and to can for future use. The pantry shelves just off the kitchen were lined with row after row of jars of fruit and vegetables.

I don't have many memorable thoughts about the garden other than that I was often expected to remove weeds. A pleasant memory is when I would walk along the rows of carrots and look for one to pull out of the ground to eat. I can still savor the sweet taste of a fresh carrot.

Beyond the garden a long fence separated our property from the world outside. On the other side was open ground distinguished here and there by oak trees positioned for maximum use of the land to harvest a variety of seasonal crops.

In the distance was a muted image of the Sash and Door Company. It was silhouetted on the horizon by a curl of smoke that flowed from a chimney. The company was a town fixture and offered employment to many. Its presence was noted each day by a loud high-pitched whistle that signaled the end of the workday at 5:00 pm, Monday through Saturday. If I was out and about with my friends it was a signal to start for home. I was expected to be home when dad arrived from work. I don't recall whether I was on time ever being an issue. I do remember my rapid run a few times to insure that I arrived on time.

My home provided privacy and a quiet way to live. I remember it with warm feelings and many happy memories.

# CHAPTER TWO – PETS

The years Christine and I have been together always included ownership of a cat and/or dog. Our divergent personalities have resulted in different approaches for their care and often these disparities to humorous moments.

# EDDY

On April 3, 2004 we had Sasha, our 13-year-old Rottweiler, put down. It was a heart-breaking decision. She had been an everyday companion, particularly for Christine. I suggested it would be in our best interests to delay ownership of another dog for at least a year. Christine agreed an absence for a period of time might be a good idea.

On April 5th when I arrived home from work she told me she had talked with a breeder of Goldens in Wilcox, Nebraska. My first question, "What's a Golden?" When it became clear she was talking about a Golden Retriever, I was speechless. It had been only two days since we made the decision about Sasha.

"What happened to our agreement? You know, no dog for the next year or so?"

"I never agreed to a year. I saw a picture of the puppy and thought it would be good to get another dog right away."

"Picture, what picture?"

"I saw the picture on the breeder's website. I also completed an online application to determine our suitability for ownership."

I locked in on the suitability concept.

"Suitable! We raised Sasha for 13 years. We went the extra mile for her. I don't mistreat animals, other than moles. Why do we need to be evaluated for suitability?"

The breeder had told Christine, "You are in luck, a sale of a male puppy has been cancelled and is now available. You and Robert would be perfect owners. I need an answer within the next 24 hours because there are many other potential buyers."

"No, absolutely not!"

Christine countered with a slight smile, a steely stare and silence. I stared back. You could have heard a pin drop. I couldn't stand it. I paced back and forth and ranted. "You are more concerned about having a dog than about me."

I reminded her how much money the dog would cost: "The expense will impair our ability to retire soon."

I raised safety concerns: "We will constantly have to be on the look out for bald eagles. They will swoop down, snatch the puppy and feed him to baby eagles."

She remained silent. I stopped, looked at her, smiled meekly and laughed. "Call the breeder and tell her we would love to buy the puppy."

I walked down to my shop, sat among my many woodworking tools and looked around. I decided to buy a new wood-turning lathe.

Our new puppy arrived on April 7, 2004, at 1:00 p.m. on a Northwest Airlines cargo flight from Omaha. Christine was ecstatic. I was still in shock.

We named our new puppy Eddy, like an eddy in a river. I have adjusted; in fact I have become quite fond of our new Golden. I dutifully watch for bald eagles to insure he is safe from attacks.

## LIFE WITH EDDY

Eddy has been with us for seventeen months. I have owned several dogs in my lifetime but I've never had the pleasure of one like Eddy. When he sees me he greets me with a wag of his tail. When asleep he senses my presence, he opens his eyes and appears to smile. He often rolls over on his back with legs extended skyward; a suggestion he would like a tummy rub. I always comply.

Life with Eddy has been an adjustment. It's like raising a child and often results in disagreements. On occasion I thought we would need canine family counseling. One area of disagreement related to the river that flows past our home.

In the spring the river is high due to mountain snow run off. Eddy had been with us for a few months. We thought it would be a growth experience to allow him to explore the Roy Family estate. A leash would not be necessary. Eddy sprinted to the river edge and leaped into the swollen waters. We watched in disbelief, as he was pulled downstream and disappeared around the bend. I stumbled down the rock- strewn shoreline. I rounded the bend and to my surprise and relief saw him sitting on the bank, He cocked his head to one side and looked me in the eye.

He seemed to say, "What took you so long?" He sprinted past me. I slowly maneuvered back upstream wet and bruised, and rounded the bend. Eddy sat beside Christine like nothing had happened.

In the fall a run of Chinook salmon migrate up the river to spawn. Upon completion of this ritual they die and their remains are scattered up and down the riverbanks. We were concerned Eddy would eat a decayed carcass, which would cause salmon poisoning or Salmonella.

One afternoon we observed a bald eagle across the river with a salmon carcass on a large flat rock. The eagle, wings spread for balance, with surgical precision, used its knife-like curved beak to dissect and eat the fish. A short time later the eagle left, and was replaced by another. With the same intensity it ate the rest of the decayed fish.

That evening we sat on the riverbank and observed the activity of the wildlife—one of our favorite pastimes. Suddenly Eddy leaped into the water and swam across.

We shouted, "Eddy come, Eddy come." He ignored us. We pleaded with requests such as "puppy treats" and "let's go for a ride."

Without as much as a backward glance he swam over to the large flat rock. He climbed up and with nose down covered every square inch of its surface. Finally he looked up, leaped into the river, swam back across and sprinted past us to the house. We looked at each other and simultaneously asked, "Do you think he ate any salmon?"

We walked up to the house. Christine toweled him dry in his usual four legs skyward position.

She said, "Let's take him to the vet."

"I wouldn't worry about it; I'm sure he didn't eat any salmon."

· A heated dispute ensued,

Exasperated I said, "Why don't I wade across the river and examine the flat rock. The river is reasonably low. I'll put on my chest waders, wading shoes and with my walking stick I'll get over and back without difficulty."

I thought she would nix the idea out of concern for my safety, but I was wrong. She enthusiastically endorsed my brilliant plan.

In the middle of the river with my natural beaver-gnawed walking stick I slipped, stumbled and edged my way across as the current aggressively pulled against my legs. I occasionally looked down river for a possible life saving rock or an extended tree branch to grasp should I fall and tumble out of control.

Finally I reached the infamous flat rock. It was bare and discolored, maybe from the decayed salmon or maybe just naturally. I looked across the river. Christine stood on the far bank, Eddy obediently at her side.

I made it safely back. She was satisfied that Eddy had not eaten any salmon. She suggested my wading method might be needed in the future. I stared at her, grunted and walked up to the house. I muttered, "When there is a cold day in hell."

I never waded across the river again to look at discolored rocks. However, it took one more Eddy crossing episode to come to an understanding with Christine.

During the warm weather months we often relax in a canopy swing on the riverbank. One evening Eddy ran by and jumped into the river, swam across and disappeared into the woods.

Christine said, "We need to go after him."

Without further comment she walked to the house. The river was swollen with snow runoff so I was confident she would not ask me to wade across. I was sure Eddy would return in a few minutes.

I gently swayed and dozed. I sensed a presence in front of me. Startled, I opened my eyes and saw Christine with my float tube draped across her shoulders, my waders, wading shoes and flippers clutched in her arms.

She said, "Get dressed, go across the river with your float tube, find Eddy and bring him home."

I calmly said no. A lively discussion followed.

I held my ground. "He's all right. He will return shortly!"

When I was just about to give in to her persistent demands Eddy strolled out of the woods and leaped into the river. He swam effortlessly back across. He ran up to us, stopped and with enthusiastic body gyrations, sprayed water on both of us. He sprinted up to the house and sat down on the deck.

Without a word Christine and I returned to the house. She carried my waders, wading shoes and flippers. The float tube was draped around her neck. I smiled to myself. I'm not positive but I think she smiled also.

There has not been another request to float across the river in pursuit of Eddy, at least not yet.

# PING, OUR FERAL FELINE

Over an unknown period of time Ping our jet black feral feline survived in the forested area along the shores of the river that flows past our home. One day she adopted us as her guardians and established living quarters within our home.

Even with a domesticated existence, she made frequent sojourns into the forest to hunt for creatures living within. Her skills were astounding with many deliveries to our front porch of birds, mice and at times rabbits as large as herself. We attempted to discourage her efforts through feeding of quality cat food. Although she no longer devoured her conquests, she continued to forage in the surrounding forest and deliver her catch to the front porch.

The forest is home to large creatures like coyotes, bobcats, bald eagles and owls, all of which threaten the existence of a somewhat domesticated cat. Most of the time Ping slept in the house at night, but occasionally she would disappear around dusk and not return until morning. We always left a window open in the garage.

One of her nightly excursions ended in a failure to return. Several mornings thereafter we arose at daylight and anxiously opened the garage door in anticipation. Each time we found only her crumpled bedding. We slowly accepted the reality she was not going to return. We miss her.

# LEWIS (LEWIE)

Within a few days after Ping's disappearance I heard snippets of a conversation between Christine and our friend Sharon about ragdolls. I surmised the discussion had something to do with Sharon's Saturday Market business.

A short time later I found an article on Christine's desk entitled The History & Development Evolution of The Ragdoll Cat. Its first paragraph created a wave of anxiety. "The origins and development of the Ragdoll breed are difficult to establish and shrouded in myths. Nonetheless, there are certain things we do know for sure." The next statement eroded any desire to owner a Ragdoll: "As time went on the breeder's statements and claims about the breed became strange, supernatural and very hard to believe. Ragdoll cats have human genes, they are immune to pain and represent a link between us and space aliens." I realized Christine planned to buy a Ragdoll.

A week later we sat on two small chairs in a room surrounded by a litter of Ragdoll kittens. The owner of Ragnificent Ragdolls, her daughter and another women sprawled on the floor among the kittens. How Christine became aware of Ragnificent Ragdolls is a mystery. Somehow she made contact and learned there were kittens for sale. An interview with a prospective buyer was required and designed to take place in the living quarters of a marauding band of the young Ragdolls.

The kittens played and meowed for attention. Several clawed at my pant legs and attempted to climb up on to my lap. I picked up a kitten, stroked it gently under the chin and uttered nonsensical soothing throaty cat-like sounds. The kitten purred and curled up in my lap.

At the end of the visit the owner announced she would be honored to sell us one of the male kittens at a discounted price of $550. I was stunned by the price. It was hard for me to accept that for $550 we were buying a cat called a Ragdoll, created by a breeder who claimed the Ragdoll had human genes, was immune to pain and represented a link with space aliens!

I had a flashback to when I lived at home with my parents. There was never a non-human allowed to live inside the house, but a male and female feline couple lived under the house and every so often produced a litter of kittens.

They were ferocious defenders of their appropriated living area. We fed them regularly, always with caution because of a predisposition to attack anyone who came within a three-foot radius of their domain.

I thought about this long-ago memory and my current experience and realized reality had shifted dramatically. I grudgingly agreed to fork over the $550.

Since we lived on the East Fork of the Lewis River, we christened our newly acquired Ragdoll Lewis. As weeks passed we started to call him Lewie, which seemed to be a better fit.

Eleven months have passed since Lewie became a member of the Roy household. Initially it was a difficult adjustment to have another responsibility that required daily care and at times crisis management. When Lewie escaped to the outside world and refused to return I chased him. I had to remind myself of my newfound awareness that as time passes reality changes and I needed to adjust. I believe I have. Lewie has become my best friend!

## EDDY AND LEWIE

Lewie glanced at Eddy. "How do you like living here?"

Eddy sprawled, eyes closed. "You woke me up. I'm tired. Let's talk another time."

"That's what you always say–another time. Why do you always ignore me?"

"Ignore you, that's impossible. You are constantly running around the house, hiding and attacking me from behind furniture, meowing and hissing.  Living with you is weird."

"Oh yeah! What about the times when I'm sleeping and you come by and bark, bop me on the head with your paw and slobber all over me?"

"Like you mind. You always leap on me and try to take a bite out of my neck."

"Now that you are awake how about my question. You know–about living here."

"Overall I like it. How about you?"

"I like it too. I would like to go outside more. You get to go out all the time."

"Yeah, but it's for your own good. You're clueless about what's out there that could harm you, like the river, eagles, owls, coyotes and who knows what else."

"Hey, I can take care of myself. Besides you are always around and I know you wouldn't let anything happen to me."

"Don't depend on me. Half the time nobody knows where you are. Robert and Christine chase you around the yard and yell at each other about how to corner you and bring you back into the house."

"I don't want go back in the house. Do you see how smart I am? I go under the truck and refuse to come out. They can't get me there!"

"Oh that's brilliant. Sit under the truck. I bet that's a lot of fun."

Lewie: "I get confused about what Christine and Robert want. Christine seems to have more rules than Robert. Although in some ways she takes better care of me. She wipes out my eyes, cuts my toenails and brushes my fur. Robert never does."

Eddy: "Yeah, Christine is that way with me too. The rule thing drives me crazy, especially when we go for walks. They argue about whether I should be on a leash when we walk up the road and through the forest. I don't want to be on a leash. I want to chase deer, rabbits, squirrels and whatever else I smell or see."

"Remember when Christine tried to put me on a leash and take me for a walk? I hated that. All I remember was the leash wrapped around my neck. I clawed, hissed, and rolled on the ground to get it off me."

"Boy that was funny. You wrapped yourself up in that rope as you clawed and hissed. I barked until tears came to my eyes."

"It wasn't funny. I could have choked to death. Would you laugh if I had died?"

"Oh don't be so dramatic. That's your problem–you always take things too seriously. But you don't have it so bad. You wake Robert up every morning at 5:00, purr in his ear and lick his face. He gets up, stumbles down stairs with you in the lead, you roll over on your back on the kitchen floor, he rubs your stomach, utters nonsensical comments and proceeds to feed you. Who do you think you are anyway? I don't get fed until hours later!"

"I'm hungry. You could do the same thing but you snore away, too lazy to get up. So don't complain."

"Oh yeah! You're only interested in yourself. After you eat a few bites you rush upstairs, demand to get in the bathroom with Robert and then jump up on the counter and scratch at the window for Robert to open it for you. Guess what? He always does. You are so spoiled."

"Do I sense a widdle-bito-bit of jealously from Eddy-weddy? Hey, that hurt. Get your big furry paw off me!"

"One of these days! One of these days! Pow! It will be all over for you!"

"Oh, I'm shaking in my paws. You're all talk. I watch you. You're friendly with everyone, you bounce up to people, tail wagging. To get attention you roll over on your back. Then you get a belly rub with adoring gibberish utterances. I get nauseated as I watch you."

"Yeah, I like those belly rubs." Eddy looked at Lewie with a smug smile. "I bet you'd like a few more yourself. You ought to try it more often. It would be a riot to watch you. Everyone would think you'd gone off the deep end or something. That reminds me. I heard Robert and Christine talking–something about Ragdolls having human genes and a link between humans and space aliens. What's that all about? Is there something I have to worry about, like you becoming a deranged blood sucking alien?"

"Oh for God's sake. I'm a cat that's all. I might add though I do have superior intellect and I'm prettier than most. Qualities I'm sure you have noticed."

"And you're delusional!" Eddy looked at Lewie, then sighed, rolled over and snuggled up to Christine.

Christine stroked Eddy affectionately. "Good morning Eddy."

Eddy to himself: "I love living here,"

Lewie walked over to Eddy and curled up next to him on his back, paws pointing skyward. "Eddy, no matter what we say to each other I love living here and having you as my brother. I would miss you if you were not here. Thanks for talking to me. It was fun."

Eddy: "Yeah, I feel the same about you. Let's talk again soon. Just don't become a blood-sucking alien while I'm asleep."

# CHAPTER THREE – BIRDS, FISH AND YOURS TRULY

My childhood years were spent living and playing in the North Woods of Wisconsin and the foothills of the Western Cascades of Oregon. Fishing mountain lakes and streams was one of my favorite pastimes. I acquired an appreciation for forested wilderness and the wildlife that lived within and along the shores of meandering waterways.

## THE EAGLE

Gazing out the upstairs window I see
An Eagle
Majestically perched on a tree branch
Bordering a stream below,

White neck, head striped in black,
Yellow hooked beak,
Rhythmic chatter,
Piercing eyes transfixed
Watching flowing waters,

Rotating head stops, silently gazes,
Suddenly wings unfurled,
Drops, razor sharp talons prepared.

Explosive splash on water surface,
Wings move powerfully through the morning air.


Clutched firmly
A rainbow colored prize undulating up and down.


# THE LAKE

It is a sunny day. A gentle breeze pushes water against the boat moored to the dock. The rhythmic lapping is the only sound in the quiet of the afternoon.

I'm sitting on the porch of a cabin on the shores of a mountain lake in British Columbia, Canada. This is my 22nd summer at the lake. Over the years many changes have happened, but it seems like time stands still. The cabins, the boats, the people and the daily routine are the same.

I have been here a few days and have difficulty remembering what day it is. A nap or fishing seems to be my next decision. Guess what? It will be here the next minute, hour, week or year. I think I will sit for a while and see what happens.


# CAUSE AND EFFECT

Imagine a sunny morning in a small boat at anchor. The fish are not feeding on surface offerings so I'm fly fishing with a full sink line and one of my favorite flies, the peacock nymph. On my fifth or sixth cast, I feel the familiar downward thrust of my fly rod. A large trout has consumed my fly.

My line tightens. The fish catapults out of the water. Glistening in the light of day it turns over and returns. The screaming sound of my fly line being pulled from my reel and the fish's acrobatic attempts to relieve itself of the obstruction protruding from its jaw ensues.

Out of the corner of my eye I notice a loon swimming toward me. The loons have learned a fish attached to a fly line is ripe for the taking. I review my options.

There is only one choice: quickly catch and release the fish. I reel it in and let it go seconds before the loon arrives. I smile with satisfaction. I caught and released a mint-bright four-pound (estimated) Kamloops trout and outsmarted a fish-stalking loon. My smugness is short-lived. I look around. The loon is nowhere to be seen.

It surfaces with a trout (my fish I'm sure) in its mouth and attempts to swallow it whole. Due to the size of the fish, the loon cannot complete the task and drops the fish into the lake. The fish, alive but injured, swims on its side 100 feet or more on the surface. The loon spots the fish and moves toward its morning meal.

Suddenly, out of nowhere, a bald eagle, wings furled, legs extended, talons curled and ready, with perfect timing snatches the fish from the lake. As it flies away the fish comes loose and drops into the water. The bird turns and swoops but fails to retrieve the floating prize.

Three more eagles arrive on the scene. Two of them are the companions and offspring of the eagle who tried to recover the fish from the lake. The fourth is competing for the lifeless form floating on surface.

The mate and young offspring dive-bomb the intruder and divert attempts to snatch the fish from the lake. These tactics allow the original eagle to pluck the lifeless prize from the surface.

Meanwhile the loon—legs churning, wings flapping on the lake's surface—moves rapidly toward the fish only to see it fly away clutched in the eagle's claws. I swear I heard it utter several expletives.

I gaze at the shadowy shoreline. I wonder if similar events occur among the wildlife that live in the forest. I pick up my fly rod and began to cast. It dawns on me and I start to laugh. I was the instigator of the loon, Eagle and fish competitive interchange. I caught the fish! Cause and Effect.

My fly line lands on the lake's surface and as my fly slowly sinks below the surface I say to myself, "Let's see what else I can cause to happen this sunny morning."

# BABY SWALLOW

The story of baby swallow started two days ago upon our arrival at our lakeside cabin. We noticed parent swallows feeding their one offspring in a nest high up in the rafters on the porch. The young bird looked ready for flight. Not to be! The next morning it was hanging by one wing, entangled in a string-like attachment protruding from the nest.

Christine came to the rescue. She climbed onto the porch table and placed the baby bird back in the nest. Then the nest along with the swallow tumbled into her hands.

Upon my return from morning fishing, Christine greeted me with the nest and the swallow clutched in her hands along with a request to return them to the rafters. I thought she was kidding but her insistent demeanor told me otherwise. I made several attempts without success.

Realizing that the nest was not going to stay aloft, we put it and the baby bird on the deck table. As I attempted to return our new feathered responsibility to its nest I noticed fishing line leader wrapped around one of its wings. Upon further inspection I observed that the leader was an integral part of the nest and interwoven in the overall construction. Unfortunately much of the line protruded, with loops inside. The baby bird's wing had become snared in one of leader line loops.

It was hard to determine whether the wing was broken or merely restricted. Using fly tying scissors I cut the leader in several places and gently pulled the individual strips from around the wing. The young bird flapped both wings, much to the joy and laughter of Christine and me.

We still couldn't return the swallow and nest to the porch rafters, so Christine placed them in an aluminum colander filled with grass on the porch table.

The parent swallows flew around in a frenzy, chirping sounds of distress. We were apprehensive about possible parental abandonment.

Christine and I attempted to feed our new responsibility. I gathered small insects caught in the strands of a spider web, dug earthworms and mixed them together in a liquid concoction of raw egg and water and offered it, drop by drop, through a needle-like syringe. To no avail! However, after several hours of continuous fly-bys, the parents started to feed their young offspring.

This incident became the topic of discussion and curiosity of everyone, particularly the children, in the nearby cabins. Christine and I, along with camp hosts Parry and Joan, initiated flyaway attempts by tossing the young bird into the air. Each attempt caused rapid flapping of wings and flights of a short duration. A couple resulted in splashdowns in the lake. To my surprise the feathered infant swam, feet churning, wings flapping on the water surface, back to the shore. Each time we returned our young bird-swimmer to its homemade nest.

The next day Christine and I were on the lake enjoying the evening fly-fishing. When we returned to the house, the nest was empty and the parents no longer hovered. We looked around outside but found no sign of our infant bird guest. Our hope was that with continued devotion and care by the parents that our young friend was able to fly away.

But a nagging unpleasant thought occurred to us. Our neighbor told us she had chased the camp cats, Rusty and Cheyenne, from our cabin deck. We don't want to unfairly malign these feline residents. We have had many joyful moments responding to their playful and good-natured demeanor.

Initially I found the swallow episode annoying. I had come to the lake to fish, relax and get away from day-to-day responsibilities. However, as time passed I became concerned about what would happen to our young feathered friend. I was impressed and surprised by the human qualities that the parents exhibited toward their offspring. I don't know the final outcome but it was a stark reminder of how programmed we are in efforts to insure we continue as a species, human or otherwise. Life is priceless. We shouldn't take it for granted.

## THE STEELHEAD

Spring, summer, fall and winter steelhead return from the ocean to the river of their birth. They swim upstream and lay roe for creation of new life.

First a female fish meticulously constructs a sizeable depression, called a spawning redd, in the gravel on the river bottom. This task is skillfully done through repetitive back-and-forth motions with body and tail. After she deposits the roe, a male moves slowly over the nest for fertilization. The female swims upstream and uses her body and tail to move gravel downstream to cover the nest providing, protection from predators and increased water velocity.

A few weeks later, young steelhead fry emerge. A year or more after that, they have grown to sufficient size and instinctively move down river toward the ocean. They spend the next two to three years in the salty waters growing to seven to ten pounds or more. Through some little understood survival signal, they return to the river of their birth.

## STEELHEAD FANTASY

It's 6:00 o'clock on a quiet Sunday morning. The day is cloudy with wisps of fog intermingled among the fir trees that border the river that flows past our home. The river moves with increased volume and speed due to the heavy rains of the past few days.

I stare out the upstairs window. I fantasize—I see myself, fly rod in hand, casting a bright orange and pink fly into the wintergreen waters. I attentively follow the fly, barely submerged below the surface.

Suddenly I see a long dark shadow aggressively engulf its presence. It's a large steelhead that realizes the newly acquired prize is not eatable but rather firmly attached to its jaw.

Realization stimulates immediate survival energy and rapid movement down the river. My fly line, with a familiar screaming sound, rushes from my reel. I attempt to slow the fish's down-river journey. I stop the rapid removal of line. As it tightens, a chrome-colored body, gleaming in the light of the day, is forced out of the water.

This is followed by powerful movement up and down the river along with acrobatic surface eruptions and with me, heart pounding, trying to keep up with this amazing, beautiful steelhead.

I gently move a wild female steelhead toward the shoreline. When she is at my feet I place my hand around her tail and firmly hold her in place in the shallow water. She shudders, gills moving rhythmically. I lift her from the life-sustaining waters, remove the bright orange and pink fly and gently return her to the river. She slowly moves back and forth at my feet, then, with newfound energy, moves rapidly into the swift flowing waters.

The rhythmic beeping of the coffee maker interrupts my reverie. I sit at the kitchen counter, sipping a freshly brewed cup of coffee. I think about my imagined fishing episode. I vividly picture large female steelhead swimming relentlessly upstream and in a wondering whisper say to myself, "Someone or something has done good here." Then again I imagine casting a bright orange and pink fly into the wintergreen waters.

# BARB SAUR

Barb Saur. After I retired from Clark College I signed up for a Creative Writing class offered in its Mature Learning program. I have now taken the class every quarter for 14 years. I took part in the first Elderberry Wine book, and am excited to be a part of this one. Time will tell if I am a better writer or just have a better editor

# ROAMING FROM LONGFELLOW TO PARIS AND BACK AGAIN

When given the prompt by my instructor to write an essay on Light and Shadow, lines from Longfellow's "The Children's Hour" came to me and would not let go.

Between the dark and the daylight,
When night is beginning to lower,
They took me to light and shadows in Paris.

My imagination carried me to the bright lights emanating from the Eiffel Tower, then to deep shadows under the bridges over the Seine. In my reverie I saw the river reflecting the City of Light in a kaleidoscope of colors and shapes as it slowly wove its way through the magical city and neighborhoods. Montmartre came into view, and the white dome of the Sacre-Coeur visible from most any point in Paris.

Pigalle, the red light district where bohemians work and play at night, is quietly busy; daytime on the right bank sees much setting up of canvases and paints, like Dali, Monet, Picasso and even Van Gogh in years gone by.

My dream goes on. The Moulin Rouge Cabaret greets me; its big red windmill invites me to come on in, drink and see the show. Its bright color gives me a new understanding of "red light district." But wait—is that Irma La Douce standing there on the corner?

I accept the invitation and as I walk into the smoky fragrant room there's action and music and dancing; voices everywhere shouting over the music. I almost expect to see Toulouse-Lautrec sitting at a table sipping Absinthe as he sketches the patrons and dancers. This dream still seems real, as if I am there living it.

My musing ends by going from Paris back to Longfellow:

And there I will keep you forever,
Yes, forever and a day,
Till the walls shall crumble in ruin,
And moulder in dust away!

# THE VEIL

Midnight November 6, 1929. A blood-curdling scream echoed down the halls, followed by a low moan and a shout of joy.

"It's a girl!"

"She's a beauty, she must weigh 8 pounds. Part of the placenta is over her face; quick, clean it off."

"A veil over her face, they say that means she will have psychic powers—you know—be clairvoyant."

"Phooey on your black magic, don't pay any attention to her. What's her name honey?"

"We—we haven't decided for sure, I need to talk to Jack first. Is he here?"

"Oh, he's out in the waiting room. We'll get him when you are back in a room. Right now we have some work to do here," the nurse said. "Give her another shot of that ether, we need to get her cleaned up. Relax honey, you'll be together soon."

The ether put her to sleep and the next thing Lucille knew she was in the dismal room with Jack looking down at her, smiling and flush with pride.

"Oh, Jack, have you seen her? They say she's a real beauty, 8 pounds and 6 ounces. I haven't seen her yet—will they bring her in soon so that I can see and hold her? What did they tell you about her? Did they say she had a veil over her face when she was born and might be psychic? Is that a good thing? I hope they got it all off. Should I be worried about her maybe being 'clayervont'? I wish they would hurry and bring the baby, I want to check her out for myself. What are we going to name her? I thought Jacque Nan Nelsen, what do you think? Doesn't that sound like a nice name? First name for you and my mother's name in the middle, isn't that sweet?"

"I'm so proud I'm about to burst," Jack said, "If you like that name it's good enough for me. Wait till you see her, she's round and sweet with a teeny button nose. And what a set of lungs. Everyone in the hospital has said they never heard a new baby with such a loud cry. I didn't see anything on her face so they musta' got it all off. By the way she has a lot of hair, not bald like me. You just gotta see her."

Lucille began to cry. "There must be something wrong or they would have brought her in for me to see before now, is there some-thing you're not telling me Jack?" She sobbed uncontrollably.

Jack held her and patted her lovingly, reassuring her that their new baby was okay and that she was just having a reaction to the ether.

"I know now where this little girl got her lungs, boy what a bunch of cry babies. Here is your little doll all cleaned up and ready to meet her mama. You gotta wipe away those tears and smile pretty for your new daughter."

"Oh, thank you," Lucille said as she reached for the bundle in the nurse's arms. "I just want to hold her and check her out. You precious baby–can you believe it Jack? This is our little Jacque. I have to look at her feet and hold her hands just to feel how real she is. She is perfect, and there is no veil over her pretty face!"

As Jacque grew, Lucille often referred to the veil that the nurse had said made her daughter psychic. She really believed there was something to it: Jacque seemed to know some things before they happened. Lucille noticed that her little girl was particularly intuitive. Especially when her youngest sister was born and she told her Mom and Dad (who badly wanted a boy to go with their two little girls) that it was going to be another girl. "I was right!" she declared, when Joan was born!

# A POST CARD FROM
# VANCOUVER, WASHINGTON,
# U.S.A.

Vancouver, Washington, is often confused with the Canadian city to the north. It is also described as "that town across the Columbia River from Portland, Oregon." It has always struggled for identity. Even Washington State is known as "the other Washington." There have been several movements afoot to change the name to Fort Vancouver (a change I would favor), but the closest we have come to changing the name is to add U.S.A!

Vancouver, Washington, U.S.A., is a historic city on the southwest border of Washington, proud of its heritage, growing out of its boundaries and changing daily. In 1792, British Captain George Vancouver sent a party to explore 100 miles up the Columbia River. Lt. William Brougton led that trip and established a point on the river in honor of Captain Vancouver. Lewis and Clark stopped here on their way to the Pacific in 1806, and camped over night on the beach near our waterfront. In 1825, when it was decided to establish a Hudson's Bay Company in the Northwest to trade with the Chinook Indians, Dr. John McLoughlin was sent to establish Fort Vancouver and was the first factor here. McLoughlin was responsible for the name "Fort Vancouver," in deference to Broughton's original map, and it was so called long before the Canadian Vancouver was established.

Forty-one years ago, in 1969, it was a "one-bridge town" on the I-5 corridor linking Vancouver, B.C., Seattle, Portland and points south through to California. In those days it had a Woolworth Variety Store complete with lunch counter, a J.C. Penney store, a local dry goods company called the CC Store, the Sassy Dress Shop, and many other small businesses on Main Street. Some people would have called it a sleepy little town on the banks of the Columbia. I just called it "home at last."

Approaching the city from the south, over the Columbia, you can see that the Fort, established by the army in1849, has benefitted from a restoration project that started thirty years ago. On the slope just above the Fort, a majestic row of white Victorian houses catches your eye. If not for the fact that you are on a freeway traveling 55 mph, you could imagine you were back in the 19th century arriving for a soirée at the General's House. "Officer's Row," as it's known, is a reminder of Vancouver's historic past and connection to the U.S. Army. General George Marshall served as commander there, and General O.O. Howard before him; General Ulysses S. Grant spent a night or two there early in his career, checking out the troops. In some of these imposing houses, museums have been established in the names of those famous men; in others there are professional offices and apartments for rent.

On the parade ground just below the officers' quarters, troops marched for over a century. Recently the Army buildings that had served as an Armory for a small contingent of the Washington National Guard were closed and moved to Seattle. When I came here forty-one years ago it was still being used as a U.S. Army training ground.

Located next door to this complex of history is Pioneer Field, a small historic airfield. It is a testimony to how the town has progressed from that first landing of Lewis and Clark, and the tenacity of a few dedicated flyers! I only mention the airfield in passing, because of its physical presence next to the Fort.

Tucked between State Highway 14, the railroad berm, and the Fort is the "Old Apple Tree." Said to be one of the first to be planted at the Fort by Dr. McLoughlin, it has been preserved and revered since before I became a resident. It was saved from the highway builders by a small group of zealous Vancouverites. The highway was built around the Old Apple Tree, which has been designated a part of the National Historic Site. I believe this one item, more than anything else, symbolizes the spirit of our community and its pride in our history. A community that would protect an old apple tree growing in the middle of a highway is where I want to live.

Much change has taken place in forty-one years. Main Street became a series of card rooms, thrift and discount stores, pawn shops, empty store fronts, office buildings, and antique shops. My love of Vancouver has never wavered and I love living here, however. With the advent of the shopping mall at Jantzen Beach across the I-5 bridge from downtown (in Oregon, where there is no sales tax), followed a few years later by the larger and more luxurious Vancouver Mall near a second bridge on a new freeway (Interstate 205), our quiet little town is emerging as a sleeping giant!

In recent years Vancouver has reclaimed the downtown area with a four star hotel and classy condos and apartments, all around the rejuvenated Esther Short Park. We are the third largest city in Washington, and fast becoming second only to Seattle. It's strange, isn't it, that people still confuse us with "that city in Canada," or that "other Washington"?

# MY GRANDMA'S HOUSE

My grandma's house
All covered with blackberries now
Once rang with children's laughter.
The windows that sparkled when viewed from outside are broken,
The swing hanging from one of the massive box elders is gone.
That swing was my window to the world,
When I pumped up high I was flying–
Pumping it half-way I was a circus act
Twisting and whirling.
When I just let it take me slowly and softly
I mused on the world around me–
Wondering where did stars go in the daytime,
Why was there thunder and lightning?
What would I be
A singer–
Like Margaret Whiting?
"Barbara!"
My reverie stopped.
Grandma was standing in the kitchen door,
"Come in now, we are ready for dinner."
Her apron was dusted with flour.
Her sweet face smiled brightly
No blackberries growing on the house then.

Singing a happy song,
I danced into her arms.
I loved my grandma's house!

# FAMILY INHERITANCE

They said I would inherit some day
But what would they bequeath me?
A diamond ring, a golden tray,
Or a silver pot for tea?

I must admit much time was spent
In musing what 'twould be.
Imagining what great treasure
They would bequeath to me.

When finally my gifts I knew
The wondrous things they chose,
My mother's shining spirit true,
My father's runny nose.

# CHANGING SEASONS

A few dancing pink and purple fuchsias
("Dark Eyes," I think).
Blue lobelia blossoms,
Hanging from the end of their weathered stems,
Try valiantly to put on a show.
A red Bromeliad points bravely to the western sun—
Blotches on the green leaves say, "The end is coming."
Pansies, bought to brighten up the dark corners—
Wilt down in their tiny cramped pots.
A garden of neglect,
The gardener, aging as the flowers—
"Is it too much?" she asks,
"Trying to cheer up the corners?"

# THE SNAKE

The river calls to me.
Dark green water shiny like satin
Curling around the bend.
Calling out like a lover.
I respond and sink into
Its frigid darkness
The water embraces me and I embrace it.

Remembrances of my first swim
A child in Burley, Idaho,
On Rotary Beach,
Swim lessons, no fear.

On the banks of the river
I catch my first trout.
It wriggles and writhes
To get off my hook.

The river winds its way
By way of the irrigation canal,
It waters my pinto beans.
The canal moves slowly
From farm to farm.
At the dam it flows back
Into the Snake River.
Tossed over giant rocks
It rushes, churns, and bubbles.

Finally it runs peacefully
And is satin once again,
Snaking through the canyon,
Quickening to join the
Mighty Columbia.

# JAN SCHAEFLER

Jan Schaefler. I have wanted to write ever since I was a young girl. I never considered that I had writing talent, so I never pursued that path. Even when I received encouragement from teachers and instructors, I did not see writing as something I could do. Along life's way, a supervisor at worked inspired me to write things I didn't know were there. Although I have a lot to learn, it's never too late to follow that dream.

# YESTERDAYS GONE BY

In times past, my life was lived in utter despair;
Contentment and happiness were exceedingly rare.
The thorns from my youth had imprisoned my mind
Keeping me from countless riches to find.

When I so desperately tried to grasp life in my bare hands,
I found only pebbles sieved from the sands.
As particles fell rapidly to earth,
Each speck flowed out to sea in the chilling surf.

Escaping any real chance of hope
And feeling no longer could I cope,
I saw before me a fluttering butterfly
Letting me know to leave behind the days gone by.

The Spirit of God had entered from above
Filling my essence with gratification and love.
Doors opened to prosperity and freedom
On my way to whom I was meant to become.

A peacefulness began to settle within me,
Setting the restraints of my mind free.
Like the elusive butterfly
So are the yesterdays gone by.

# MY TIME HAS COME

In the stillness of the day, I sit quietly and ponder
Through endless potentials and possibilities, I begin to wander.
I fear that should I fail, will I lose my mind?
But then I ask myself, what if it is success I find?

What if I reach for the stars, and the moon is as far as I can go?
What if the moon becomes too much, and I want to say no?
What if all the way back down I begin to fall?
But is it not a success to go half way than not at all?

Is it not better to stretch my arms to reach into the sky,
Than to sit and do nothing, then ask why?
I know the only limitations are the ones within.
If they continue to hold me prisoner, I shall never win.

There is a story that the Spirit keeps knocking on my door to tell.
Through sharing with others, there's no need to fail.
Not everyone would care to read it,
But, somewhere there's a soul who'll want to heed it.

Somewhere is a soul who is sinking in despair
Who believes life is beyond all mortal repair.
It is that very soul that the Spirit leads me to reach.
Touch the heart and through my encounters, teach.

So, I set out to sail though the waters may be rough.
With God's hand upon me, I must be tough.
I must not give up, but rather continue plunging forward.
For it is success and all that it holds I need to evolve toward.

To soften the heart of that one soul and what is ailing
Is worthy of my efforts and possible failings.
Thus, I must do what God has asked me to do.
My time has come; my mission is due.

Should I reach that one soul, it'll be worth my while.
I will have traveled the distance and then one more mile.
It will bring true meaning to my time,
And at long last, success will forever be mine.

# CHERYL SIMONS

Cheryl Simons. I am originally from Colorado but my husband and I moved to Kalispell, Montana, in the early 1970s. We lived on a ranch outside of Kalispell for 14 years, where we had many adventures while raising quarter horses, cattle and four children. We moved to Vancouver in 1988. I worked in the utility industry for 25 years as a manager of finance and accounting. My hobbies include reading, writing, painting, riding with my husband of 43 years on our Harley and spending time with my children and grandchildren.

# LOVE-HATE RELATIONSHIPS

I sat in the crowded airport terminal waiting for my husband's flight to arrive and I couldn't help but notice the young father with the two cute little girls. I'm a people watcher. I can't help it, I'm interested in people and I've seen a lot in my 80 years. This was back when everyone could go to the arrival and departure gates and you saw a lot of interesting things. Young couples hanging on each other, kissing and hugging one last time before one of them had to leave. Sometimes one or both of them looked rather relieved when no one was watching. There were families welcoming a child returning from college or the military or Grandma's house. It was interesting to see if the child's boyfriend or girlfriend had come to the airport with the family and then to see the arriving party try to decide who to approach first. It was obviously a tough decision, especially for the boys. Should he kiss his girlfriend in front of his mother? Business people traveling with their important looking brief cases and carry on luggage. Most of them looked exhausted and harried. The people traveling alone were especially interesting. What's that woman's story? She looks lonely, sad and preoccupied–maybe visiting a sick relative? There's another one–she looks excited with a blush of anticipation. Going to start a new job? She's dressed up, trying to look sophisticated, wearing new shoes that obviously hurt her feet. Interesting.

Anyway, this nice-looking young man with the two little girls was meeting someone very special. He carried a bouquet of red roses that had obviously cost him a pretty penny. The little girls were about 8 or 9 and 6 and all dolled up. Both had their blond hair in pony tails with ribbons that matched their dresses. They were pretty little girls and very well-behaved. Each held a piece of paper that said "Welcome Home Mommy!!" They were anxiously awaiting the arrival of this flight from L.A. I couldn't help but watch them. He was nervous, kept looking at his watch. The girls sat there quietly and patiently.

The flight arrived and I could hardly wait to see this woman. I was more interested in her than in my own husband! Not nosy mind you, just interested. For some reason my husband was one of the last people

263

to get off. I kept waiting for him and of course for the mystery woman. The young man and I were among the last people still waiting. The little girls kept asking "Where's Mommy?" He didn't know, she should be here any minute. Finally my husband appeared. I was sort of sorry that he was there, you know, now I wouldn't be able to see her. As we left I saw the young man ask the departing stewardesses if there were any more passengers on the plane. I saw one of them shake her head no.

Of course, my husband had to stop at the Men's Room before we left and I waited in the walkway. I watched as the man stuffed the roses into a trash receptacle along with the girls' signs. The little one was crying, asking where her mother was; the older girl was stoic, walking stiffly beside her father. I felt so bad for all of them, but I felt even worse for intruding on their private moment. I remember this tableau every time I go to the airport and wonder what happened to the mother and ultimately to the rest of the family.

## *Jessica*

*I had every intention of going back to Rob and the girls. I was packed and had made arrangements for the lady upstairs to take me to the airport. I'd given her a dime bag of pot to help pay for her gas. My bags were sitting by the front door when Jason walked in. He wasn't supposed to be home so early. God, he was gorgeous! He made me weak in the knees just looking at him. He was tall, slim and dark and had a dangerous air, the complete opposite of sweet, boring Rob. He had a swagger and a slow smile that turned me to jelly. "Where're you going babe?" he asked. He pulled me to him and held the back of my head while he kissed me passionately. "Are you sure you want to leave me?" No, I wasn't sure. I was addicted, he was a habit that I didn't want to break. But his wife showed up the other day. Yes, his wife. I didn't even know he was married, so when this strange woman knocked on the door I was completely taken by surprise. She'd been looking for him for several months. Apparently he was behind on his child support payments and she needed money. Child support payments! I didn't know he had kids either. His wife waited for him. He wasn't due home from rehearsal for several hours, but she refused to leave. He had a gig playing guitar at a local bar and hoped to be discovered. I hoped he'd be discovered too—maybe we'd have enough money to pay the rent this month. He didn't seem surprised to see her. I guess he figured she'd find him sooner or later. After she left with what little money we had, we had a huge fight and of course made up in the usual way afterwards. Like I said I'm hooked on him.*

*So I surveyed my options and decided that I was better off with Rob. At least he was steady and reliable and most importantly, employed. I called him, collect, and told him that I wanted to come home. He was surprised to hear from me and acted mad at first, but I was able to tease and cajole him and make him laugh. He was so easy to please. He said he'd buy me an airplane ticket and asked when I wanted to come home. I said, "Give me a few days to get some loose ends tied up. How about a week from today?" "Okay," he said, "give me your number so I can give you the flight details." I said, "I'll call you in a couple of days, I don't have a phone." He agreed, sounding excited and anxious to get me back. "That was easy," I thought, "I guess he's still crazy about me." The thought of spending the rest of my life with this dull man was almost more than I could bear. But things here with my lover were sketchy at best. And of course there are the girls.*

*I called Rob, collect again, and got the flight details. I was supposed to leave in five days. Five days here in sunny L.A. with my love trying not to think of what I was going back to. Those five days and nights were intense! When Jason walked in, my resolve vanished. I'm nuts about him—I can't help it. I just can't leave him. For the first time in my life I'm happy, excited and I look forward to every day with him even without any money. So I guess I'm not going back to Portland after all. And who am I to judge? I'm married and have kids too. They're probably better off without me anyway. I was never much of a wife and mother. They need too much from me, all of them, and I feel like they're draining me dry. But I did have every intention of going back.*

## Rob

I am such a pathetic sucker!! I can't believe that I fell for it again! At this moment I honestly hate her!! I knew it was too good to be true when Jessica called me wanting to come home. I didn't know where she'd gone when she left us, but assumed it was somewhere warm and sunny. She'd been gone for six months. She'd met that musician when he stayed with his sister across the street from us. Jess was always restless and I couldn't seem to make her happy, but man did I try! A house, furniture, car, everything and anything she wanted even when I couldn't afford it. When we had Lindsay I thought it might settle her down, but nothing changed. Then when she got pregnant with Amanda she was devastated. She worried about her figure, which I told her was perfect, and it was. I always felt so lucky to have such a beautiful wife. I'm just an everyday guy. I go to work, mow the lawn, pay my bills, and take care of my family. Slow and steady, that's me. I'm not very exciting, I know that, but I'm not a bad guy. I guess I wasn't all that surprised when I came home and found her gone. She'd sent the girls to the next door neighbor's house and left me a note saying she was sorry, but that she just couldn't do it anymore. I sat down and cried. Yes, I cried like a baby. I cried for us, for the girls and for what we could have had and I cried for myself. Then I pulled myself together and picked up the girls at Marcia's, along with the pieces of my life, and started over again.

When she called I went through every emotion imaginable. I was surprised, then pissed and then after hearing her voice I was back in love again. I am so gullible–but God I loved that woman! So I made reservations for her and waited for her to call again. I was sort of surprised when she called back. I thought that she might change her mind, but she said she was ready to come home. I felt like a kid again! I spent the next few days cleaning the house, fixing things up so that she'd be glad to be home. I bought new sheets for the bed and some fancy bath towels. I bought lotion and bubble bath for her in her favorite fragrance. She probably didn't know that I remembered, but I did.

I probably shouldn't have told the girls until she was actually here, but Lindsay knew something was going on. So we made a banner and signs saying "Welcome Home Mommy!!" and waited for the days to pass. We got up early the morning she was supposed to arrive and made sure everything was perfect. I stopped on the way to the airport and the girls helped me pick out some roses for her. We all went to the airport and waited, and waited. I kept thinking she would walk into the waiting area at any moment, but nothing. I asked the flight attendants if they were sure there wasn't anyone else on the plane. They said the plane was empty. This old lady was waiting for someone too and she kept watching us. I wanted to tell her to mind her own business. I could tell she was sorry for us and I didn't want her pity.

I didn't know what to do. I didn't know where Jess was or how to contact her. I was worried that something had happened to her, but knew in my heart that she hadn't gotten on the plane at all. I was furious and felt betrayed and stupid! The first thing I did was to stuff the damned flowers into the trash and then I took the girls' signs and threw them away too. Well, we're back to square one. Just the three of us and we're probably better off any way. Now we just have to go home, take down that silly banner and get on with our lives. No more tears!

## *Lindsay*

*I'm not surprised she didn't come home. She was always looking out the window and not paying attention to Mandy and me unless we made too much noise. Dad and Mandy and I can make it on our own. We don't need a mom, we're okay. I'm almost nine and can make peanut butter and jelly sandwiches, so we'll be fine. I cried a lot when she first left us but not anymore. I still love my mom but I kind of hate her too! I hope she never comes back!! Mandy still cries and asks where Mommy is, but she's little and doesn't understand. I didn't want to make the stupid banner or the signs either! I even had to help Mandy make her sign. She didn't know how to spell Welcome and left off the "e" any way. She's such a baby. I'm mature for my age. At least that's what Dad and Marcia next door say. I'll ask Marcia how to make tuna sandwiches so I can make more than one thing. Marcia brings us food and stuff and hangs around talking to Dad. He doesn't notice, but I think she likes him. Dad is nice to us but he's always so sad and busy working and taking care of things. I hope he doesn't decide to leave too. I don't know what we'd do then. Maybe we could live with Marcia.*

## *Jessica*

*That was ten years ago. Where have the years gone? Time flies even when you're not having fun. Jason never did get discovered, but he discovered someone new and younger. His wife told me, "You're not the first and you won't be the last." I should have listened to her. I've always been attracted to the wrong kind of men. Some things never change. I haven't talked to Rob since the time I stood him up at the airport. The girls are teenagers now. I hope they're all happy.*

## *Rob*

Here I am ten years later. I can't believe that I've come so far–and that I was so unaware of Marcia next door. She's not a knock-out but she's pretty and a good wife and mother to the girls. They both love her and so do I. We've got a good life. We're comfortable, no drama, no excitement. I hardly ever think of Jess and when I do I hope she's happy

## *Lindsay*

*I'm a freshman in college now. Dad and Marcia helped me move into my dorm room. It's small but we fixed it up so it's homey and my room-mate is quiet like me, not a partier. Mandy is a lot more popular than I was in high school. She's the fun one, I'm the steady one. She still misses our mother and talks about going to L.A. to try and find her one of these days. Dad says we both look like her. I don't like that idea, but Amanda loves it! She has some sort of fantasy created where Mom was a tragic, misunderstood princess. I missed Mom at first, but am glad that things turned out the way they did for my dad, Marcia, Mandy and me. I kind of hate my mom, but I still love her too!*

# THE LAKE

Those of us who live by the lake year-round look forward to summer—to the return of old friends and the arrival of new acquaintances. The people who visit our little part of the world fill our lives for the time they're here. We come to know them, their likes and dislikes, their idiosyncrasies. We look forward to their arrival and at times we look forward to their departure as well. Some are demanding, but most are happy to be here; content to relax and enjoy our slower paced world. We watch parents teach their little ones to swim or fish. Fathers and sons embark on new adventures or relive old memories. The summer air is filled with squeals of delight and the quiet murmur of evening conversations. Our visitors see us in the summer months when the lake glistens like a jewel; the trees are all decked out in varying shades of green; the flowers are in riotous bloom. We know the lake has more facets that are hidden, only to be revealed when gray clouds race across the sky.

After the summer people leave the trees don their gold and russet crowns. The afternoon sun seems to make them glow from within. These are the times we love; the quiet days when we hear the passing geese and the loons that live on the north shore. We spend the autumn months making repairs and buttoning things up for the winter. The warm afternoons and cold crisp evenings remind us that we have much to do before the snow arrives.

By December the trees have lost their leaves, and the flowers have bowed their heads to wait for their winter coverlet. The snow comes in quietly. The skies are dark gray and seem to touch the horizon. The lake reflects the gray of the sky and holds many secrets beneath its surface. Our days are short, spent close to the warmth of the hearth. Now we wait. The snow continues to fall; creating a new, whiter robe that blinds in the sun. The lake is frozen solid; the fish sleep under the ledges by the shore. We sleep as well. The nights are long and dark. Some adventurous souls clear the snow from the lake's surface so they can skate or play hockey. Their voices echo across the lake and against the hills. The laughter and shouts proclaim that life goes on.

Spring sees a gradual warming and an increase of daylight. The ice on the lake begins to melt and cracks form, allowing the light to reach the slumbering fish. Everyone and everything feels the imminent change. The grass awakens and the crocuses lift their heads searching for the new sun. The trees raise their arms; their fingers newly covered in green, seek the warmth from above. Robins stop by on their journey singing their distinctive song. We rise, stretch our unused muscles and get ready.

The summer people will start arriving soon; the onslaught will begin in earnest in June. We will share our little part of the world once again. Those of us who live by the lake year-round look forward to summer—the return of old friends and the arrival of new acquaintances.

# HERB STOKES

Herb Stokes. Upon retirement, Herb and his artist wife, Marianne, moved from New York to the Intracoastal Waterway in North Carolina. They did the boat and beach scene for a few years but after a wonderful summer trip to Portland decided the Pacific Northwest would be their home. Herb took a creative writing course at Clark College soon thereafter and he hasn't stopped learning yet.

# MUCHACHA

The pueblo of Copala, Mexico, squats in the folds of the western foothills of the Sierra Madre, like a woman making tortillas by an open fire. In the fall of 1920 the population is 658 souls. Morning comes late because El Sol must first arc himself over the mountain before hurling his cosmic rays onto the red-roofed mud and stone houses and gray cobblestone streets. A green iguana labors up a bank with an unhurried plodding gait but is watchful for both prey and predator as she moves to her hunting grounds in the trees.

Lupe leaves her bed while it is still dark outside to start the fire in the oven that will bake the bread for the villagers to eat with their morning eggs and coffee. It is a job her husband, the town baker, usually performs, but this morning, after a late night at the cantina celebrating his youngest brothers' waning days of bachelorhood, he does not hear the alarm jangling on top of the massive dresser.

The cantina was a way of life for Hector before he married Lupe, before he became a serious suitor. But Hector was in no hurry for marriage. Like most villagers he was a farmer who worked in the fields during the day, being baked by the sun, and relaxed in the cool cantina at night. Cantina girls preferred single men; married men counted their change too carefully. Most of his single friends were regulars.

Lupe plans to move to a larger city when the opportunity is right. Her plans have worked out so far. It started when she decided to marry Hector. After a two-year courtship he said they would become engaged on her next birthday. On her birthday he didn't show up. A week later he appeared at her door with candy and a five-day beard. Her mother told him she was out. The next morning Hector was back at her door. The mother said Lupe had come in late and was still sleeping. Come back later. Hector returned in the early evening. The mother said she went out again.

Hector started to raise his voice about her whereabouts until Lupe's father appeared in the doorway. After three days Lupe made an appearance. She had spent the time washing her hair with perfumed shampoo, shaving her legs, and learning the art of makeup from her little sister. Hector couldn't wait to propose.

Lupe continues building the fire in the oven while Hector sleeps. In a corner of the oven closest to her she starts a second fire – a small one, just enough to make coffee and cook eggs. She wakes Hector and goes into the other bedroom to rouse the children and get the boy ready for school.

Hector stabs his fried eggs with the jagged end of a piece of oven-toasted bread until the saffron-colored juice bleeds from the yellow eyes over the shiny white face. He mashes a mound of cornmeal and jalapenos into the mix and lifts it, dripping, to his mouth with a wooden spoon. Some residue from the eggs sticks to his black handlebar mustache. The wanton aroma of brewing coffee brings Lupe back to the kitchen. She refills his cup and pours one for herself, then scrapes two eggs from the pan onto an ancient blue ceramic dish and joins him at the breakfast table. She sees the crusted mustache.

"Must you use a spoon for your eggs, husband?"

"Breakfast is not the time to hound me; can't you at least wait until lunch?"

"Why, what are you planning for lunch that will annoy me?"

"I'm planning on not being here."

"And you think that will annoy me?"

"Of course, how else will you amuse yourself if I am not present to find fault with?"

The easy banter helps relieve the normal tension of a husband and wife, with two young children, together in a small house almost every hour of every day.

"Where will you be for lunch?"

"Concordia. The truck needs the gasoline. I will help fill the barrels and store them in our underground area here and also buy supplies for the baking. The Mayor asked me last night in the cantina. You will have to watch the loaves, they will rise soon." The town has recently purchased the truck from the army. The truck is used by the entire populace for medical emergencies, bringing in supplies, taking foodstuffs and hand-made products to market, and transporting the residents.

"If you can find some chocolate that is not too expensive bring it back for Elena. She still grieves for her cat taken from the yard by el coyote last month."

It wasn't until the coyote snatched two laying chickens that Hector became interested in reinforcing the wire fence; too late to save the cat. He caught the indirect rebuke.

Lupe can still hear the empty barrels banging against each other in the open truck; the sound reverberates across the valley as the truck winds its way through the mountain.

*    *    *    *    *

Eight years earlier, at eighteen, Lupe had decided to marry Hector. She told no one about it. Not her friends, not her family, and especially not Hector. Of the few available young men in the village, she thought she could do the most with him. He was tall and thin; not likely to get a big round belly from too much beer. She would not stay a farmer's wife forever. Lupe was attractive but not really pretty. But she was intelligent and strong-willed, had a good figure and knew how to keep a man interested.

A couple of years after Hector and Lupe's marriage the baker's wife and son died of influenza. Lupe waited a respectful interval, then approached the baker and convinced him to take Hector on as an apprentice by including in the agreement that she would cook meals and clean his house for three years and that Hector would not open another bakery in the village. The baker depended upon Lupe for advice about women he thought would make a good wife. She always discovered a flaw she said would make him unhappy in the long run. Mostly it was a problem with the woman but sometimes Lupe even discovered problems with the woman's family members that caused him to forego a romantic involvement. Before the three years were up, she had persuaded the baker that it was time to relocate to a larger village where he would have a greater choice of women to select for a wife. This enabled Hector to open his own bakery.

The most difficult problem she encountered during this period was making Hector understand the benefits of becoming a baker. He complained about the early rising, the heat from the oven, having to wear an apron like a woman, not seeing his friends during the day and having to learn something of which he had no knowledge.

Lupe pointed out they would make more money; that he would finish work by 1:00 p.m., before the sun was at its hottest, and would be able to take a long siesta. The white apron was a symbol of his new prominence and dignity. If he felt he had to visit with his friends, out in the fields under the blistering sun, he could waive his siesta to do that, and since he was an intelligent man he would learn to bake–besides, she would help him. And finally his clothes would not stink of chicken manure which would make him more appealing and her more receptive to making love in the long evenings.

*    *    *    *    *

She checks the newly risen loaves and is about to place them in the oven when she hears a voice over a loud speaker from the direction of the town square. A familiar sound that began when the rebels and the government took turns appealing to the residents to support their cause. Her son, Miguel, age seven, is three blocks away in the town school. Elena, age five, is in the front yard hunting for caterpillars to feed to the ever hungry chickens. Elena tries to make a pet out of every animal she sees. Lupe can't make out what the voice is saying but Elena hears the voice say to come and see the animals. She runs to the end of the street, then turns left and runs three more blocks to the square.

A small truck is parked with a trailer behind it that contains two large cages. One cage holds three brown bears and the other is separated into two sections, each holding two half-asleep lions. At one time, years ago, the bears stood upright in pristine coastal streams feeding off the salmon making the upstream run to where they first found life. The lions dream of the hot yellow plains where they ran down zebra and wildebeest and fought viciously for the right to mate. Now both are fed half-rotted horsemeat and live in cages not high enough for them to stand on their hind legs and stretch the tiredness from their bodies. The driver rolls the canvas sides up so potential customers can see the beasts while a phonograph record plays, telling about the other thrills of the traveling circus that will arrive later in the day. Several people surround the driver asking for the free tickets promised to the first five who show up.

Elena approaches the cages from the opposite end. No one notices her. Her large dark eyes widen when she sees the beautiful cats, like her own gato that was taken by the coyote. Only much, much bigger! Her heart leaps when she sees the lion's golden eyes. She has never seen golden eyes before, eyes the color of the lion's tawny coat. Elena moves closer to the open cage. The lions do not move; they look past or over her, She looks in her dress pockets for something to give to them. She finds a few corn kernels buried deep in the seams and steps forward.

Lupe is about to put the loaves in the oven when something disturbs her for a second, then goes away. She cannot identify it immediately. It comes back seconds later. She doesn't hear the clucking sounds Elena makes when she is in the yard with the chickens. That doesn't frighten Lupe–there is nothing in the village that could harm a child. Even the well has a metal grate with a clasp that a child cannot undo. But like all mothers she wants to know where her child is at all times.

The girl takes another step towards the cage. Her hand is open revealing a few kernels of corn. She hopes the lions will eat them. One more step and she is at the edge of the cage. She has their attention now but they just study her and blink their large yellow eyes. She sticks her hand through the four-inch space between the bars and drops the kernels inside the cage. The closest lion reacts. He is on her immediately, clawing her head and face with one strike! As she falls he reaches through the bars and hits her again on the back, sending her under the trailer. The lions are on their feet, snarling and roaring, thrusting through the bars for her, but she is beyond their claws.

Lupe hears the lions and then the screams from the crowd. She runs toward the square, connecting the roar to her daughter's need to touch and hold animals; she prayed to Dios she was wrong. An Army officer has pulled Elena from under the trailer and carried her across the square to a storefront next to the church where a full time nurse, paid by the State of Sinaloa, tends the public. Copala does not have its own doctor. The crowd points Lupe to the nurse's office.

Lupe bursts into the room. Elena is on a table, her face and head wrapped in towels soaked with blood. The nurse presses the towels in place while the officer tears strips from a large roll of thick cotton gauze. The child, who was quiet up to now with shock, screams when she hears her mother's anguished voice. The child sees the huge head of the lion snarling at her with teeth the length of her hand. She feels his hot, moist breath on her face and smells his foul odor. Her face burns where the claws ripped through flesh, shredding it like soft cheese in a grater. She kicks and twists, then tries to put her hands to her face. The nurse injects her with morphine, then treats the wounds with mercurochrome while her mother rocks her back and forth in her arms. The morphine acts as a sedative as well as an anesthetic.

The officer volunteers to drive the child and mother to a doctor in Concordia, in the truck that towed the animals, but the nurse says the most important thing now is to stop the bleeding and prevent infection. Bouncing around on a mountain road for four hours will not be helpful.

Lupe does not recognize her child's face when the nurse pulls back the bandages to treat the wounds and suture them. Clots of dark blood cover small mounds of mangled flesh. At one place on Elena's cheek, some teeth and gum are exposed. The nurse breaks open an ampule of smelling salts when she sees Lupe about to faint. She applies new bandages after suturing the worst wounds. A doctor will remove the temporary stitches and then use finer thread and smaller needles to reduce scarring.

The officer is about to leave when Lupe takes his blood-soaked sleeve in her hand to thank him.

"Senor, wait!"

"Captain," he says gently. "I am Captain Diego La Madrid."

"Thank you Captain for, for…" She breaks down.

"Senora, I know the wounds look bad but believe me there are doctors who can do wonders now—you would be amazed."

"Oh, but did you see her fa..."

"Yes, but I have seen worse, Senora—during the war."

"Where would I find a doctor that can..can fix…that…?"

"I will write it down."

Lupe places the sheet of notepaper inside her blouse, afraid to trust it to her apron pocket. She wants to wash the Captain's jacket but he refuses. He says the hotel will take care of it. She cannot explain that she wants her hands immersed in the water that contains Elena's blood. She wants her hands to wring out the blood and then pour the stained water into the brown earth of her yard—not into a drain that empties into a scum covered sump—but she doesn't know how to say it. He starts to salute her as he leaves but she catches his hand and kisses it.

A few days later Lupe and Hector wait to hear when the circus owner will come to the village to discuss the accident. Lupe still has Elena's face covered and mirrors removed so the little girl can't see the damage. To distract her they buy a tame white rabbit that can tolerate being clutched to the bosom of a little girl and fed on pellets from her hand. It is placed in a cage with fresh water and grasses at night, after Elena falls asleep and relaxes her grip on "Pedro."

A day before the owner arrives the Mayor sends word to Hector to meet him in the cantina; that means Lupe cannot be there. Decent women do not go into the cantina. After a couple of rounds of tequila and beer the Mayor explains the meeting with the circus owner, Don Carlos Garza, and Padre Tomas from the church, will take place in his house the next day Don Carlos, the Mayor explains, is a war hero and a friend of the new Mexican Presidente Alvaro Obregon. He does not mention that Don Carlos will make a donation to the church and also to the mayor for brokering the meeting.

As a matter of fact Don Carlos sold war material to both sides during the war but never donned a uniform, and attended Obregon's inauguration only because he had made a large contribution, for future business purposes, to have his picture taken with El Presidente

That night Hector tells Lupe she cannot attend the meeting–it is for men only. The head of the household they told him. She protests although she expected it. "The bastards don't want me there. I don't trust any of them." She reminds Hector of their agreement: listen to everything they say but don't sign anything until we can read it together. Her reading skills are better than his–she does not say this aloud. The next evening, before he leaves, she takes both his hands in hers and makes him promise not to sign anything–swear to Dios!

Don Carlos wears a white silk shirt and white linen trouscrs with a silver buckle. His hair, now starting to show the white, is parted on the left but combed back straight, as if he stands in a strong wind. An aquiline nose complements the square jaw and thin mustache. At sixty-five he shows a paunch but holds his back straight. He shakes Hector's hand warmly, expresses his sorrow for the little girl, then shoots a look at Padre Tomas.

"God's will," the Padre says.

"Yes, God's will" the Mayor repeats.

"We can't know why these things happen but who are we to question God's actions," Don Carlos says.

"Exactamente!" The Mayor lifts his forefinger for emphasis.

"There's a reason these things happen."

"Si, Padre, you are right." The Mayor nods in agreement.

"Hector, sit here by me, por favor–this is my niece, Consuela."

"Gracias, Don Carlos. Mucho gusto, senorita."

"Is it too warm for wine? I have some black rum in the kitchen. Squeeze some lime in it," The Mayor says.

"Consuela, would you get the box of cigars on the back seat of my car. Please bring it here."

"Si, Don Carlos."

"Is everyone hungry?" the Mayor asks. "We are serving sea shrimp and green vegetables with salad; Padre would you say the blessing?"

"Si, of course."

"Come on then, we're going in to the dining room; bring your drinks. Whose drink is this?"

"It's my niece's. Hector take it in with you, por favor. Consuela sit there–next to Hector," Don Carlos says,

Later, after dinner and more drinks, Don Carlos faces Hector knee to knee and says he would like to meet Hector's son. The circus is only one of his enterprises. He is always looking for lads willing to work and learn. That's the way he started. This could be a big break for Miguel.

Don Carlos motions the padre to join them and asks if it is true the parish sometimes sponsors young ladies for the sisterhood. Padre Tomas says it is true. He has sponsored several himself. Don Carlos asks if he would be willing to sponsor Elena, if the parents thought that it would be the right thing to do. Si, the priest answers, I would be willing to sponsor her.

"Blessed is the household that gives a daughter to God, eh Padre."

"Que?"

"I said blessed is the household..."

"Oh, blessed, yes."

"Hector, I made us drinks; let's go outside." Consuela takes his hand.

Hector returns home early in the morning. They fed him rum and tequila with Cuban cigars to smoke after the brandy. The beautiful woman who accompanied Don Carlos never let Hector's glass be empty for long, and then took him on the veranda and made him forget about the promise to his wife.

Lupe meets him at the door–he is drunk. The woman's perfume clings to him like a parasitic vine on a jungle tree. Lupe asks to see the documents they gave him. He waves her off. She slaps him hard. He tries to push her away but falls across the bed and does not get up. While he sleeps she finds 3000 pesos in his pocket; the most money he ever had in his life. She knows then he has signed away their rights for other compensation.

When he awakes that afternoon, Hector finds a note on the breakfast table. It says Miguel is at her sister's house and she has Elena with her, but does not say where they have gone. She wrote that he had dishonored his family and she was ashamed to be his wife and had no interest in seeing him. Hector realizes it is the worst day of his life.

Lupe feels uncomfortable back in the nurse's office. She feels Elena's hand trembling as they remember the trauma they experienced the last time they were there–a little over a week ago. But she needs the nurse to call the bus company in Concordia and ask the bus to stop and make a pickup here in Copala for the trip to the coast. Lupe will not ask to use the two other phones in town–one in the mayor's office and one in the church. She does not want the mayor or the padre to tell Hector where she went.

On the bus ride down the mountain Lupe takes the sheet of notepaper and again reads the name and address of the doctor in Ciudad Mazatlan that she will go to see the next day. She wonders if 3000 pesos will be enough. If it is not, she will find work; some work, any work. Nothing on earth will stand in her way to make her daughter smile again. She will find a way to overcome this heartbreak. Lupe has a good feeling when she reads the name on the card:

Doctor Jorge La Madrid

Ave. Camaron 1727

Mazatlan

Underneath the address the Captain has written "my father."

# HOSPICE

When she woke in the hospital from her drug-induced sleep, she saw her husband still sitting there, holding her hand. He was a short man, in his late fifties, swarthy, with thick glasses, a neatly trimmed dark mustache and hair cut close to his head.

"What time is it Hon?" she said.

"Oh, hi dear. It's eight o'clock. How you feeling now?"

A little better," she lied. "Is it morning or night?" Her mouth was dry. She tried to lick the stickiness away from her lips.

"It's morning, dear."

"Could I have some water? Have you been here all night again?"

"What? No, I've taken some breaks. Here's your water, dear."

"I can tell by the way you're sitting your back is bothering you."

"I'm fine. Do you want some more water?" She had trouble finding the straw with her mouth. He held it to her lips.

"I must look a mess." Her too-blonde hair had come undone at the back and now partially covered her face. The cancer made her face more delicate by pulling the skin tighter over the cheekbones from weight loss. Later it will become skeletal, the eyes sunken and frightening.

The darker roots of her blonde hair showed through where it had parted indiscriminately. Her paleness and fragility brought out the cool blue of her eyes.

"I want to wash my face. Help me to the bathroom, Hon." He held onto her while she ran a washcloth over her face, then brushed her teeth. She shooed him out after he set her down on the seat. Later, back in bed, she asked: "Were the kids here?"

"Kim was, Rob's flight is late; he'll be here some time this morning but he'll miss visiting time. Kim's having a bite to eat in the cafeteria. She'll be back in a few minutes. Would you like something to eat dear?"

"Maybe later." She wanted to call the nurse to find out when she could get more pain medication, but she hesitated to ask in front of him. She wished he would leave for a while so she wouldn't have to pretend she felt better and could cry and moan without seeing his stricken face turn ashen gray when she did.

"Did you find my checkbook?" she asked.

"Kim found it. I brought the list with the monthly bills."

"Okay, good. We'll go over it later when my head is clearer–if it ever is." She allowed herself a small chuckle.

A nurse entered the room. She smiled pleasantly at the couple then placed a small instrument in her patient's ear to take her temperature. The wife tried to look into the eyes of the nurse to convey her longing for more painkiller but the nurse looked only at the instrument and the connections on the IV tubes, then left so abruptly there was no chance to speak about it.

"Listen Hon, now don't get upset, but I think it might be better if I went into hospice. You and the kids won't have to try to sleep sitting in chairs and visiting hours are not restricted." She had to stop to take a breath, then continued." You can even sleep over in a bed. Our friends can come visit almost any time." She took another breath then held her hand up when she sensed he was about to interrupt.

"Also, this way, since other people will be around, you will be able to get some peace at home." She also knew she would be able to self medicate for the pain.

He stood up. "You listen to me, Katherine Louise McCabe, if it's peace I wanted I sure as hell wouldn't have married you and I won't have you bossing me around telling me to do something that don't need to be done either!"

She realized she had frightened him. He was still wishing for a remission. Her body told her it was too late for that.

"OK Mac." She squeezed his hand. The inevitable move to hospice would come up again soon enough. She would talk to Kim. Women, she thought, were better at these things.

# BURIAL DAY

The terrible day was almost over. Jean had buried her husband, Paul, killed in a car accident five days earlier. He was returning from a hunting trip and was hit head-on by a van passing a slower vehicle on a mountain road. When she first heard the word "accident" on the phone she thought he had been shot by another hunter; she always had that concern when he went hunting.

Family and friends left, to return to their humdrum lives. Jean had always wanted more excitement from life. God, If only she could return to that wonderful humdrum life!

Kevin, her six-year-old, went into his dad's game room after everyone left. He spied a well-used gym bag that he hadn't noticed before. The police found it in the trunk of Paul's wrecked vehicle, along with tools, sneakers, fishing rods, tackle boxes and old clothing. Jean hadn't had the time or courage to sort through it all yet. Kevin found something interesting at the bottom of the bag, wrapped in an oily rag–a .32 caliber snub nosed Colt revolver.

Jean found him sitting in the center of the room, his hands gripping the handle. She felt panic taking over her mind and body.

"Kevin, please, please put the gun down. C'mon sweetheart, you don't know how to handle it."

"Do so." He aimed it at her. "See?" Then he pulled the trigger.

# THE CHILDREN'S STORY

## *A Holiday Tale*

Once upon a time a young woman from a lower middle class family won a glass slipper contest with the help of a kindly old wand-waving lesbian, or fairy, as she called herself. That part of the story is too absurd to repeat here, boys and girls—maybe we can check back when we get to read about sibling rivalry and alternative sex.

Anyway, the prize was to marry a prince with a foot fetish and live happily ever after, which turned out to be about three years. Then one morning, following her unsuccessful wild boar hunt, she returned to the palace early and saw that the prince had developed an even greater interest in her underwear than she had. "Oh shit!" she mused. "No damn breakfast bacon and now this!" The prince reluctantly changed back into his dull olive drab shorts and sought release by swimming around the moat for several laps. When that didn't work he went off by himself behind some trees near the duck pond and god only knows what he did in there.

She had signed a pre-nuptial agreement, against her mother's advice, which allowed the prince to do all the crazy things men are apt to do if they are not held liable or responsible for any of it.

Moral: Sometimes, boys and girls, you should listen to your mother. Especially if you have to move back in with her, with no job prospects and two whiny kids.

# NEW YORK WIND

It was a biting wind
A New York wind
I'd had enough of it
To look for a bar.

But Fifth Avenue is not the
Place to drink
You shop on Fifth.

One block west to
Sixth and 52nd Street
Around the corner
The wind drove battered newspapers
Through the air "at gusts of 50 MPH"
Leaving the stench behind.

Overhead signs swung menacingly
From shuddering brackets.

I turned my head to draw a breath
And protect my eyes from the street grime
Peppering my face.

I almost passed the place
Bushmills Irish whiskey
To heat the blood.

Two men in a corner watching TV.

She was halfway down the bar
Sipping from a shot glass
Then emptied the rest over the ice:
A drinker's move.

I bought a round
She switched to Bushmills
From the cheap bourbon
We moved closer.
I took the cigarette she offered
Breaking my promise again.

She dropped some coins in the box
Old blues singers–Nina Simone and Dinah
Women weeping when men went away.

We had another round
Just to drown out the wind
I could make her laugh
A pretty second generation Latina.

Swapping stories of broken romances
Sometimes it was our fault.

She cooed along with the singer
Rocking on the stool
Touching my leg.

She stood up and held out
Her arms but there was no room
To dance so we held each other.

Swaying to the rhythm
Listening to the words
Feeling sorry for the singer.

We had another round
Just to keep out the wind

Holding each other
Listening to the music
Swaying to the sound

Having no other place to go
And neither wanting to face
The Wind.

# MAZATLAN, MEXICO

The daughters of the Maya.
Are taught to beg
When only four or five.

A soiled palm upraised
Holding pieces of gum
For any price you please.

Smiling
Instead of pleading
With olive black eyes.

The light not yet put out.

Still a game played with strangers
Run back with the coins to show mama
Squatting under a shawl
On the corner.

With palm upraised.

# LOVELOST

A green eyed woman with auburn hair,
Has me caught in her soft snare.

She's taken my thoughts away from me,
And placed them where they ought not be.

Across a river, into a wood,
Where once a house of stone had stood.

Now blackened rocks are what remain,
But no one's there that can explain.

So lost was I within her hair,
That I saw auburn everywhere.

In every thought and dream as well,
Nothing there was could break that spell.

Until she stopped and turned away,
And there was naught that I could say.

For well I knew that love's not fair,
I've gone and drowned in auburn hair.

# SUMMER SKY

On summer nights, atop the hill,
We watched the stars and sighed,
I sat beneath the willow's branch,
While Maggie sat beside.

We did not speak and barely breathed,
Remembering how Kate died,
Then one of us would speak her name,
While the other cried.

A million billion points of light,
on a cosmic ride
Streak farther and farther away from earth,
Nestling our babe inside.


# THE WAY

So much of life I do not know,
And think the time to learn has flown,
Most doubts I raised are mysteries still,
My question list has only grown.

From the man titled CEO,
To one with a bricklayer's hod,
The more I see the ways of Man,
The less I know the ways of God.

# THE PROMISE KEPT

When I said I would do this for you
It seemed a long way off
But it has come.

There is more to you than just
Quiet ashes.

I did not realize I would feel
Your burnt bones
Scraping against
The sides of the urn
As if seeking a way
To become part
Of the world again.

We move through a familiar seascape:
A breakwater of granite boulders
Moored sailboats, masts moving like metronomes
Keeping a beat to the ocean's rhythms.

Past the channel's flashing buoy
Beyond the flooding race
I release you to the sea.

# WILLIE'S WILD RIDE

Willie ride his bicycle
Across the railroad track
He ride it past the green corn fields
Then he ride it back.

He ride where men were huddle roun'
A pot of bubblin' stew
He ride past people holdin' signs
Wantin' work to do.

He ride beyond the light of day
He ride till moon come out
He ride until his Mama cry
And ride till Papa shout.

He ride in a thunder storm
He go as fast as hell
He hide under Burnside Bridge
But he don't feel so well.

He ride when the puddles gone
Until a wheel come off
Rain come back when walkin' home
Then he catch a cough.

Willie's home—in bed with flu
But wanderlust has hooked in deep
They're still mad—sold his bike too
Willie rides—though in his sleep.

Seems that's the way life's gotta be
O World, O Willie
O You an' me.

# BEFORE RISING

Finches roosting in a white birch
Impatient for the new day to begin
Announce dawn way too early.

I'm still half in the dream state
My thoughts as shapeless as sand.

I dreamt autumn had returned
And with it came the old melancholy
That always catches me off guard.

Something about the dry dead leaves
With no will of their own
Rattling down barren streets
Piling up against a hundred barriers.
Like unwanted memories building a dam

Black skies with haunted heavens
A stubborn northeast wind
Sheeting the road with water.

Rain lashing my windows
And drumming against the house
Too loud to be a beguiler of sleep.

Before a ghostly autumn drags me down:

Set me on a pair of skis
Where there's the white of winter
And the glisten of ice
Crusting on top of snow
On a hillside glinting silver
In the starlight.

# COLT IN THE MEADOW

The dappled colt saw me for the first time when I crossed the meadow.
He belongs to my neighbor but the colt knows only that he belongs to the mare.
We watched each other with interest–his long face searching mine–
Looking for kinship but not realizing any at the time.
He flung his ears straight up and eyed me with head high
But did not recognize my shape or walk.

As I approached closer he backed away from the fence
Until his rump touched his mother's flank
And so emboldened he stopped–
Locked his knees to discourage panicked flight,
Then shook his head, flared his nostrils and snorted.

Being a reasonable person I stopped and whistled to his mother
So she would know it was just me that came by to see them.

I turned and walked away
Admiring the colt on his bravery
For protecting the blind mare from a stranger.

# THE SAPPHIRE RING

Lost
While inside his breast pocket
For safekeeping.

Bluer than most
But not as blue
As her shining eyes
Reflecting a
Cloudless summer sky.

Also lost
While close to his heart
For safekeeping.

# LOOKING FOR LOVE

The little green lizard
struts across the woman's porch railing
with a proprietary air, then suddenly stops

and flicks down a flap of
vermilion colored skin from his throat
and freezes in place.

He bobs his head up and down several times
before moving on.

Wordless—soundless
but with such eloquence of expression
does he signal his desire for a mate
that, without conscious intent,
the woman touches fingers to her throat,
then catches herself
and with a rueful smile, nods back.

# TURNING

I watched green leaves turn to gold,
Then read what Frost had to say.
That's when my warmth was turned to cold,
He said: Nothing gold can stay.

All the gifts that I kept golden,
Were so carefully locked away,
Gifts to which I was beholden,
And would retrieve another day.

They'd retreated from my fire,
That night on a cold floor lay,
But were indifferent to my ire,
As I watched the gold turn gray.

# FEEDING DOLPHINS

(This poem won first place in the Oregon State Poetry Association's
Fall 2009 contest.)

I wade out into the cool water
Of the rising tide that's being lifted by the moon.
They sense the ripples of water I push aside
With my thighs.

But I cannot tell if they are out there
Until I see their dark forms slipping under
The waves in the moonlight.
A large male makes a wide turn
Then slides up in front of me.
I hear him breathing noisily. The eye shining with intelligence.

We wait: He floating between earth and sky;
And me with feet planted in watery sand.
I must be as mysterious to him
As he is to me.

He gently takes a fish from my hand
I think he can find better than my stale offering
But he presses against my leg and nods for more.
I wonder if he feels my warmth through the salty element.

We are not finished with each other yet
He nudges me for another fish
I run my finger over a scar on his rubbery snout.
His pod circles us. He senses them, then turns back to me.

What is this affinity that passes between us?

I need to touch something wild.
He wants to know if we are kin.

# SHADES OF SUMMER

She was the kind of girl
you didn't bring home to meet the folks.

Chances are my old man would hit on her
which would piss mom off
and the kid brother might take a shot at her
which would piss me off.

No  this one I kept to myself.

At quitting time she came by the shop
To pick me up.

No peck on the cheek shit
full on the lips then she would get my lower lip
between her teeth and bite softly
until I was ready to bust.

Off we would go
as my crew went bug-eyed
while pretending not to look.
With her car radio set to LOUD
until we hit the beach.

Fighting through waves to get
beyond the surf
shivering under long shadows
sharing one wet sandy towel.

Dozing in lukewarm sun
until the night hid sins.

Then making love
on the nudie beach
under a bright moon.

While lovesick grunion
pulled by the moon and scaly passions
squirm in the high tide shallows
in a milky way of sperm and eggs.

Under the hard eyes of human hunters
who grab the fish by hand and drop them
by the dozen into burlap sacks.

Some fish escape on the receding tide
Some will be devoured in the ocean
Some will be back when the moon
And passions rise again

On a warm beach in California.

The following was written in response to new charges, and convictions, of molestations of boys by priests, this time in Chicago, Ireland and Germany, again with the aid of bishops and a cardinal (Cardinal George–a so-called Prince of the Church) who allowed predatory priests to be transferred to other Chicago parishes so they could continue raping children. To date the Papacy has still not publicly condemned a bishop or cardinal for any of these practices. 3/28/2010

# VATICAN CITY

I do not see
A Holy See
Where one is
Supposed to be.

A secret city
Without pity
That's the sad
Nitty-gritty.

Molestation
Protestation
Not absolved
By His ablation.

Pedophiles
Stole the smiles
Of little boys
By priestly wiles.

Priests who preyed
That should have prayed
Lost to lust–
Their minds waylaid.

To allow a child
To be defiled
Makes Church's princes
Be reviled.

Our money used
For the accused
No money left
For the abused.

May those who knew
That it was true
Find Hell on earth
And years to rue.

# THINGS THAT SHOULDN'T SPEAK

(This poem won third place in the Oregon State Poetry Association's
Spring 2010 contest)

Save us from people who love us,
Said the butterfly
As the collector lovingly stuck a pin
Through its body
To hold it fast
To the mounting board.

We would not sting you
If you just wanted some honey
But you take everything
Including our home and unborn children.

It's too late for me now
But I can see your fly line leader
In the distance
Said the Steelhead trout
As she was being reeled in
From the gravel bed
Where she was about
To deposit her eggs.

You trick us to fly near your decoys
Then you shoot us out of the sky
Dogs carry us in their mouths
You eat us.
Then you paint beautiful pictures
Depicting us in flight–detailing exact feather patterns,

You admire our statuesque stance, our magnificent antlers
And our graceful movements when
Just walking stately across a meadow;
Our strength and speed when running
From a bear or wolf pack.
But you most admire our severed heads
Nailed to your walls.

# AT THE CROSSING

I saw her where the freeway
Intersects 134th Street
Just above Salmon Creek.
It was dark enough for cars
To have their headlights on.

A full grown doe that should have known better
Standing quietly on the sidewalk while staring at the
Patch of woods behind a high wooden fence
On the other side of the street.

Then I noticed the yellow construction signs behind her
And how the trees had been torn down so something
Not as grand could be put in their place.

A van turned towards her
On the way to the entrance ramp that
She had just climbed
Blinded and startled she ran in front of it.

Somewhere—in the woods below—they wait.

# BEING BROKEN

My government is broken.
The men sent to fix it have returned
Wearing wide smiles between tanned cheeks.
They have new cars and money in the bank
That was donated by industries that wanted
And received favors at our inflated expense.
They say it is fixed now.

My church is broken.
The men sent to fix it travel in chauffeured limousines,
Wear tall pointed hats, red silken robes
And carry crucifixes atop golden staffs.
But they don't seem to know that it is broken.

My bank is broken.
The men sent to fix it have given the men
Responsible for the breakdown
Millions of dollars in bonuses
And have asked them not to let it happen again.
But penalties have not been assessed
Nor has anyone been held liable or responsible.
They say it is fixed now.

My country is broken.
Parasites from within have sucked out the vital juices
So now the roots have withered and are dying.
We are on the edge of a boneyard
And seem almost eager to rush down its slope
And throw ourselves onto the heap.
The men sent to fix it are nowhere in sight.

# SIX SONNETS

## MEMORY

There's no greater liar than the truth,
When corrupt memory plays the ancient fool,
And forgets the cancelled boasts of youth,
That, for some, became a drunken drool.
I can still remember, still remember, when
Reason is bright alert, yet calm, besides.
The words come back as muted music then,
Desires ebb and flow like ghostly tides.
It's dreams of you my mind enhances most,
Thus frees what pain has sought to enslave.
Though truth comes hard because it's you I lost.
Damned memory will wait there by my grave.
Quince-bitter thoughts chill my evenings, love,
Life's caprice kept me, while it sent you above.

## AUTUMN SONNET

Autumn's ancient core is buried deep
Among the roots and pods, in fertile slumber.
The patient farmer wakens it from sleep,
To reap the fruit beneath the birthing umber.
Earth takes a respite under winter's robe,
Until spring explodes and shakes the world!
Becoming the blessing that greens again the globe
And so revives dry roots where they lay curled.
When the leaves of summer turn to dust
And ghosts of pagans celebrate the moon,
When the brightest colors turn to rust,
Then will autumn's bounty follow soon.
Build up the fire and lay in drink and food
To stay the chill of autumn's somber mood.

# ORDINARY FLOWERS

Ordinary flowers bloom below,
Lupine and daisies dozing side by side.
Then a fresh sea breeze begins to blow,
That pushes two lace curtains open wide.
Spring's chilly entrance brings her full awake,
Life also stirs within her ancient heart
And fills it with a different kind of ache,
Like lovers feel when they're about to part.
The family waits outside the spotless room,
A bell cord's on the bed to ease her strife.
Once cords of flesh fed life inside her womb,
And in her daughters'—passing life to life.
Go, gently, when the sand has filled the clock,
As gently as the boats that slip the dock.

# WILD HORSES RUNNING

I heard them—before I saw them on the hill,
The horses broke over the ridge in front of me.
The stallion watched then saw I meant no ill,
But kicked his heels for all his mares to see.
They galloped past and made the earth move too,
A tremble only—but still they shook the ground!
Awkward colts now made their spring debut,
On stick-thin legs that have been newly found.
Manes and long tails swirled like banners of silk!
Multi-colored streamers of brown and black,
Roans then reds and some as white as milk;
Running like they're never coming back.
They flowed across the prairie like a stream,
Then gone in seconds—but still I hold the dream.

# THE LOVE LIZARD

I taste your breath while you are still asleep
No lizard is there that creeps as sleek as I
Nor one as long of tongue and green of eye
Do you know that in the night you weep?
I can swallow air to change my shape.
Then transfix you with my detached tail.
Use my loosened skin to form a sail.
Make you delighted with my jeweled cape.
I touch my serpent's tongue to your white feet;
Then hear about you telling utter lies
About supposed endangered butterflies.
That night I wept red blood for your deceit:
The lie that lizards put them on the list.
But they, like you, hide dimly in the mist.

# DISGRACE IN DIXIE

Katrina is the name they gave the storm,
That broke the dikes and drowned us in the flood.
Our leaders knew a great flood would transform,
New Orleans into a sea of mud.
Still angry are we who watched them drive away,
While we were forced to stay and face our fate,
They who still had faith knelt down to pray,
Those who left us said they could not wait.
They dumped us in the stifling Superdome,
To bear the heat and thirst for many days,
The old and weak that should have found a home,
Died in filth beneath their loved ones' gaze.
Big Easy's streets became choked with slime,
While George Bush praised Brownie* one more time.

*"Brownie, you're doing a heck of a job," he said to Michael Brown, the head of FEMA (Federal Emergency Management Agency). Brown resigned, reluctantly, shortly after the facts were publicized about the almost criminally substandard response by his organization to the disaster.

# POEMS HA-HA

## LONG BEFORE I MET YOU

Long before I met you, dear
I lived a pirate's life.
Then I dove for pearls one year
And learned to use a knife.

Which came in handy in cannibal land
'Till I was caught and bound.
But a princess came and took my hand,
We crawled along the ground.

We crawled across a mountain peak
And under a shining sea.
She said, with a tear flowing down her cheek,
What would she do without me?

She took me to her father's house
Then said we must be wed!
So I agreed to be her spouse
And sleep in a prince-sized bed.

Then soldiers came in sailing ships;
They attacked our castle at dawn.
But, frightened away by a solar eclipse,
They fled across our lawn.

I knew about shadows, by sun and moon,
And that light would surely return,
Although the sky was dark at noon,
Just listen to me, and learn.

We won the war; they crowned me King!
A new bed for my rank!

A king-sized bed with a hand made spring!
Instead of a wooden plank.

Now, my dear, you know it all,
You'll have to get off my lap.
I hear the voice of nature call;
Grandpa needs his nap.


Re solar eclipse–Grandpa said he borrowed the idea from
Sam Clemens, who stole it from a Greek that swiped it from an
Abyssinian.

## A LOT'S IN A NAME

I sometimes wear a wide-brimmed hat,
A shiny revolver strapped to my hip,
An old leather jacket that's seen combat,
A 20 foot long studded bullwhip.

I search for treasure all over the place,
My college students know little of this,
I'm just the man with a craggy face,
The kind the girls don't want to kiss.

I've found neither treasure nor someone to love,
But that's what happens when you're not a myth;
When luck turns around and gives you a shove,
And you are Indiana Smith.

## LAMB IN A STEW

Mary had a little lamb
With snow-white fleece.

Now I have a lamb too.

Mine comes with mint sauce
And garlic potatoes.

But Mary's lamb is missing!
I will help her look for it–right after dinner.

# OF MICE AND MEN AND CATS AND DOGS

Somehow my cat discovered
That I am the hand behind the wand
That tantalizes him with feathers
And drags the cloth mouse, stuffed with catnip,
Around corners and under chairs.

Perhaps I will have to become more sophisticated
And challenge him with card tricks, juggling,
Disappearing mice–or effect an escape, in handcuffs,
From a cardboard crate.

My dog knows that I really don't want
That old stick back; he plays along anyway.

But my cat has quit playing the fool.

# CHRISTMAS MOUSE

Stanislaus, a gray field mouse,
Loved cheese almost as much as I,
This bold mouse got in my house,
His sneaky presence I did decry.

I set out to make him flee,
And knew I had sufficient choice,
A baited trap or cat could quickly,
Still his cheese-besotted voice.

No more happy squeaks I'd hear

From his fattened little face,
No more midnight snacks down here
By the cozy fireplace.

Then I saw him curled up tight,
Green cheese rind between his paws,
He'd been sick throughout the night,
Tainted cheese the certain cause.

I cupped him in my outstretched hand,
My sick savior quivering there,
Warm pink nose, runny eyes and
With such soft and delicate hair.

This gentle, meek, tiny beast,
Had eaten food meant for me,
Cheese gone bad, to say the least,
That had poisoned him, you see.

Thank you, friend of Robbie Burns,
Then, of late, a friend of mine,
I'll count the days this world turns,
And will think, each time I dine,

Of thee, wee timorous mousie,
No longer living in my housie.
Buried by the white oak tree,
That could have, should have, been me.

# THE FAN

She said she was a big Elvis fan and that
he would never be forgotten.
I remarked that's what they said about
Lamont Davies.

"Who?"

"See what I mean."

# THE SAILOR HOME

## (A 19th Century Scottish seaman back from a voyage)

### 1

I dinna say I loved ye, lass,
'Twas ye that said those words to me,
Upon the eve of Candlemas,
That winter's night in old Dundee.

### 2

Soon I left to find a life,
And found I truly loved the sea,
Wedded–though not to a wife,
For a ship was wife to me.

### 3

Heart and head and muscle and bone,
The jealous sea demands them all,
No mistress–just the sea alone,
On ships with masts past treetop tall.

### 4

We cross'd the Horn in search of whales,
I learned the sea's a flighty wench,
Breezes grew to be full gales,
Whilst waves became a deadly trench.

### 5

When, on the day I turned nineteen,
A riot struck Manila town,
Our Captain shot the Philippine,
Who tried to burn our mainsail down.

6

The crowd found a sleeping shipmate,
In an alley on King's Way,
They slit his throat with heathen hate,
And threw him in Manila bay.

7

Then, chasing whales in open craft,
Where icebergs loom in fogbound straits,
Harpooners stand, their arm abaft,
As death for whales and seamen waits.

8

In Barents Bay a blue whale breached,
MacDonough struck his lance in deep,
It sounded till the depths were reached,
Then rose–and sank them with a leap!

9

Four widows made in just one day,
Four corpses now turned blue in death,
God's greatest creature swam away,
Where frigid waters steal men's breath.

10

Whales can talk while singing a song,
That can be heard in oceans deep,
But when they die it takes so long,
I heard them sighing in my sleep.

11

We hunted them from tropic seas,
To both the poles and back again,
Sloe-eyed women, taught to please,
Made lonely boys think they were men.

12

Her face behind a parasol,
Except for lustrous almond eyes,
That sent a signal o'er the wall,
But hid the pain of latent lies.

13

We lived together for a week,
I knew of nothing but delight,
We loved without the need to speak,
Lost in the raptures of the night.

14

Until the next ship took its berth,
And richer men strode into bars,
Spreading wealth and raucous mirth,
Then wanting women—they took ours!

15

More blood was spilt in just three nights,
Than sixty under sail and sun,
In seven bars were seven fights,
My mates and me in every one.

16

O Rangoon's jails are stinking holes,
Where white's no better man than yellow,
Our jailors hit with bamboo poles,
Then throw us in the pits below.

17

There was naught to do but wait,
Until the captain paid our fine,
Then docked our pay for being late,
And had us bathe in oil of pine.

### 18

But whales were waiting to be caught!
We weighed anchor on the tide,
She wore the trinkets I had bought,
And she could laugh–while I near cried.

### 19

So farewell my black-haired angel,
You gave to me more than I paid,
I'd rather have been doomed to hell,
Than leave my lying Burmese maid.

### 20

A whaling ship's the place to be,
To clear the head and cleanse the heart,
And bring to light, in memory,
Those from whom you've been apart.

### 21

When, in my hammock, half awake,
With four hard years of service done,
I thought of home with such an ache,
And of the lass whose heart I'd won.

### 22

Now I'm back from sea and ships–
I came home to marry thee!
But I can never kiss thy lips,
There in the graveyard of Dundee.

# DAN STRAWN

Dan Strawn took up creative writing when he retired in 2001. His stories and essays have appeared in *Idaho Magazine* and in *Trail Blazer Magazine*. "Everyman's Smalltown," his essay about Moscow, Idaho, was a finalist entry in the University of Oregon's 2005 Northwest Perspectives Essay Contest.

His novel, *Isaac's Gun—an American Tale*, has been picked up by Merpoint Publishing, LLC, for release in August 2010. Merpoint will also rerelease *Lame Bird's Legacy*, Strawn's self-published novel of the 1877 Nez Perce war, at a later date. On occasion Dan teaches courses for the Mature Learning program of Clark College in Vancouver.

# ABOUT BEING OUT OF DATE

(reprinted with permission)

Lately, rather than creeping up, old age has launched an all-out attack. It's not the body so much as the way the rest of the world seems to be out of tune with where my mind resides. This idea, that I'm no longer synchronized with the rest of my culture, really hit home the other day at a McDonald's in Salem.

We stopped there for a quick breakfast. Usually we have fruit and oatmeal, but what the heck, I figured, we are on the road; a fast meal at a fast food restaurant won't hurt this once.

I was still studying the breakfast options when a pimply face with a ring in its lip asked for my order.

"I'll have one of those biscuits with the egg and sausage," I said.

"Do you want a meal?" the face said.

"Uh, what?" I was still studying the board; the question didn't register.

"Do you want a meal?"

I looked at him. "Yes, that's why I came in here."

"So, do you want hash browns or tater tots?"

You need to know, I pride myself on clear communication. I was really perplexed. Where had I gone wrong?

I decided to start over.

"Neither one. I want one of those biscuits with sausage and an egg."

"Oh, so you don't want a meal?"

"Yes I do. As I said earlier, that's why I came in here."

"Okay," said Pimply Face, "Do you want hash browns or tater tots?"

Now he had my full attention, as in, "He's starting to piss me off!"

"Look," I said in a voice that caused the other pimply, studded, and ringed faces around me to look up. "I don't want any damned hash browns and tater tots, whatever the hell they are. I want a biscuit with sausage and an egg. What might it be about that you don't understand?"

Pimply Face looked at me with a blank face. One of his co-workers, evidently from a different tribe (her ring hung out her nose) touched Pimply Face on the arm.

"He doesn't want a meal," she said in a low, knowing voice that reflected her desire to help in a quiet and unobtrusive way.

I decided I wasn't going to fight this. I didn't want to eat anyway. But before I retreated I was going to give this twit an appraisal he wouldn't forget. I was struggling in my mind with a suitable adjective to precede son of a bitch, couldn't settle between stupid and dumb, when the wife showed up.

"Did you order your meal?"

"You know," I said to her, "it's funny you asked. I've been trying to order a meal for the last five minutes. This stupid, dumb son of a bitch won't give me a sausage and egg on a biscuit. For some reason I have to choose between hash browns and potato kids, or some damn thing.

"It's not the pimples. You and I had pimples once. We heard just fine. It must be the ring in his lip. Somehow that ring has impaired his hearing."

My wife looked at Pimply Face. "How much is a sausage with egg and a biscuit?" she asked.

"One dollar and seventy-two cents," he replied.

She put two dollars on the counter. He rang up the change, and the wife and I sat down at a nearby table to wait.

"Did you order our coffee?"

"Jeez, I forgot the coffee!" I stood up, walked to the counter, dropped another two dollars on the counter and ordered two coffees, one with cream.

Pimply Face laid my change on the counter. "If you'd ordered a meal," he said, "one coffee would have been free."

I returned to the table and sat down. I said to the wife, "Apparently if I order a meal, the coffee is free, and I have to choose between two items I don't want in order to get what I do want. Wouldn't it be cheaper for McDonald's to keep what I don't want, let me pay for what I do want, and give me the coffee?"

My wife took a sip from her Styrofoam cup and set it on the table. "Your friend Tom is right," she said. "You've got too much time on your hands."

# LORRETTA THOMAS

Lorretta Thomas.  I came to a love of words through reading, and started writing down random thoughts, prose, and verse while still in school. As a mom I wrote for fun and relaxation, but children and career took an always expanding amount of time, and I did not write much for many years. Retirement now allows the time to pursue that enchantment I've always had with words.

# DADDY

Daddy was a carpenter by trade, and a fix-it man if times were hard, but he was a philosopher too, deep down. He could make me see haze and mist, glitter and fog, as philosophers do, and mostly when I thought I could see clearly. And even though he used few five dollar words he could make my mind stretch, sometimes so completely I thought there should to be sound to go along with the stretching. Sometimes he would grope through the fog of an idea along with me, pausing the sandpaper block in his hand, as he pursued the thought he needed to capture.

"What do you see there in the wood, Jacob?" he'd ask, as I struggled to add curve to the carving I was working to finish. "Do you see the tree, all grown and majestic, swaying in the wind, breathing in and out, and ruling the forest? Do you see strength of time in the rings, or hear the red-winged hawk as she hunts her missing nest? Redwings mate for life, just like folks."

He was always saying things like that, things that would make me view the birds, and the forest, even the wood in the fireplace, in ways that caused me to feel somehow there were things hidden, just out of sight, just waiting.

Then there was my Aunt Liddy. Her real name was Alegra, but no one ever called her that, no one who didn't want to get smacked, anyways. Aunt Liddy's house was a two story box with nine tall windows on the front, five up and four down, and the walls of all the rooms covered with old faded photos in peeling ornate frames, ovals under bubble glass, of babies and small children. "Somebody, somewhere, loved these little 'uns, Jacob," she'd say. "It ain't right for them to be buried in the heaps at the back of some junk store, or be going off to the dump all alone, all by themselves." Some days I would wander through the rooms looking at those babies in their christening gowns, or in their shiny, crumpled stockings and patent shoes, little boys in sailor suits or small girls with collars that hung halfway down their backs, and I'd wonder who they'd been—who they still might be.

Curious that sometimes I could almost feel their breath mingling with mine in the rooms of my Aunt Liddy's house.

Most days Daddy would write a letter or poem to Mama, and then he'd walk on down the hill to the cemetery and read it to her. Some days he would read something he thought she'd enjoy from the newspaper too, or from a book. But mostly he'd just talk of stuff he wanted to tell her or thought she should know. Sometimes he did not talk at all but would sit there anyways, being close. And sometimes I'd go with Daddy to see Mama, and the ache and the talking always left me feeling smaller, younger, and thirsty fit to dying from missing her.

One day, when Daddy was out in the shop working to finish the mantel he was making for one of the fireplaces at the Sheridan house on the hill, Uncle Cecil came all excited with news of war. But the war he told of was far away, and in a place nobody ever heard of. When he told Daddy though, Daddy shook his head and talked about the brotherhood of man living right to its most eager expectation and no better, then asked Uncle Cecil why he thought that was. Uncle just looked up though, like the answer was somewhere in the dust motes drifting in the sunlight slanting through the windows. Finally Uncle Cecil said, "What is worth fighting for, Luke? What is big enough, or important enough, or necessary enough?" But Daddy just looked at my uncle and said in a sad voice, "It all is, damn it anyway, all of it."

"All of what?" I wanted to yell. "All of what?"

And so I went to war, and the stink of it gets all down in the bones, hot and thick, smelling of rot and sulfur and blood, and makes taking a deep breath hard. But mostly war is hard work, lots of waiting, running, crawling, and choking, with no stars at night, and no quiet, not ever.

There was a buddy at Hood the guys all called PQ, short for Pipsqueak, but he was okay, and we'd talk some, mostly about home, his and mine, and I told him about the baby pictures in Aunt Liddy's house. He started crying then, but tried to hide it, and said Aunt Liddy must be a nut cake but that was okay in his book. When we boarded the plane for Germany, before heading to Southeast Asia, his normally orange freckles looked all gray, and I knew he was holding in his sick.

Shoot, most of us were, thinking flying would be the worst thing ever, over all that water.

I took a bullet that left a scar in my front and my back about the size of a nickel and a dime. The front puckered badly, so it burns and cramps when I twist hard, or chop fire wood, or make love, sometimes even when I just turn over in bed. The hospital at Chu Lai smelled almost as bad as war, and Yokohama not much better, both with a sour urgent scent of pain and hurt, but different than the stink of fear and rotting jungle.

Sometimes I can't help but think of those days, the early ones with Daddy and the talks and the processes of growing, and sometimes I think of PQ with his name on The Wall in D.C., and out in Oregon on a wall there too. If I ever get east, or even that far west, when I put my hand out to touch, like I did with those long ago baby photos, it will say Arnold J. Aynson, Jr., and I won't wonder at all who he was. I'll take the deepest breath I can and mingle my air with his name, then I'll sit down and share a cigarette with him even though it's been years since my last smoke, leaving him the pack, and tell him about the sun, and the day, and all the things he'd want to know.

# NAN SCRIMGEOUR WESTON

Nan Scrimgeour Weston. Scottish by birth, she was raised in Toronto, Canada. After twenty years in Vancouver, Washington, Nan and her husband lived aboard their sailboat Pacific Rose, traveling from Texas to Georgia, spending winters in the Bahamas waters. They currently split their time between Vancouver, Washington, and Venice Florida. Nan has published articles in *Latitudes and Attitudes*, *Living Aboard* and *Venice* magazines.

# CORAL CAY

Smoke encircled the lounge and its sofas. Dim light flickered from candles in colored jars set on bamboo holders. The noise reached a crescendo as ribald jokes ended in laughter and more drinks were called for. The night's activities had only begun. Nubile girls, some scantily clad, some nude, were beautiful with skin in hues of chocolate and ivory. Each enticed the men with an inviting smile that promised later delights in the rooms atop the hill. With catcalls and encouragement to drink up, the debauchery continued for two days until the next plane was due to arrive. Juan had noted the plane's identification number and ETA on a slip of paper and placed it in a cabinet drawer by the telephone.

Juan Lopez, the drug kingpin, had claimed Coral Cay. The main house overlooked terraced gardens painstakingly nurtured in the coral ground that underlies the Bahamas archipelago. Beyond lay the crystalline Bahama Banks to the west and emerald Exuma Sound to the East. With a show of firearms, it had not been difficult for Juan's boys to rid Coral Cay of its resident families, most of whom spent only a few winter months at their paradise homes. These 1980s were the turbulent years of illicit drug trafficking. Through Juan's island headquarters cargoes passed from Colombia and Jamaica to the United States. The trade was at its apex.

* * *

Bill and May, a cruiser couple in their sixties, arrived at the Coral Cay anchorage on a late afternoon in 2006. Cruisers were aware of the nefarious activities that earned Coral Cay its reputation. With a couple of hours of daylight remaining, Bill and May decided to explore the island's ruins. After climbing the rise and traversing the remains of the terraced garden, they reached the dilapidated Big House. Their explorations revealed coral walls surrounding a disintegrated interior. They saw a bullet hole on one wall. Wires, plaster, broken glass, and aluminum cans littered the stone floor. Hermit crabs shuffled noisily amidst the rubble.

"I wonder what actually happened?" said May. Of course, they'd heard the stories that circulated throughout the cruising community. "I wonder how it all came about. I mean, we see the result—the abandoned house, the sunken airplane, but I wonder what really happened, I wonder . . ."

\* \* \*

As he headed on a northeast course from his Jamaica takeoff, Larry Thompson relaxed. The controls were on auto pilot. The flight had been scheduled to arrive at Coral Cay at 2300 hours. After three days of partying, Larry was hung-over enough to have a headache but not enough, he thought, to prevent him from flying this most lucrative of flights. He'd flown this route for Juan Lopez for over a year and was more than pleased with his take of the proceeds from the contraband. Drug bales were easy cargo providing easy money.

His mind wandered over the path his life had taken: trouble through his school years in the tougher area of Philly, Mr. Jenkins at the high school. Somehow he'd seen through the swagger Larry used to conceal his insecurity. Given the family background, it was no surprise he sought friendship and acceptance in the gang he ran with rather than from the mother he loved so dearly and the jerk she'd chosen to shack up with. "Yeah, Old Man Jenkins," he mused. "He'd stay and work with me after school." Mr. Jenkins had coaxed that hidden potential for math and science that eventually took Larry to Penn State University. But he didn't last long once out of Mr. Jenkins' influence. He flunked out and worked at a series of dead-end jobs. His one interest was flying, and he scraped enough money together to pay for lessons. When he was airborne, his troubles disappeared in the clouds below. The sense of freedom and the knowledge that he was in charge exhilarated Larry.

When he was 23, Larry's world caved in with his mother's death. He felt his mother had chosen a deadbeat character over him, but although he chose not to show her he cared, she meant as much to him as flying did. He started drinking, made his way to the Florida Keys, and found that place so many before him had reached, the end of the road.

One evening, as Larry downed beers in the Oasis, a tanned fellow, about forty with sun-bleached hair and a gold chain around his neck, took the next barstool. He introduced himself as Charlie, and said, "I understand you fly. I'm looking for a pilot. How'd you like a job flying for my boss?"

"Tell me about it," said Larry.

"You'd fly on Air Jamaica from Miami to Kingston, fare provided by my boss, and go to The Pelican Club. You'd be contacted there. The job's an easy stint, Jamaica to the Bahamas, pays well, and if it works, perhaps more jobs."

"I'll sleep on it" said Larry. They agreed to meet the next night at the Oasis.

Larry's beer money was running low and the landlord of the shack he amusingly called a cottage was clamoring for past-due rent. He decided to go for it. The job sounded simple and the money was substantial. The fact that it was astonishingly high for a legitimate job was not lost on Larry but he'd flirted with the law before in his life, and he was willing to have a go, piece of cake. "Yeah, I'll take the job," he told Charlie the next night.

A few days later found Larry in Kingston wearing clean jeans, with a new island shirt and his shaggy hair combed. He sat at the bar in The Pelican Club enjoying the reggae music and the slim girls dancing as he awaited his rendezvous. Before long a tall Jamaican arrived and introduced himself as Gregory. He suggested he and Larry have dinner on the deck overlooking the long beach. During a meal of lobster tails, rice and plantain, they discussed arrangements. "You'll be driven tomorrow evening to a small airport twenty miles from Kingston. The private plane is tied down there," explained Gregory.

"When is takeoff?" asked Larry.

"At 1800 hours. You'll fly to Coral Cay in the Bahamas. The plane's ID and charts are in this envelope. You'll land at the small runway where you'll be met by Juan Lopez. Are you with me this far?"

"Yeah," replied Larry as he took the brown envelope.

Gregory continued, "Your cargo will be transferred to another plane with a new pilot. You'll be paid by Juan and next day taken by boat to Nassau where you'll be given a ticket for a regular commercial flight to Miami, your job finished. Questions?"

"Sounds easy," said Larry.

All went well—so well, in fact, that Larry was soon the regular pilot for the runs.

On the fateful flight, Larry stirred from his hangover musings and glanced at his instruments. Fog was rolling in from the Atlantic over Exuma Sound. He switched off autopilot and resumed visual flying. He hoped the fog would clear as he approached Coral Cay. Instead, it thickened as he descended. Suddenly the instrument panel showed a red blinking light. "What is it?" Larry panicked. Too late he wondered, "Was I really ready for this flight?" An alarm was wailing, and fumes were rising in a cloud in the cockpit. "Where did they come from?" he screamed. His rate of descent increased rapidly. Perspiration bathed his forehead as he saw the lights of the Coral Cay airstrip two miles ahead. "Can I make it?" he thought. "What if I can't?"

Juan and the revelers heard the thrum of the plane as it approached the little island airstrip with its cargo of drugs, on schedule despite the fog that had blown in from the ocean. "Okay, let's go meet our man," he said as he grabbed his jacket and headed for the door.

In the cockpit, Larry saw his Mother's face outside the windshield. "Are you calling me? Do you finally realize you love me?" He was jubilant. "Yes, I'll come to you. Yes, I will. Mama . . ." he cried as the plane crashed into the Bay just short of Coral Cay.

Juan and the others heard the explosion. Confusion reigned as the entourage raced to the beach. This was one shipment that would not end up on the streets of New York, one payment that would not enrich the many facets of the drug kingdom.

Now, more than two decades later, the jungle had claimed the abandoned island homes. Others had arrived in the interval and built new residences. The plane remained on the bottom of the sea where cruisers from the anchorage often snorkeled to explore its deteriorating fuselage.

Bill and May raised their anchor and continued their passage south, having noted in the ship's log their discoveries on Coral Cay. There was, however, something they did not uncover, something left for another cruiser to find some day–a yellowed sheet of paper in a toppled cabinet drawer. It contained a barely discernible series of figures and letters and a number, the note Juan had written that told him what plane was bringing his contraband and when it would arrive. The pilot had known his destination but had he known it would be his last flight?

# THE IMMIGRANTS

"These damn foreigners. They come here illegally, go on welfare, use my tax dollars, and we'll all end up having to speak Spanish," complained the heavy-set trucker to his companion as they quaffed beer at the dimly-lit bar. They didn't see Dimas, the Mexican dishwasher, behind the flimsy partition. "Man," thought Dimas, "if they only knew." He recalled his entry into the great US of A two years earlier.

He'd said goodbye to his parents in their little village. Tears trickled down his father's sun-baked face, lined and wrinkled. His mother's tight hug needed no words to express her sadness at this last son's departure. Yet each knew there was no future there for the young man. Jobs were scarce and wages were not enough to sustain even a meager living. The United States, far to the north, was his only hope of a decent life. Each of his four brothers had left in a similar manner. Three had married, and as grandchildren arrived, the money they sent to sustain their parents had dwindled. It was his turn to share in their support. To do so meant heading to the great land north of the Rio Grande. He took a soft bag with his few belongings and set out to meet the truck scheduled to stop at his village.

The truck arrived an hour after the expected time. A gruff fellow lowered himself from the cab and grumbled incoherently as he stretched out his palm to take the money Dimas had saved. He motioned Dimas to join the three young men sitting on a wooden bench on the bed of the truck. Hours later, darkness was falling when they arrived at a small city. The nine passengers jumped down, shook themselves to relieve their cramped muscles, and entered the hostel where they were to stay the night.

The same routine marked the next three days. Under the hot sun, the rickety truck crawled up and then down the twisting road, skirting dusty hillsides on its slow northward trek. The racket of the ancient engine made conversation impossible. Each man was left with his private thoughts of the life he was leaving behind and the unknown future that lay beyond.

Dimas befriended a young boy, Marco, who'd joined the truck's passengers on the second day. He sensed the lad's fear as he climbed aboard and sat hunched on the wooden bench next to Dimas. They'd chatted briefly at the hostels. Dimas learned that he and Marco shared a similar background. It gave Dimas a sense of purpose to take Marco under his wing, and Marco in turn was thankful to find a friend in Dimas.

The last night's stay was in the border town hostel. Passengers from other trucks joined the emigrants, all headed for the same destination. After a meal, the hostel manager directed the men to a room full of cots. On each was a threadbare blanket. Lights were out within twenty minutes and each man fell asleep. Dimas wondered, "What is each of these men thinking on his last night spent in his land?"

The next day they met with the gruff courier who'd pocketed Dimas's savings. He told the men they would be driven in a truck that evening to within two miles of the border. He assured everyone that for the sum paid, they would be guided across the border into the Arizona desert. From there, another truck would provide transport to a large city. Someone there would usher them to a safe house until they could be dispersed to one of a few other large cities where they would be given employment and housing. Each held this dream close.

At dusk the men waited in the village square until the truck arrived. The courier herded the emigrants into the flatbed with the familiar wooden benches. Upon reaching the border, the trucks stopped away from a large fence. The men gathered in the darkness, apprehensive yet excited to begin the border crossing. The courier whispered that once the sweeping spotlight passed the area, they were to climb the fence in groups of five. Each was to clamber down the dry gulch of the riverbed, the great Rio Grande, and run across. They'd be met by another "mule" who would guide them on the U.S. side. "Are you ready?" whispered Dimas to Marco.

"I guess so," Marco replied. With that, the new friends left Mexico, no time for a formal farewell.

Dimas paused from his dishwashing to listen to the two workers continuing their contemptuous complaints about the "dagos." He wondered if his life was really better than it would have been in his Mexican village. The United States Border Patrol had captured him twice and returned him to Mexico. Then he'd successfully crossed, making his entry over a year ago. He'd secured a job in this tavern, no questions asked, and he was able to send money home to his mother, his father having died in the meanwhile. He'd met Maria and planned to marry her as soon as they could save enough money to move out of the hovel they shared. Her job as a maid at the little motel down the street brought in a few tips to bolster the less-than-minimum wage she received. Perhaps his American Dream could yet be realized. He'd not heard from Marco after the second time the Border Patrol deported them. His money depleted, Marco had decided to return to his village and forget the immigrant dream of life in the United States.

At the same time, Joanne Wright was settling into life in Portland, Oregon. A Canadian citizen of British birth, she'd met Steve Wright, an American businessman whose company had transferred him to the oil company where she worked in Calgary. Their romance flourished and soon they were sure their love was real. Joanne had to decide whether this love was enough to justify leaving family and friends in Calgary, where she'd lived many years. She made the decision and the wedding date was set. Family and friends surrounded them and wished them well in their efforts to obtain the precious visa that would allow Joanne Wright, née Clark, to enter the United States when it was time for Steve to return to Portland.

Joanne spent many months going back and forth to the U.S. Embassy completing the myriad immigration forms. It seemed every visit led to a further requirement which she endeavored to fulfill. Once she'd left the Embassy in tears. "Oh, Steve, that dour, rigid Immigration Officer required even more information. Now I have to get proof of the date I arrived in Canada from Britain, and you know how long ago that was! I have to contact Canadian Immigration and complete their forms. I can't see ever getting into the States . . . and she's so unpleasant," sobbed Joanne.

She did, however, obtain the required information, meticulously complete the complicated forms and obtain the required TB x-ray from the U.S. Medical Officer. She finally received notice of her interview date. As Joanne exited the Embassy the final time, wearing a smile and carrying the precious Resident Alien Card, she said to Steve, "We made it. I have the Green Card. We can go."

On a bright June day they presented the Card to the Customs Officer at the Blaine, Washington crossing. He gave her a smile and said "Welcome to America!"

Legal immigrant and illegal immigrant—each has a story. But one can rest easy at night; one will always be awaiting the tap on the shoulder.

# THE THIEF

The only child of an American missionary couple, Madeline Jackson was ten in 1922 when the family left their home church in a small farming community in coastal Georgia to serve the Lord in China. In Honan Province Madeline's sweet personality won the hearts of the hillside villagers. Through hard work and compassion, Rev. and Mrs. Jackson, a nurse, founded the House of Hope Orphanage, a facility sorely needed in the region. There they educated the children and fostered Christian values. After a few years, ill health caused the family to leave the orphanage in the care of another missionary family. With heavy hearts the Jacksons returned to Georgia.

In 1936, equipped with a degree in theology, Madeline returned to China. She had often told her classmates, "I'll return to Honan Province some day as a missionary." Friends cautioned Madeline to think twice before deciding to serve in such a remote region especially with rumors of conflict rife. On her return she discovered that the missionaries had left and the orphanage had closed. The number of children without parents had grown as disease and conflict worsened. She set about the challenging effort of reopening the House of Hope.

She was gentle yet resolute in her focus. She was a ready listener and had been trusted with confidences from a young age. Her ability to see both sides of an issue and give a fair assessment when asked earned her admiration. Her adventurous spirit helped her cope with the many unusual problems she was called upon to resolve in that far-flung mountainous area. She loved each child in her charge, and she taught and guided the students in the life principles she espoused. All her actions bespoke Love.

The war news filtered slowly to the orphanage. A villager who had been taught years before by Madeline's parents sporadically received news through a forbidden BBC shortwave radio. One day he ran to the door to alert Madeline. "Miss Jackson, the soldiers are coming. You and the children must leave immediately. I have heard stories of their barbarism. Go quickly with God's blessing." Madeline organized their escape and prepared to lead her charges to safety.

"Come along, Children. Hold hands and be careful of the rocks underfoot," she said as she led twenty-two children away from the House of Hope. The Japanese army had invaded China even as far as this remote region. The little legs of the children carried them at a much slower pace than that of their pursuers. Soon the enemy overtook and captured them.

Madeline and her charges were taken to an internment camp. Although they escaped the ruthless treatment suffered by those left in their village, they spent the ensuing war years in harsh conditions in the camp. Even there, Madeline's exceptionally loving character came to the fore as she helped the incarcerated. She organized school classes using the meager resources about the camp; she comforted mothers who had reached the end of their coping abilities under the brutal Japanese rule; she helped administer medical assistance even as supplies became nonexistent; and she acted as Detainee Representative to the camp's authorities. "What resource does this marvelous woman call upon to enable her to comfort and aid us?" many wondered.

When World War II ended, Madeline returned to the marsh country of coastal Georgia, and in 1977 she retired as Principal of the local high school. Over the years her unfailingly understanding nature and her knack for leading youth in a nonjudgmental way endeared her to all. Many attended her retirement party. Among those was Dr. Jim Moore, whose wife had recently died. He guided Madeline to a corner of the room and said, "Miss Jackson, I remember you as the quietly confident young woman who returned to our town after the War. I noticed you immediately and felt drawn to you, but I was engaged to be married. My heart still turns over when I see you. You remain the attractive woman who guided our three children through their school years. They still speak lovingly of you as they follow their own life paths."

Love has a mysterious way of surfacing. Before long, Madeline and Jim married.

In the summer of 1990, a well-dressed Chinese businessman visited the Chamber of Commerce in that Georgia town. "Can you please direct me to Rest Haven Home?" Lee Lin asked the receptionist. Shortly he entered the facility and enquired if he could visit Mrs. Madeline Moore. He had traveled far to fulfill his dream of seeing the loving House of Hope teacher he remembered from his childhood. He wanted to thank her for the sustaining character she'd been throughout his years of happiness at the orphanage and during his years of challenge in internment.

"I'm sorry to tell you that Mrs. Moore is unable to receive visitors," the Director of Rest Haven told Mr. Lin. "After the death of her husband, she exhibited signs of dementia and now has advanced Alzheimer's disease. This scourge has robbed her of her sweet personality. She is now held in a special section of our Alzheimer's unit under a 24-hour guard. She rages violently; she uses obscenities and will harm others without reason. She is our most difficult resident. Mrs. Moore is no longer the person you remember. I'd advise you to live with your memories, Mr. Lin." Mr. Lin thanked the Director and slowly walked away, a saddened man.

# ELIZABETH WILSON

Elizabeth Wilson. I was born in El Paso, Texas, on April 8, 1922. I earned an AA degree at Clark College, a BS degree at PSU and an MS degree at Lewis & Clark University. I write essays, short stories, nonsense and poems because it's so much fun!

# I. SEASONS AND HOLIDAYS

## A GLIMPSE OF PARADISE

Old fashioned roses, dark red,
climb o'er the wall of the shed.
A tall clump of lilies sways on
slender stems sway with ease.

Daisies, breeze tossed, catch my eye
'neath a bright blue cloudless sky.
Dappled shade cast by the tree
cools a garden bench for me.

Eden must have been like this,
blue sky, shade, the soft air's kiss,
beauty everywhere I turn,
violets and lacy fern.

Is this the way the angels wise
give us a glimpse of paradise?

## SUMMER, THEN AND NOW

Today is like the ten days past,
Mornings cloudy, overcast,
By noon the sun comes out at last
Bringing summer's hot, red blast.

My parents wilted in the heat,
And searched for any shaded seat,
And let the children run the street
In scanty clothes, bare legs, bare feet.

Today, I turn the A.C. on

And tell the heat, "Begone, begone."
I take a nap, sometimes quite long,
Until night breezes come along.

Now that's today—when I was young
I did as my poor parents done.
SWELTERED!

## GOOD-BYE SUMMER

The summer's long and lazy days
Reluctantly give way
To chilly morns, to autumn haze,
And fewer hours to play.

## AUTUMN OUTSIDE MY WINDOW

The green-crowned tree across the street
Is turning orange and brown.
Soon she'll be quite indiscreet
And let her leaves fall down.

## PREPARING FOR HALLOWE'EN

I'll don my coat, my scarf, and hat,
And find a pumpkin patch.
I'll buy a pumpkin big and fat.
In fact, I'll buy a batch.

Bad Jack-O-Lanterns they'll become,
All with scary faces.
On Hallowe'en, when dark-time comes
I'll put them in their places.

The witches, ghosts and goblins,
A Trick-or-Treat brigade

Will come in droves, then leave with grins
And goodies from their raid.

Inside we'll drink hard cider while waiting for the ghouls.
Hard cider can be tasty stuff—us old folks ain't no fools!

## AN INVITATION

The trees are gaunt and tall and bare.
Their leaves are scattered everywhere,
And Halloween is almost here
Filled with gruesome things to fear.
A pair of pumpkins I did buy,
To carve with features all awry,
Then put two lighted candles in
each one to show its ugly grin.
I'll save the innards for a pie,
And oven roast the seeds to dry
To eat when winter winds blow cold
When I'm curled in a blanket's fold.

I think I'll go to Mexico
away from all the ice and snow
In the shade I'll drink iced tea.
Would you like to come with me?

## WINTER RAIN

'Tis Nature's plan to bring the rain
To wash the mountains, fields and plain,
The wayfarers like you and me,
Each tiny seed and barren tree.
The mountains gain a coat of snow.
From thence in spring the waters flow
To waterfalls and rushing streams
And make a wonderland it seems.
The crops that grow so we may eat

May ripen in the summer's heat
But will not very long survive
If winter rain does not arrive.
So when begins the winter rain
Tell Nature, "Thanks." Never complain.

## SEASON'S GREETINGS 2007

Rudolph can soar past my chimney this year.
I want for nothing but comfort and cheer.
My stockings lie mated, all put away.
None will be hung to await Santa's sleigh.

Hustle and bustle, all that frantic hype,
Are part of my past. I am glad to wipe
From the task of this eighty-fifth season,
To keep my mem'ry, also my reason!

Around me is quiet, ne'er stir the mice.
It's hum-drum, but Hi-Ho—my life is nice!

## A CHRISTMAS CONFESSION

'Twas a week before Christmas. Two bright blue eyes
Saw Dad and Mom hide a brown wrapped surprise,
A secret for Christmas, high up on the shelf.
A place Brother knew he could not reach himself.

When Sister came home, the boy told her this tale.
Sis knew she could find a good way without fail
To conquer the problem and take down the box.
Both skinny and tall, she was also a jock.

On Saturday, early, Dad left in the car
To golf at the Men's Club. He rarely made par.
The children said, "Now's our chance to climb SO high,
"Cause Mom is outside hanging laundry to dry."

Children are clever, but sometimes not bright.
This next adventure proves I am right.

Upstairs, in the closet for linens and stuff,
Said package lay waiting, 'twas quite safe enough
From anything but two curious children,
Unstoppable, even by all the King's men.

Sis climbed on a chair, plus a stool. Much too low.
They piled on four books and Mom's Bible. Oh, NO!
Sis did reach the package by stretching tip-toe.
Bible, books, chair, and stool slipped—down they did go,

Sis wasn't hurt, but the package split open.
The gizmos and balls inside were unbroken
Mom, finished her chore, came in and heard giggles,
"There's something AMISS, my warning flag wiggles!"

At the top of the stairs Mom found a big mess,
And two guilty children who had to confess.

### THE MORAL

Don't snoop at Christmas or you'll lose
Something you'd like, something you'd choose
Over anything in the world,
Two trick balls and gizmos that whirl.

## 28 DECEMBER 2009

Mid-afternoon the snow began to fall.
Wind blew it westward
In a momentary blizzard.
Then the wind abated.
A curtain of white fell to earth.
By night the street was covered.
Trees, branches bent with snow,

Stood alone. No one was about
To see the beautiful winter scene.
But from my window I could see
There was no moon this night,
The street lamps were hidden,
But in their glow snow-laden branches
Painted a magnificent sight
Against the black velvet night.
I knew driving was treacherous.
News reports were nothing but warnings to drivers
And reports of hours and hours taken
For normally short 20-minute trips.
I am at home with no plan to go anywhere,
I can revel in the beauty of Nature's winter spectacular.

# 29 DECEMBER 2009

'Twas the morn after snowfall—
The cat and I rose
To look out the window
And view how much snow
Had fallen since bedtime
The ev'nin' before.
What to my half open eyes should appear
But a black knitted cap
On a warmly dressed gent
Shoveling the drifts
From all my cement.
He spoke not a word
But kept at his work
And finished the job
Then turned with a jerk,
He waved his right hand as he jumped in his truck,
And quickly drove off with a clunkety chunk.

# 2010

The New Year is here,
It's two thousand and ten.
The problem that comes
With a change in the year
Is silly, but mostly
Because we forget to force
Our worn minds to accept
New info when dating a check.
My Goodness Sake,
A charge made on 12/12/09
Just cannot be paid
If the check date's 1/10/09.
Letters or e-mails
We send to our friends
Will only confuse them
They may think we're dead,
And sending old letters from
Heaven or Hell
OH WELL! Life goes on . . . and on . . . and on.

Deborah Guyol

# NEW YEAR'S DAY

It's New Year's Day
The sky is gray,
I wonder what
I'll do today.
I called my daughters.
They're not home.
This must be
Their day to roam—
Renewing friendships
Old and dear
And wishing each
A good New Year.
What will I do
This New Year's Day?
Go back to bed
And dream away.
HAPPY 2010!

# II. FANTASY

## FANTASY

Without the world of fantasy
There would be no talking tree,
No cows that leap, nor wee fairy–
A talking donkey could not be.

Mice could not sew, nor could cats grin.
A swan would never be a prince,
A pumpkin could not be a coach,
The midnight hour would have no charm.

Oh what a dreary world 'twould be
Without the help of fantasy–
Without a gallant knight of old
To rescue maids lost in the cold,

To serve a king both kind and good
And bless the poor like Robin Hood.
My dying wish for you will be
To love and cherish fantasy.

## THE OTHER SIDE

There is another world out there–
A world I cannot see.
A world of magic creatures
Like goblins, toads and ghosts.

I think that I shall visit there
When bedtime is my boat
And dance with all the fairies
'til morning calls me home.

My mother thinks I'm balmy,
My father thinks I'm touched.
But I'm a'goin' back again to see
The other side of nowhere.

Come, I'll take you there.

## THE COMPLETE DAY

What novel shall I read today?
I feel it should be something gay,
Nothing erudite or gloomy.
A sweet fairy tale will suit me.
I have decided what to read—
A book with dragons full of greed,
And gallant knights who win the hands
Of maidens brought from many lands.
When that is done I will retreat
Within the hall for bread and meat
And Elderberry wine so sweet.
All this will make my day complete.
If you believe this silly tale
Try tar and feathers on a rail.

## FAIRIES

Have you heard the fairies
Sing of home and happiness,
Of the fairy King and Queen?
You and I can join them—
Dear friend, come with me.
We'll play beyond the rainbow
And when our play is done,
We'll take a nap on fleecy clouds,
Quite sheltered from the sun—
Dear friend, come with me.

A butterfly can take us
To where we want to go
Up there where the fairies live
Just beyond the rainbow—
Dear friend, come with me.
You can't hear the fairies sing?
And you don't want to go?
Goodbye, I'm off for fairyland.
I shan't come back you know.

## MY SECRET HIDE-AWAY

I have a secret place to go
No one can find me here you know.
In my big book of fairy tales
I visit goblins, gnomes and elves.
But I love most the fairy folk
And how they love to dance and joke
And hide behind a blade of grass
To catch the butterflies that pass.
When I am crosswise, out of sorts,
I read of trolls with lots of warts
Who scare the billy goats away
Trip-trapping cross the bridge to play.
For every mood I have I find
A mystic waif within my mind
To keep me company each day
Until I put my book away.

## IF

If I had a million
I'd hide it in my shoe
And never tell a single soul
About my secret place.

If I had two million

I'd hide it in my socks
And weight it down for safety
With a bucket full of rocks.

If I had three million
I'd take an airplane ride
And hide my riches in the clouds–
I think the sunny side.

If I had a billion
I'd give it all away
To poor folk on the edge of town
Who had no food today.

# THE WHOPPERDILLY – LESSON ONE

A Whopperdilly does what a Whopperdilly do–
If he's driving down the avenue and runs a red light through
He'll swear by all that's holy that the doggone light was blue.
Yeah, a Whopperdilly does just what Whopperdilly do.

The truth just isn't in him; he'd rather tell a fib.
With big round eyes he'll look at you and mouth untruths so glib
You almost think he's honest. Then you begin to doubt,
But he disappeared before you got him figured out.

His bed is by the river where he much prefers to play,
But if you ever see him, stay very far away
Because his Whopperdilly mind will think you want to stay–
You'll be in his cage at night and tethered through the day.

A zombie, ghost, or vampire cannot strike in me such fear
As a sneaky Whopperdilly attacking from the rear
To claw my back with talons while he bites off my ear.
Stay home and keep the doors locked when a Whopperdilly's near.

A Whopperdilly does

What a Whopperdilly do,
So never let a Whopperdilly
get ahold of you.

## LESSON TWO – IF YOU SEE A WHOPPERDILLY

Should  you meet a Whopperdilly this is what you'll see:
His shiny legs are big steel pipes, ratchets for each knee,
His eyes are two black bowling balls, his long mouth is a zipper,
His arms are monstrous rods and each hand's a spiny gripper.

Don't mistake the Whopperdilly for a friendly guy–
He's ugly and he's nasty; he has an evil eye,
Enormous ears that flap when he moves his pointy head,
'Neath his scraggly beard beats no heart–for he is dead.

I've never been an artist, his picture I can't draw.
If you're artistic, make a sketch and take it to the law.
Whopperdilly must be stopped, and quickly sent to jail,
And kept there for eternity–no visitors, no mail.

## LESSON THREE – IF YOU HEAR A WHOPPERDILLY

Whopperdilly's legs when he moves go Clank, Clank, Clanking.
If he's moving fast, both his ears go Flap, Flap, Flapping.
Oh, you'll hear his feet softly Shuffle, Shuffle, Shuffle.
These are sounds of warning Whopperdilly can't muffle.

Sometimes, if he's near, there's a Snuffle, Snuffle, Snuffling.
That's his long old schnozzola a'dripping and a'dripping.
If you hear Clank, Flap, and Shuffle, take care, he is near–
If you can hear him Snuffle, it's too late, he is here.

Oh, children, stay alert–the Whopperdilly wants you.
Everything you see or hear just may be a clue.

"Clankety Clank" go his legs, his feet "Shuffle, Shuffle."
Flappety Flap" go his ears. His nose, "Snuffle, Snuffle."

## LESSON FOUR – IF YOU SMELL A WHOPPERDILLY

Whopperdilly smells like naught you've ever smelled before.
Hi odor permeates a room, its ceiling, walls and floor.
You gasp and run outside for air, choking all the while,
Whopperdilly's zipper mouth will widen in a smile.

There are no words descriptive of the odor he exudes.
It's worse than any garbage dump, or smell of rotten foods.
Whopperdilly never bathes and launders not one thing.
A Whopperdilly's odor out-stinks everything.

It would be so sad one day if Whopperdilly chose
To take you to the big black pond (where no wise person goes).
You'll struggle and you'll holler, but your parents will not hear.
Hold your nose and kick his shins to show you have no fear.

Be sure you kick him hard enough to make his two legs leak.
When Whopperdilly's fuel is gone, then he becomes quite weak
'Tis then you can escape from him, if you are still alive.
But as a rule he smells so bad that nothing can survive.

## LESSON FIVE – (NEVER) TASTE A WHOPPERDILLY

My recipe for Whopperdilly is a rare treat.
You strip the Whopperdilly, toss out the nose and feet.
You marinate the legs in lye until they turn red,
Remove the hair, beard, ears and shoes. All of which you shred.

The pincers, ratchets, arm rods, you grind 'til they are dust.
By now the eyes have rolled away. Chase them if you must.

Throw out the big red legs, and all the stuff you shredded.
I wouldn't taste it, nor should you, or you will be dead.

## LESSON SIX – TRUST YOUR SIXTH SENSE

Whopperdilly doesn't know you have another sense.
He's scary and he's ugly. He's also mighty dense.
Your Sixth Sense is inside yourself, everything you know.
It's a feeling in your gut that tells you how to go

If your world is upside down and everything is tough.
Use your head, and what you know, to smooth the road that's rough.
This now will end our lessons. I thank you everyone
This venture has been tedious, but it has been fun.

# III. CAT TALES

## SMOKEY AND THE BUTTERFLY BUSH

I was an "in-the-house" cat, de-clawed and de-sexed, an "IT." I grew from a tiny kitten to maturity with a master and mistress who lavished me with affection. When I was a tiny kitten they named me KeKe (Hawiian for Baby) and I remained KeKe for ten years.

In my tenth year, my aforesaid mistress produced a man-child, much smaller than I, and sickly. His arrival destroyed my way of life. There was no routine, the child wailed night and day. His parents often forgot to fill my dish, or leave water. The pediatrician and the allergist said, "He has an allergy to cats." Poppy-cock, that child was Damaged Goods! They should have sent it back. Instead, my mistress put me in a carrier and delivered me to Elizabeth. I never saw the mistress again.

For days I hid under Elizabeth's bed. Late every night I pussy-footed through the dark house. I found a dish of cat-food, the flavor I had always eaten. I found a litter box, identical to the one I had used for years! However, it was a week before I was willing to see, or be seen, by daylight, then only briefly. I began to sleep ON the bed, then ON the chairs. By the end of week three, Elizabeth's lap was a very nice place. I decided Elizabeth could stay. She kept food and water available, my litter box was clean, and her lap was nice. She thought KeKe was a ridiculous name for a handsome, full-grown cat and gave me a new name, "Smokey." That was quite okay. I respond when I choose. What I'm called doesn't matter.

My world expanded when Elizabeth opened the back door and allowed me to explore our fenced yard. I had never been out of doors in my life. The grass, the trees, the open space, the warm sun on my back were awesome. From that day forward, within the fenced yard, I roamed, chased leaves, chewed grass or, best of all, sat for hours under the Butterfly Bush. I sat there and watched the world go by, the world beyond the fence.

Two days ago I hid under a bush right by the gate. Elizabeth was pulling and pruning ivy around the fence. When she brought the yard debris through the gate it was easy to slip into that world beyond the fence. Elizabeth, though, was quick to discover my absence and attempted to catch me. It became a game. I hid in the shrubs, or waved my tail and ran off faster than she could scramble after me. She couldn't corral me. I was curled up under a shrub well out of her sight, or her reach, when she called a neighbor to help her. I could hear Elizabeth and her neighbor talk about "automobiles" and "unleashed dogs," and that I had no claws and couldn't protect myself, or climb trees . . . blah, blah, blah. By the way, what is an unleashed dog? And why would I need to climb a tree? Elizabeth and the neighbor went around the house to look for me. I was bored huddling under the bush. In fact, I was bored with the game. I crept from the branches, shook off the leaves and climbed some sunny steps on a concrete stoop. From that vantage point I should have been able to see Elizabeth. I didn't. I wondered, had Elizabeth also tired of the game? Was she no longer looking for me?

I had no idea where I was. I was hungry. I wanted to go home. I was lost and lonely. The sun was warm on the concrete. Half asleep and half awake I heard voices—Elizabeth and her friend. They came around the corner. Elizabeth gasped, "Smokey!" I knew she was cross. She picked me up, her arm tight around my belly, my fore-legs dangled in front, my back legs and tail dangled behind. It was most undignified. She ignored my complaints, and gripped tighter. I was carried thus, through the gate, across the yard, and dumped, not gently, under the Butterfly Bush. I tried to explain it was just a game. I guess she doesn't like games.

I can defend myself. I am clever, resourceful and a worthy opponent, despite my lack of claws. I can bite. I don't I need claws. A while back I bit Elizabeth's hand. It oozed blood for three days and didn't heal for weeks. Has she forgotten?

Just tell me two things. One: What is an unleashed dog? Two: Why would I ever need or want to climb a tree?

Elizabeth and I have made up. I learned Elizabeth doesn't like games. She's learning that sometimes I play little games.

Yesterday I loafed under the Butterfly Bush. It's a great place, thick with leaves and purple flowers. The long branches bend low, almost to the ground. I sleep there almost every day, sometimes well into twilight. Last evening, just after dusk, Elizabeth called and called, I ignored her–it was my little game. Maybe it was "our" little game, she knew where I was. The air was still and warm. I would spend another hour under the Butterfly Bush, then go inside. A chilly little breeze came from nowhere, quickly followed by a brisk wind. Perhaps we were in for a storm. The wind turned the long branches into whips. I thought, "What if Elizabeth closes the door? What if I'm out here until morning?" With that, I left the Butterfly Bush, crossed the lawn in two jumps, ran up the steps and through the open door. She waited there, I purred, I rubbed her ankles (she's a sucker for attention). Elizabeth loves me and, in my own furry way, I love her. I love games too, but sometimes games are not wise.

I could hear the rain during the night. This morning is disaster! I can see out the window, Sheets of water are falling – rain! – the porch, the steps, the grass . . . all wet.

"Oh Butterfly Bush, your wet branches bend low, water courses down your leaves onto the dusty bark at your feet. Your bark is muddy and cold. I will not sit under your lovely shade today, Butterfly Bush."

Elizabeth opened the door wide. "I love the fresh smell of rain," she said.

"Prrmp, meew, I shall curl up on the pillow by the fireplace, the fresh smell of rain is not for me."

# CATTITUDE

Something is going to be different today, I can't put a whisker on it.
I am not sure I'll like it.
Right now, I think not.

I watch as she dresses.
Most mornings she puts on robe and slippers.
I yawn, stretch, and follow her to the kitchen.

She knows I watch, but makes no move to scratch my ears,
Or say, "Good Morning, Pretty Boy."
She usually does.

I sit at the door and wait. I want out.
She won't open the door
Until she completes the ritual.

Every morning there's this ritual.
She hobbles, kitchen to front entry, opens wall box,
Sticks finger in box, box beeps and flashes green. End of ritual.

She closes box, hobbles to kitchen,
Opens door and lets me out.
"What did you say?–She's just turning off the Security System?"

Does she know how insecure I am until I get outside and dig that
hole?

Today, she's dressed for the street.
Instead of water for coffee
She pours water in two white dishes on the floor,
She opens a green bin and scoops pellets
Into two whimsical Kitty dishes next to the water,
Last, she replenishes the litter box.
I hate that box, but . . . it's clean.

I use it immediately.
"Phew, Kitty, phewww, pheww!" she says, and fans the air.

I don't care.
I'm not desperate, but I would like to go out.
I sit at the door.

She hobbles, kitchen to front entry, opens box . . . completes the ritual.
In the kitchen,
I wait by the door.

I hear her voice, "Hi Millie, I'm ready. Where shall we g . . ."
A door closes.
I'm left with food, water, and that BOX!

The bed is warm, it's a good day to sleep.

# IV. CONTEMPLATING TIME

## GOING AWAY

Where are you going
My very best friend?
Can I go with you?
I'll stay to the end.

What? You won't let me.
I'm asking you why?
Because it's a secret?
I know that's a lie.

You've promised me truth
Till you die, till you die.
We'll walk to the ends of the earth,
You and I.

If this is not friendship there's little to say
What stands in the way?

## THE BOOK OF LIFE

"The book is long," the woman said,
"It took a lifetime to be read.
I started it at one or two;
Now, at eighty, I am through.

"My eyes were bright, I could see far,
They twinkled like the morning star,
But now they've dimmed, the print seems small,
And I can scarcely read at all.

"This book of life, my joys, my fears,

I leave behind. Don't weep, my dears.
The book's complete, there is no more
For death knocks loudly at my door.

"For every soul there is a time
To leave this life, and this is mine."

## A SONNET TO PLASTIC SACK

What is less rare than a plastic sack,
One crushed, and soiled, reused for waste,
One ragged and torn, blown by wind,
Awaiting breath on the freeway face?
Quite lifeless, flat and prone it waits
Until it's lifted and can soar,
Almost alive, in traffic draft.
Soon, torn to shreds, 'twill rise no more.
I too am like a plastic sack.
My Spirits crush, my soul is soiled,
At Death I'll seek an errant wind
To give me life once more, ere cold.
Like plastic sacks, am I but waste,
to be torn to shreds and rise no more?

## HEAR WHAT I WANT TO SAY

To you I speak in Words,
A few whispered Words.
Do you hear my Words?
Or what I want to say?

At this, life's last hour,
In darken'd bower—
Do you hear my Words?
Or what I want to say?

Do not grieve for me.
I lived, now I'm free.
Do you hear my Words?
Hear what I want to say!

## TOMORROW NEVER COMES

Each morn wakes me with a kiss,
"Today you are the Queen."
Each day I make this promise,
"Tomorrow I will clean."

Since there is no Tomorrow
And I have just Today.
I don't feel any sorrow
When cleaning I delay.

"Tomorrow will bring sunshine,"
The weather man could say.
I will play, not clean my grime,
'Cause that will be Today.

Tomorrow never comes, you see.
Waste not Today on drudgery.

## DEATH ON THE FARM

The washing machine goes splash, splash, splash.
The junky old car goes crash, crash, crash.
And this old lady has no cash
To pay the junk man well.

The birdies in the tree just warble away.
The children down below frolic and play.
And this old lady cannot pay
The ice cream man come Saturday.

The horse in the barn has no more hay.
The chickens in the yard have no more scratch.
The pigs in the pen have no more slop.
And this old  lady can buy naught.

The poor old horse ran away.
The chickens were fried on Saturday.
The pigs were slaughtered come payday.
And the poor old woman passed away.

# A DAILY LOVE NOTE FROM HIM FAR AWAY

What shall I write, when I've nothing to say?
A note you'll receive on some future day.
I sit, pen in hand, while time ticks away.
What shall I write, when I've nothing to say?

What things have I done to tell you about?
To rouse your interest, or raise your doubt?
That I cut my thumb, or still have the gout?
What have I done to tell you about?

I know! I'll tell you the snow is all gone.
The rain has stopped falling, I see the sun,
The flowers have buds, the birds sing a song,
But none of that's true, the snow is not gone.

Today I will write when I've nothing to say:
I miss you, I love you, and have a Good Day.
xxoxxoxxxooo

# DOROTHY DEE WORKMAN

Dorothy Dee Workman was born on the prairies of South Dakota in 1927, grew up in New Jersey, Buffalo and Boston. She married a South Dakota farm boy who became a preacher, had four children, lived in several South Dakota towns, and spent two years in South Vietnam working with native tribes. She got an MA in counseling in 1975, and worked as a mental health counselor, moving to Vancouver in 1985. Widowed after 54 years of marriage, she decided to follow an early dream of becoming a writer, and enrolled in a Mature Learning Creative Writing course at Clark College. Her interest in Haiku poetry is a result of many visits to Japan, where her oldest daughter lives.

# HAIKU JOURNAL
# OF AN ORDINARY LIFE

## INTRODUCTION

Once every ten years or so I decide to keep a journal. I still have one of the five year diaries in which I wrote about ten entries in 1939 and fifteen entries the next year, none of them earth-shaking. Since then I have written various detail of my life, but not in a systematic way!

Thirty-some years ago, while visiting my daughter in Tokyo, Japan, I became acquainted with haiku poetry. Haiku is a set form of unrhymed poetry–three lines, the first with five syllables, the second with seven syllables, and the third with five. This is not an ordinary verse form in this day and age, though it was an integral part of communication, both written and oral, in early Japan where it was developed. The rules for the Japanese version, in addition to line length, included the use of a seasonal word in each haiku. For instance, pumpkin would indicate fall; cherry blossoms spring, etc. Also the verses were to be subtle, and not personal–as befits Japanese character.

When in Japan for a visit, I began to compose haiku to help me remember the events of the day. Since then I have kept a daily journal on special occasions, such as my visits to Japan, trips to South Dakota to visit family, once even a cruise to Alaska. As I read those journals again, I am reminded of the pleasures, as well as the pains and embarrassments I experienced. I also become aware of the pleasure involved in the writing each day.

Having taken many small steps in the past few years to enable me to make use of whatever days of my life remain, I decided this year to write at least one haiku each day. I don't have a good record of follow-through on New Year's resolutions. I begin this year expecting to enjoy the process.

# JANUARY 2009

## January 1

I just pace the halls
Not ready to rock–or roll
In this brand-new year.

Wondering what the year will bring–and what I will bring to it.

## January 2

Keeping company
Something yearned for years ago
No yen for that now

Even in this retirement village, once in a while a single lady and single man will become an item–of course, many more women than men. I haven't yet spied a single man that gets my heart racing.

## January 3

Bed is so cozy
Don't know where to start the day
I'll just take a nap.

Still not ready to rock and roll.

# January 4

Unproductive cough
An unusual ear ache
Nap again on tap.

This new year is getting a slow start from me.

# January 5

So pleased I saw it
Pristine snow cover last night
Now gone with the rain.

At last, my interest is aroused—by the old familiar sight of snow.

# January 6

Facing it squarely
First step to erasing it
Financial chaos

Perhaps this is part of what has kept me slow—I remember the poem—"We are rich we have nothing to lose—we are old we have nowhere to rush."

# January 7

Like cherry blossoms
Who share their beauty briefly
The snow quickly melts.

Snow reminds me of pleasure of cherry blossom season in Tokyo last spring.

# January 8

Thrill to see the moon
From my apartment window
Almost fully round.

Wonder why the moon seems so wonderful. Sun is equally amazing, and yet we see it every day (well maybe not every day) and yet I take that for granted.

# January 9

No writing today
All creative energy
Used up in my dream.

Sometimes wonder who is creating those dreams inside my head.

# January 10

Morning adventure
Pour milk into a white cup
Oops! It overflows.

I don't see as well as I like which often adds interest to day's little tasks.

# January 11

Where is my heart's home
Is it wherever I am–
Or where I will be?

I have lived so many places–from South Dakota, East Coast, Vietnam, Washington state–all have been home to me at one time or another.

# January 12

Jazz exercise class
Swing and sway the hour away
Me with two left feet

I enjoy it—even when I trip over my own feet.

# January 13

Don't fly in my dreams
Never have done it; maybe
I'm not creative.

I have read that creative people will often find themselves taking flight in their dreams. I never get off the ground.

# January 14

Still "nobody knows
The troubles I have 'seeing'"
My favorite hymn

Or the trouble I have hearing, for that matter. Hopefully I will continue to do fairly well in the area of thinking.

# January 15

Frosting on the grass
Disappears soon in sunshine
Sweet spring harbinger.

This has been a good winter—snow-wise and frost-wise—as far as I am concerned.

Wonder this morning
If old haiku-ists don't die
Do they fade away?

Some mornings I just enjoy staying in bed and composing haiku in my imagination.

## January 16

I hate getting old.
Watch what you're saying, missy.
Some days you love it!

My main conflict in life is with myself—conflict between my optimistic self and the self who always drags her heels.

## January 17

Today payback time
For yesterday's two a.m. wake-up,
Yesterday's full day.

Some days I think I am young again and can burn the candle at both ends (although as Edna St. Vincent Millay says, that does make a lovely light).

## January 18

The shit hit the fan
An awful-wonderful day—
I faced it squarely.

I balanced my check book!

Some folk pet dog pets
I have a frog pet to pet—
Soft squishy plush frog.

I collect frogs—ones that I don't have to feed or take out for walks.

# January 19

Expecting little
You're seldom disappointed.
A worthy motto?

This motto from Tony Hillerman's memoir *Seldom Disappointed*. I'm not sure it's the best motto for motivating an active life. Although it seems to have worked well for Tony.

# January 20

Stay in bed and dream
Or clean up dirty corners—
Both satisfying..

Actually I chose the former—just wouldn't face the corners.

# January 21

Do you want to know
Vicissitudes of aging?
I just love that word.

I don't really care if you wanted to know about the vicissitudes. I just wanted to use that lovely word.

# January 22

Barack Obama
Our 44th President–
Sing praise for the day.

I am hopeful that new administration will restore American sense of rightness. Also pleased with the Inaugural poet. She read an occasional poem–a poem on a special occasion. I write occasional haiku–though my occasions are pretty mundane compared to a presidential inauguration.

# January 23

The retirement  homes
Excellent places to meet
Many new "old friends."

You can never be too rich–or have too many friends.

# January 24

Last week in wheelchair
Today, she used her walker.
It gives me courage.

Seeing someone else–even older than I am–keep on trucking is an inspiration to me.

# January 25

She's going downhill–
Why do I feel so helpless?–
That could well be me.

Another friend not quite so up reminds me to keep on picking daisies while I can.

# January 25

Mother Nature's gift
Bushes, grass, trees, wrapped in white
Winter's ermine coat.

I've lived in lots of snow places, and still miss a good blizzard.

# January 26

If I don't get done
Getting them ready, they'll be
Mailed post-humously.

I've had the books since last August that I plan to mail to the grandchildren. Although I'm not expecting my immediate demise, the books still are in a neat pile by my desk.

# January 27

A past memory?
In my dreams, I walk freely–
Future prediction?

I am grateful that I am still a sturdy walker, and I am greedy for more. Jogging would be fun.

# January 28

When the moment comes
Necessity, energy
Shake hands, go to work.

Time to do the laundry–I do it.

# January 29

Many English words
Don't fit in haiku format
Do you remember
Su-per-cal-i-fra-gu-lis-
Tic-ex-pea-a-li-do-shush.

I have no idea how that word is spelled. I remember the pleasure of hearing the word in the song.

# January 30

What do others see
That pulls to Mona Lisa—
The smile? Roving eyes?

Maybe I would know if I had seen it in Paris. So far I haven't made it to Europe.

# January 31

Itchy arms and legs
Transformed in dark before dawn
Rare case of shingles!

I started the month pacing the halls, and end with weird thoughts.

# JUNE 2009

## June 1

How does the dog know
She is eager to pet him?
"She's a dog person."

My friend seemed to know the dog wanted to be petted; the dog seemed to know she was a person who would pet a dog. A complete mystery to me.

## June 2

It seems rather odd
To be called a "frog person"–
I confess, it's me.

The frogs I have don't have to be fed, walked or have bathroom facilities. I have more than I need–and I still smile whenever I open a gift frog.

## June 3

Amphibians here,
Staring up at dinosaurs.
Why are they leaving?

Frog and toad relatives have been around on this earth for a long time. Scientists are puzzled by the disappearance of many species over the last two decades.

# June 4

If you live through it
All experience is great.
If you don't, bad luck.

This from a quote by Alice Neel, a Bohemian artist during the 1930s and 40s. "All experience is great if you live through it. If it kills you, you've gone too far."

# June 5

A fly hit my face,
Just as nonplused as I was.
Neither one to blame.

I have no idea how the fly felt about the encounter. I hope it was not fatal for her.

# June 6

A nice healthy walk–
Took time to smell the roses,
And chat with some friends.

What more can I say?

# June 7

Taking down the tent,
Men doing their jobs smoothly–
A pleasure to watch.

A huge canopy had been erected to shelter the flower-laden tables for a memorial reception. Taking it down required the coordinated efforts of several workers.

# June 8

Both the same to me–
Outer space or inner space–
Both provide themes.

Sometimes my haiku floats up from my memory; sometimes from something I see or read. Although in some ways my memory probably came from something I have seen or read in the past.

# June 9

Thirty-nine–holding?
Eighty-two and still counting.
Exquisite birthday.

Friends took me out for dinner at a restaurant that gave a birthday celebrant a lovely big fresh baked chocolate chip cookie with a scoop of ice cream and a candle on top. My friends sang happy birthday. As the woman across the aisle left, she wished me happy birthday, and said she was thirty-nine and holding. I am happy to claim eighty-two.

# June 10

My birthday flowers,
An e-card on computer,
Happy Birthday tune!!

A surprise scene of beautiful flowers, along with the music of Happy Birthday from my grandson Paul. I have secretly wished for flowers on my birthday, and it was a pleasure to get them in this special way.

# June 11

The end may be near.
Still each day a beginning
For the rest of life.

The connection between endings and beginnings is a common metaphor for a life well-lived.

# June 12

Sunny morning walk,
Pink rhody blossoms falling,
Red in full glory.

The rhododendrons are especially gorgeous this year (although I have vague memories of saying the same thing every year).

# June 13

I have mixed feelings today-
Folks used to dress up for church,
Now anything goes!!

I don't "dress up" as much as I used to either—but I think for the most part I am tastefully attired.

# June 14

If girls were flowers,
Oldest—Indian Paint Brush,
Then Iris—Sweet Pea.

Susan asked me, "If your girls were flowers, what would they be?" I don't know why these particular flowers floated up. As I think about it, the flowers I picked for the three do fit in some ways, although humans are considerably more complex than flowers.

## June 15

Don't wait for the mood.
You won't get things done that way.
Just sit down–do it!!

Pearl S. Buck wrote over 100 books. She said, "I don't wait for the mood. You accomplish nothing if you do that. Your mind has to know it has to get down to work."

## June 16

So many leave us
With no chance to say good-bye.
Remember–"hello."

In the four years I have been living here, there have been several who have died, or moved away without leaving a forwarding address–Betty, Jane, Roy, Shirley, Harriet, Harold, Jerry, Mary, Jane, Kearney, Helen. I wish I had gotten to know them better. Good-bye, old friends. I remind myself to keep contact with friends that are still here.

## June 17

The house seems empty–
Our company is leaving,
Some never return.

Though there may be still many others around, it takes a while before they fill in the gaps left by those who have gone.

# June 18

Email from afar.
The Land of the Midnight Sun–
Norway in summer.

My sister sent an email telling about the wild scenic beauty
of the country, the home of our family ancestors. I had dreamed of
visiting Norway sometime to go cross country skiing–but that would
have been under the Midnight Moon.

# June 19

Unexamined dream
Like a letter unopened–
And I have thousands!!

Freud, in his book about dreams, suggested that a dream
not analyzed would be like not opening a letter. (He had his own
interpretations–something about cigars, for instance.) As I think about
all those dreams over the years, they seem more like junk mail; some of
them interesting, but not enlightening.

# June 20

Some things just happen
Without known rhyme or reason.
My frog collection.

Putting some of my collection on display here at Waterford, I
have been asked when I started collecting. My love affair with frogs may
have begun while my husband and I were in language school in South
Vietnam, where we were serving a short term with Vietnam Christian
Service. There was a ditch outside our window which filled with rain,
thus bringing to life a wonderful frog chorus. However, my collection

didn't start until ten years or so later. Frogs kept accumulating, and all of a sudden I had a collection.

## June 21

Where has my oomph gone?
I keep walking, though slowly.
Never an "oomph girl"?

If I am remembering correctly, an oomph girl was a cute perky, cheerleader type. I never aspired to that career, though I wouldn't mind a little "perky."

## June 22

Is God evolving,
Or have humans made progress
In morality?

A New York Times book review had a column about a book by Wright, *The Evolution of God*. Although I have not seen the book, the author's point seems to be that God has been evolving over the centuries, and because of that evolution, humans are becoming gentler and kinder!

## June 23

Too much violence
In James Patterson's mysteries.
I'll stick with "cozies."

Reminding myself not to be pulled in by the hype about the best-selling author, James Patterson. Just saw an ad on TV about his newest book, *The Bikini*. (The token bikini-clad woman on the cover.) A cozy is a sub-set of the mystery genre, which does not include all the blood and gore.

# June 24

We are born to grow
In mind, body, and spirit.
If we shrink, we die.

"Human self-hood is made to grow. If we stay still, we shrink and atrophy."

# June 25

Hear birds, see green growth,
Smell fresh bark dust, feel the breeze,
Taste summer's medley.

Early morning circuit of the grounds brought sensual pleasure.

# June 26

Memory and history,
Not the same, but related.
We can use them both.

Memory doesn't always provide a true history. For example, my sister and I will sometimes remember the same event differently. We each experienced it from our own perspective.

# June 27

Indirect death cause,
Houdini, famed washboard abs,
Fails to suck them in!!

One of Houdini's demonstrations was to tighten his abdominals and have a friend hit him as hard as he could. Once someone hit him in the belly, and his abs were not washboard hard. Houdini died of kidney failure. (The friend said he had asked Houdini to "suck it in." No one knows whether the story is true.)

## June 28

Each one dies sometime,
But rarely with the fan-fare
Of Michael Jackson.

Really quite incredible. No wonder his ranch is named Neverland. That is indeed where his life story is played out.

## June 29

Talk about living–
Even while we are dying,
We who are well fed.

I heard a powerful sermon on Sunday, the kind that leaves you feeling you should do some important thing–but not sure what that thing actually is. The aim is to see that everybody is fed–physically, spiritually, emotionally. A big task–and each one of us can do only a little.

## June 30

It's only Tuesday,
But already end of month.
Keeps me off-balance.

The perception of time is filtered through feelings. Thus, for me, each week starts out slowly on Sunday, and then speeds up until Saturday. A new month does the same thing–slow on the first, and then gradually moves faster, until the grand finale of the last of the month.

# DECEMBER 2009

## December 1

The Full Cold Moon Month
Starts out with the clear vision
Of that silver globe.

I have finally discovered a vantage point in my apartment to get a glimpse of the moon–if I stay up late enough and if the sky is clear enough. That happened on this first full moon of the month.

## December 2

EE TAH DAH KEE MAS
Does the Lord know Japanese?
Does she know English?

The Japanese phrase used as a word of gratitude at the beginning of a meal is just one of the few I have learned. Every once in awhile I take a brief stab at learning more Japanese–and it is such a completely different language that I have not been able to retain what I learn more than a day at a time. I'll never tell jokes, or talk about the meaning of life in Japanese. (Of course sometimes my English fails me for jokes and life's meaning.)

## December 3

Be yourself–wise choice.
Everyone else is taken.
What's more to be said!!

An obvious bit of wisdom, that we sometimes fail to follow.

## December 4

Gonna stay in bed–
Just sleep away, fade away.
Shucks, I gotta pee!!

I don't often write in child dialect. This haiku just came full-blown as I lay in bed, deciding whether or not to just fade away. The child in me would be the part to stay abed, so the dialect is appropriate. I didn't stay in bed, so the adult took charge.

## December 5

G.W.–example
Of one who doesn't see grays–
Things are black or white.

George W. Bush has bragged that he doesn't do nuances.

## December 6

Her father's hanky–
The kids would  get it from him,
Find a dry spot and blow!!

This practice would not fit in today's strict guidelines–use a new tissue, blow, throw it away, and wash your hands. Were we really sicker in those old days?

# December 7

What's wrong with me I do not know—
In spite of those three naps I take,
I sleep long hours at night; then wake

And still have many miles to go.

Not haiku and not a sonnet, though I have borrowed Robert Frost's iambic tetrameter. The piece came as I woke up after ten hours of sleep. It's both a blessing and a curse that I sleep so well.

# December 8

Axis of evil—
Free cell, solitaire, Cheetos—
What will rescue me?

Each of us may have her own axis of evil. These happen to be activities to which I am addicted when I could well be doing something more satisfying. (There undoubtedly is deeper evil in my life which I conveniently ignore.)

# December 9

The upbeat tale of
Old lady and ugly frog—
Because I can hear!!

Had my new "hearing enhancer" when I went to a Christmas party with friends. Gave me the courage to enter in the conversation with my own story, even though I still often don't hear the jokes that others are laughing at.

# December 10

Picked up a stray germ–
Nose-blowing, coughing frenzy–
An old-fashioned cold.

I had felt invincible lately–missing out on many potential disasters–but I guess the possibility of the germ is always with us.

## December 11

Living the question
To at last live the answer,
How close have I come?

Some erudite philosopher came up with this one. Since I have no idea what the question is, I won't know if I finally end up living the answer!

## December 12

Never was perky,
Though I could sometimes claim pert–
Now not even pert.

This thought comes when I take a shower.  I use Pert shampoo–and though I still am not Pert, I do have "Pert" hair.

## December 13

The sun shines thinly,
The breeze blows chillingly
On my paper route.

I walk out to the paper vending machine for the Sunday paper, which includes the TV Guide. The chilly walk reminded me of the year that my son delivered a morning paper in South Dakota. We figured he could use his bike for delivery most of the time. The year was the record blizzard year that is still talked about, and he couldn't use his bike for several months.

## December 14

To die with dry skin
And three bottles of skin cream–
What an irony!!

I had been using a skin moisturizer after a bout of a dry skin rash, and when I saw the same brand at Costco, I bought the two bottle set at a good price. I realized that I had not used up the first bottle, and still had the two unopened ones under the bathroom sink. (A post script is that now I have finished the first bottle, and have found that the other two–though the same brand–are a skin cleanser, not just a moisturizer. Continued irony!!)

## December 15

Challenge of knowledge–
Science has gathered it further
Than human wisdom.

There is so much information on the internet, in books and newspapers that it is impossible to put a coherent knowledge base together. The New York Times boast was they had all the news that's fit to print. I can't even manage to get three days worth skimmed, much less digested.

## December 16

Life slipping away
Or the normal  ebb and flow
Of the daily tides?

A recurring pattern–one day feeling cheerful–for no reason; the next feeling blue–for no reason!!

# December 17

My own eponym
Haiku Dorothydean–
From my mind's jumble.

My Word for the Day brought more famous eponyms–
Orwellian, Byronic, Draconian. I thought of "Workmanian," and
dismissed the idea. "Allisonian," from my maiden name, has a nice
ring to it. However "Dorothydean" is somehow more personal.

# December 18

What are we doing?
We aim to make "Senior Years"
Compelling and fun!

Not always an easy process since each of us has different views
of what is compelling and fun. Waterford does an excellent job of
providing challenges for so many.

# December 19

Early morning rounds–
What if I walk–and don't sit?
Hooray, I made it.

I am aiming to increase the distance I can comfortably
walk without sitting down to rest. Today made it once around the
campus–about one third of a mile. I'm not doing well in the persistence
area.

# December 20

An essay each week
Instead of a haiku a day
In two thousand ten?

Probably not—I expect I will stick with a haiku a day, and hopefully throw in an occasional sonnet or essay.

# December 21

Most letters have one—
W has three—as in
George "double-you" Bush!

Don't think this has anything to do with my antipathy towards George W. Bush—that his name often includes the three-syllable W.

# December 22

Solved a mystery—
The source of all those stray kkkkkks
On computer screen.

I noticed several months ago that the index finger on my right hand is slightly curved. The letter "k" is under that finger on the keyboard. The curve means the finger rests more heavily on that key than fingers on the other keys, resulting in the procession of kkkkks if I am not careful. At first I thought I was developing arthritis in that finger. However, I remembered that those stray kks have been with me ever since I have been using a computer—which has a more sensitive key board than the old typewriter; I decided that this must have been present for years, and probably will not result in any crippling deformity of the whole hand.

# December 23

Story-teller's goal
May be a sacred duty
Or a playful task.

I'll opt for the playful task. Any sacred duty eludes me.

# December 24

Nostalgia attack—
Christmas Eve, glass of white wine
And my memories.

A quiet Christmas Eve with no family, no stocking hung—my small tree, an ornament with a tatted cover, my Christmas frogs, the glass of white wine, and the memories.

# December 25

A special Christmas—
A daughter holding her place
In my life—and hers

Kris fixed a good dinner—turkey, Margie's potatoes, sweet potatoes. We ate and talked—no snow on the ground now, but lots of talk about past Christmas snows.

# December 26

Eileen remembered
The autumn blanket I loved,
And found one for me.

It is a special pleasure when someone remembers what you like, and actually goes out to find it for you. An extra bonus in this case—Eileen actually found that blanket on sale.

# December 27

An auctioned painting–
"Saint Dorothy" would sell for
More than one million!!

I had never heard of Saint Dorothy and had a momentary thought that it would be interesting to have her picture painted by an Old Master. I knew, however, that the asking price would not fit into my budget–and also, sour grapes, the picture would probably be too big for my apartment walls. Saint Dorothy, from what is now Turkey, was a young woman, martyred in 311 A.D., when the Roman Emperor Diocletian was persecuting the Christians.

# December 28

She has gone away,
My dear pal of the fireside–
Loyal wife, mom–friend.

Jean was my first friend when I moved into Waterford. We often had dinner together, and would sit by the fireplace in the winter months after we ate. I had been to see her two weeks before she died. I think she still knew me–and she was no longer really present in this world.

# December 29

Forlorn patch of snow–
Jealous of its mid-west kin–
They can last for weeks.

There had been a lovely blanket of snow on the ground–which almost before it quit falling had begun to melt in rain and warmer weather. If snow has feelings, it might be jealous of the wonderful snow that has fallen in South Dakota, my old home state. That snow seems like it lasts forever.

# December 30

Quantum leap from bed–
Almost to another year
Cause for gratitude.

The word quantum can mean a huge amount–or the smallest particle of an element that can exist. Sometimes getting out of bed in the morning can seem like both definitions–a giant leap out of my slumber–or the smallest part of my activity for the day.

# December 31

Celebrate this Eve
But on Eastern Standard Time
Drinking pink champagne.

I had never been excited about champagne, and I loved the pink variety. Whether I liked the taste or just the color better I don't know. I would need to do a blind taste test of white and pink, and even that would not be the final word since there are many whites and many pinks. I did learn that taking the fruit skins out of the liquid immediately gives the white varieties. Leaving the grape skins in contact with the liquid for awhile gives the colored variations. I learn something new every year!!!

# JANUARY 2010

## January 1

Decide to build it–
Or slap together the days.
A New Year awaits!

I've never had much luck with New Year's Resolutions, and I don't know if the image of plans for building my days will do me any more good, but the image appeals to me.

## January 2

"Nine hundred word thoughts"–
Seventeen syllable thoughts,
A challenge to write.

An article about the New York Times rules for their contributing op-ed writers recommended 900 word limit–a real challenge to pull together a thought–beginning, middle and end. In some ways the haiku limit of 17 syllables is easier. (The phrase, op-ed, means that these articles are usually printed on the opposite page from the editorials.)

## January 3

Always on the road
To becoming a writer;
The end not in sight.

I have been a reader as long as I can remember. I have been a closet writer almost as long. I enjoyed writing those obligatory thank-you notes for Christmas gifts, even if I did not particularly enjoy the gift.

## January 4

It's the little things,
The niggling gnats, biting fleas,
That eat up my days.

Often when I get to the end of a day which seems to have kept me busy, I try to figure out what I actually have done. And all I come up with are those small little chores that produce nothing but the passage of time.

## January 5

Moving on–simple
All are slip-sliding away
To the next life stage.

Whether we wish it or not, we are on that slippery slope of life.

## January 6

What am I stomping?
My failure of persistence
In my daily tasks?

In some early counselor training class I learned that a repetitive motion, when a person would ordinarily be sitting in a relaxed posture, often had some hidden meaning. I became aware that my right heel was stomping nonexistent ants. As is often the case, I am annoyed with myself for not getting more done.

# January 7

What does it all mean?
Everything is meaningless!
Is that the whole truth?

In my daily Bible reading, I came across one of the examples of the Wisdom of Solomon (who was purported to be the wisest man ever). I don't know what he means about everything being meaningless. Doesn't seem that way to me.

# January 8

Not a radical–
Just followed "the way things are"
It is not too late!!

My tendency has always been to stick with the status quo. My sister remembers that when she was ten or so, she got up on a stool and pretended to be preaching a sermon. She says I made her get down–because women couldn't be preachers! (I don't remember that!) I have long since made many changes of beliefs–which might have seemed radical at one time for me.

# January 9

From stretchy panties
To white cotton bloomers, to
Japanese beetles.

The mind (at least mine) does move in mysterious ways. Putting on a pair of stretchy panties reminded me that stretch fabric wasn't available in the old days, and in my childhood  back in New Jersey, I wore white cotton bloomers.  Clothes used to be hung on the line outdoors to dry. One day I put on my clean bloomers, and felt a strange sensation of something crawling. It was a Japanese beetle. At that time in my life, it represented my whole knowledge of the Asian world.

## January 10

What a real nuisance–
Insufficient hearing for
Casual chatting.

Although I pretend to myself that I am a loner, the fact remains that I would like to be able to enter into conversations with others on more than a superficial level.

## January 11

"Great Decisions" group–
Obama's special envoys–
Good or bad–who knows?

I go to the discussion group because I like the opportunity to learn more about world politics and finance. The DVD that is shown at the beginning of the hour is information that I can digest–the discussion that follows is useless for me.

## January 12

The bad girl Charlotte,
Came early, forgot her purse,
Kept whole bus waiting!

Sometimes I find myself being judgmental about others–even those who obviously are handicapped by various ills of old age. I suspect part of my reaction to Charlotte had to do with my own fear of losing touch with reality.

# January 13

Time to let them go–
Impatience, regrets, anger–
And live this day free.

Reaction to my negativity of yesterday.

# January 14

Interesting life–
Wish I'd noticed it sooner.
Glad I see it now.

Some famous person said this–don't remember who. I expect many of us, not so famous, could also make this statement.

# January 15

Actually true?
A season for everything?
To see–or not to see.

I find my skepticism increasing–although I can sometimes see the value of the negative.

# January 16

Time to start living–
Stop this waiting for Godot,
Waiting for insight.

As I read this haiku at the end of the month when I am putting it all together, I don't know what I was thinking–perhaps I was waiting for insight.

# January 17

Not just about life–
Art: discovery, design,
Accepting chaos.

Going through a career-choosing workshop in my twenties, one of the comments made about my style was that I was so comfortable with chaos that I might have a problem finishing projects. That has many times turned out to be true. However, maybe because I accept chaos, I can call myself an artist.

# January 18

The heart has reasons
That reason knows nothing of.
Wisdom of Pascal.

What more can be said?

# January 19

Up before dawn's crack–
Have you ever heard it crack,
Or even crackle.

Before dawn is my favorite time of day.

# January 20

Puzzles in my dreams–
Crosswords, free cell, Sudoku–
Impossible tasks!!

Wonder if working puzzles while I sleep is improving my mental abilities, or depleting whatever brain power I possess.

## January 21

If the truth be told
All of us are somewhat odd–
Yes, you and me too!

After a life time of attempting to be "normal," I have finally come to the realization that we all are somewhat odd–rather than just an exact carbon copy of a human.

## January 22

A waste of my time,
Rehearsing my short essay.
Never got called on.

The main reason I was not called upon to recite was that I didn't try to listen to instructor and therefore didn't raise my hand at appropriate time. Pays me back for not being willing to volunteer and expecting others to read my mind. And according to the experts who study brain function, memorizing is a kind of brain exercise which keeps the mind flexible.

## January 23

Week's start was upbeat–
Its final day was down beat.
Every hour, heart beats.

Through all the ups and downs that life offers, the heart continues its regular (for the most part) beating.

# January 24

One ton temple bell
In a Japanese garden,
Moth sleeps in silence.

This is my rendition of a centuries-old haiku by Basho, a famous Japanese writer. I first saw it used by Billy Collins in a long narrative poem which reads like a meditation.

# January 25

Whatever we wish
We're all in this together–
This mad, crazy world.

Reading the newspaper–earthquakes in Haiti and Chile, the ground underneath us in Washington potentially shaky, we are indeed all in this together.

# January 26

Those interruptions–
Pungent, bitter, sweet or sad–
Each adds spice to life.

The unexpected phone calls, the emails from a cousin you haven't been in touch with for years, may at first be an unwelcome break into the rhythm of life–but often, in retrospect, represent the spice of life.

# January 27

Now the die is cast–
We're all on the homeward trail
For better or worse!!

"We're on the upward trail/ Singing, singing, everybody singing/ Homeward bound"–this was an old camp song I learned from counseling at summer camp in the Black Hills. My aim was to able to have enough stamina and breath to sing as we walked up the hill to our cabins from the swimming hole (cold mountain water!).

## January 28

Clear bright pinks, greens blues,
Oranges, accents of black–
Kept me entertained.

Cataract surgery was really quite pleasant; no pain, only colorful entertainment–all with the hope of better vision.

## January 29

What are the chances
Of a semi-miracle?
Quite common I'd guess.

I was not expecting to have any major improvement in vision because of the macular degeneration in both eyes. The removal of the cataract turned out to be a real miracle. I am beginning to see clearly.

## January 30

If I could not hear
Or see, sad; if I could not
Imagine, tragic.

I suspect that this is only true because I can still see, hear and imagine. Once imagination is lost, I probably would not have the capability of imagining tragedy!

# January 31

First things first, she said
As she got up late–and found
'Twas wrong side of bed.

As I mentioned several days ago, before dawn is my favorite time of time. If dawn has passed me by as I slept, I may initially leap from bed–but the day has already gone awry. Hopefully this is not a portent of the months to come!

# FEBRUARY 2010

## February 1

A useful motto–
I'll get up for the big one.
Old age–a big one!!

Serena Williams, who recently won another tennis grand slam victory, explained how she so often seemed to recover from a negative scoring position. "I get up for the big ones." And old age is definitely worth getting up for.

## February 2

Youth, a gift of nature;
Old age is a work of art.
You do have a choice.

Well, you don't actually have the choice of remaining young, though some folks do their best to do so. Somebody on a TV show said that if you walk down Broadway in New York City, one out of three women would have had some kind of plastic surgery! Your choice is what you do to produce a genuine work of art of your aging.

# February 3

On top of the world–
Designer clothes, skis, cell phones–
Take pictures, make calls.

The cover of the New Yorker showed the stylish couple in the midst of a gorgeous scene–not living for the moment, but with attention on the future– showing their pictures at cocktail parties–or in the distance–whoever is on the other end of the phone conversation.

# February 4

Chef's salt shaker hop–
Two purposes–limit salt
And exercise arm.

The salt shakers on the table in the Courtside Dining Room have such small holes that it takes quite a bit of arm energy to get salt out–limits our salt intake, and at least keeps some of the muscles in the "shaking" arm from disappearing completely.

# February 5

Three ghosts from the past
Driving away in a blue Ford,
Leaving me behind.

In a way, this seemed like a straight-forward dream. The ghosts in the car were my husband David and his parents, and the blue Ford had belonged to them before we bought it when we were married. All three ghosts–as well as the blue Ford–are long since gone. Why do I dream of them now?

# February 6

Met Helen Keller,
Gracious, regal, warm, friendly–
Thank you, Miss Keller.

It is rare that a famous person shows up in my dreams. I suspect
Miss Keller came to remind me to stop whining about my hearing and
vision problems. Of course she was too polite to tell me just to shut up
and keep living.

# February 7

"Violinist Linked
to JAL Crash Blossoms"–
Newspaper headline!

The headline referred to the story of a young violinist whose
career was blossoming, and whose father had been killed several years
earlier in the crash of a JAL plane. Obscure writing often occurs with
the use of words that can be either adjective or noun–like crash or
blossoms.

# February 8

Not a waste of time,
Memorizing poetry–
My own and others'.

I still remember the first poem I memorized–Robert Louis
Stevenson's "My Shadow." I have learned many since then–and probably
forgotten quite a few, though with a little review they come back.

# February 9

There are two problems
For writers; getting started
And then getting stopped.

I have experienced both problems many times–once I get started it is easy to keep going.

# February 10

A relief today–
Everybody sees the fog,
It's not in my head.

Before cataract surgery, I hadn't realized that I was in a constant fog–although I didn't really believe that everyone else saw it too. Just nice to be free of the fog.

# February 11

My hair "styled" today.
"Shave and a haircut, two bits."
Two bits won't do it.

Did have my hair cut today, and as the beautician was using the electric razor to clip my neckline, the words of the old song came to me. I wonder when a man could get a shave and a haircut for twenty-five cents.

# February 12

Taped the Super Bowl–
Fast forward game, watch the ads.
An odd thing to do.

I had heard that the ads are more fun than the game, although I have been told that the game was exciting this year, with the underdog winning at the last minute. I still haven't checked the ads.

## February 13

The little black bug
Like a friendly small puppy–
Invites being squashed.

One remnant of the eye surgery is the little black spot that appeared now and then. Eventually it disappeared–and I miss seeing it.

## February 14

When I was younger–
(Six months ago)–I could pop
Six pills in my mouth–
And swallow all with one gulp–
Now only two at a time.

I have no idea why this happened–physical, psychological, who cares?

## February 15

A single feather,
Perfect burnished gold satin,
Does the bird miss it?

This vivid image appeared in a dream–the bird that the feather came from must have been gorgeous.

# February 16

Thought 'twas just haiku
It turns out to be haibun–
"Bun"–literature.

Interesting to think of the little pieces that I write as literature,
instead of just doodles. (Of course, literature can be either good or bad.)

# February 17

If you are planning
To do something–do something–
The way to the prize.

I keep needing pep talks to keep me going some days.

# February 18

In these stormy seas–
The rat is deserting us;
Is our ship sinking?

Our manager departed suddenly, causing this image to come to
mind. Gave me minor concern about how our ship would stay floating.
Turns out he is now working for a competitor–and when someone does
that, it is considered protocol to depart suddenly.

# February 19

Do we live our lives
In quiet desperation?
There is a better way.

Another pep talk.

# February 20

I almost missed it–
The Christmas rhododendron
It bloomed while I slept.

Living most of my life in colder climates, I am still astonished at the glory of various blooming bushes and trees in these milder temperatures.

# February 21

There is a little boy–
Different from other boys–
Yet God loves each one.

A moving sermon by the preacher who was the transgender little boy who when he was born was on the surface a little girl–and eventually became aware that in fact he was a boy–and how the idea of God's love followed him throughout his life. A challenge for each of us to accept and enjoy the differences in others and in our own lives as well.

# February 22

Old plastic glass frames–
She made hers nail-polish red
With nary a smudge.

Getting new glasses after the cataract surgery, I was reminded of my high school friend who used red nail polish on the old clear plastic frames. I always admired the way she could use the polish with no smudges. (My new frames are not red!)

# February 23

The millennials–
From eighteen to twenty-nine–
All of my grand-kids.

There is always someone who will label generations and then talk about the statistics for the group. The only one I accurately remember is that 37% of the group has tattoos. Four out of my nine have tattoos! One good statistic is that in spite of hard economic times, the group as a whole remains optimistic about the state of the world.

# February 24

My new singing frog–
"I can see more clearly now"–
My current theme song!

I had declared a moratorium on getting more frogs. However, when my daughter saw the frog that sings about seeing more clearly, she knew that I would appreciate hearing it sing about seeing clearly.

# February 25

A story teller's
Sacred duty–open a path
To world harmony.

I am a kind of story teller–don't aspire to anything as grand as world harmony, though it sounds like a good idea. Trouble is that even in the realm of music, there are differences in the idea of what is harmonious and what is dissonant.

# February 26

Old woman rescued
After seven days in hell–
Came out singing praise.

One of the inspiring stories from rescue efforts in Haiti after the earthquake. I wonder if I would come out singing praise if I were buried under rubble for seven days.

# February 27

Tsunami alert.
Earthquake in Chile sends waves
Across the ocean.

A vivid concrete illustration of the way we're all connected.

# February 28

If you wonder why
I walk like an old lady–
Remember–I'm old!

I was passing judgment on myself for walking like an old lady. But I am old.

# MARCH 2010

## March 1

Road to Ithaca—
Pray that the journey is long,
Full of adventures.

I am inspired by the poem "Ithaca" by C. P. Cavafy. Ithaca is a metaphor for the final destination of a journey. The poem encourages me to make use of this long journey of life—and to live it with great pleasure and joy.

## March 2

Don't ask audience
If they can hear—use a mike,
Be professional.

It is frustrating to me when a speaker asks the audience if he or she can be heard without the microphone. Nobody, including me, is brave enough to say they can't, so the speaker continues unheard by some of us.

## March 3

My life takes more time
Now that I'm old. Is that why
Time accelerates?

Both things seem true in my life. My daily chores do take more actual minutes on the clock–and it seems like the hours are rushing by at mach speed.

## March 4

Just write down that word–
If you wait for perfection
Writer's block results.

Usually that perfect word eludes me. I need to remember that perfection is rare.

## March 5

Sport within a sport–
Athletes at highest levels.
True of writing skills.

Lindsey Vonn, the skiing sensation, talked about her compulsive training for the Olympics. I doubt that the same thing is true for writing though time spent on developing writing skills can be a big boost to the writer.

## March 6

My next waking up
Will call for an uprising
To a brand new day.

Good reminder to be thankful for each day.

# March 7

Waiting for blossoms
Don't see any signs of life
On the cherry trees.

Although I do not see any signs of either bud or leaf on the trees, the trunk of the tree is in itself a sign of life.

# March 8

All truly great thoughts
Are conceived by walking—so
Start walking and think!!

This may well have been true of Nietzsche, and I have also read that brain activity is aided by physical activity so perhaps it is true of garden-variety thinkers also.

# March 9

I walked this morning
And no great thoughts came to me—
A few mundane ones.

I'm not surprised that one morning walk didn't instantly produce any great ideas. Guess I'll have to keep walking.

# March 10

The upside-downside
Living in retirement home—
We're none of us young!!

This haiku comes from watching others around me showing more signs of aging—and worrying about my own.

# March 11

Somewhat like preacher
Going to competitor–
You never come back.

I was unhappy that our managing director resigned and left without any chance of closure for residents. Later I understood that since he was going to work for a retirement home competitor, protocol dictated that he needed to depart without any good-byes. It still seems like being abandoned. (When preachers leave a parish, they are encouraged to not stay connected so that members of the congregation will go to the new preacher for ministering. I'm not sure why that is true in a business.)

# March 12

Still an outsider
"This class is full of good cooks."
Alas, that's not me.

The quote comes from an email about the up-coming pot-luck of our writing class members. Since I no longer cook, that doesn't apply to me. And I have often felt in life that I am an outsider, looking on at life from another point of view.

# March 13

Vocabulary–
Learning new words makes your life
More interesting.

The "Yo Mama Vocabulary Builder" declares we should increase our vocabulary, not to impress other people, cultivate professional goals or build scholarly achievement, but for the pleasure of learning.

# March 14

By living fully
We can lengthen our days while
Our years do not change.

At the end of a day, a sense of satisfaction comes from living it rather than just existing.

# March 15

There's a curvature–
A bending of time–which hides
The future–good thing.

I sometimes wish I could see the future, but more often I think it is a good thing that I can't–surprises are often a pleasure and a negative outcome would have caused unnecessary anxiety.

# March 16

Without your haiku
I would not have known you
As well as I do.

A friend wrote this haiku in response to my February Journal. And interesting to me is the fact that I actually know myself better as I write.

# March 17

Financial blaming–
Need to rely on myself–
Plus be more careful.

I am aware that I need more time to keep track of my finances. When I was younger I would balance my checkbook down to the penny. Now I can easily lose dimes, quarters and dollars!!

## March 18

Phones dying or dead
Cell phone not enough volume–
I relied on technology.

I realize that I relied on these instruments to conduct business, to talk to family and friends, to make appointments. And writing letters or sending smoke signals definitely won't do it.

## March 19

Where did we come from?
Pakistan, Japan, Turkey
And South Dakota.

Sitting on the plane taking me to Japan and looking around at passengers, I became aware of the variety of backgrounds represented. I was reminded of the old radio soap opera, Helen Trent. "Can a girl from a small mining town in the Midwest find happiness as the wife of a wealthy, titled Englishman?" (And if you listened to any of the episodes, the answer was probably "no.") Can a girl from a small town in South Dakota find happiness visiting exotic Japan?

## March 20

My haibun travel–
From ancient tradition,
Primitive travel.

The original haibun from Japan was a travel book by the haikuist Basho about his trip to the far north–a combination of haiku plus commentary, his travel by foot. It took much longer than my flight to Japan.

I would not have guessed
She has toured China five times—
Beijing to Great Wall.


I talked to a family at the airport as we were waiting for plane departure. I would not have placed her as a world traveler—shows my prejudice. (I met the same family at the airport as we returned to Portland—they had a good time, though China was cold and rainy. Sounds like Japan.)


## March 21

The first day of spring
We arrived "home" in Tokyo
But not the same day.


I'm always amazed at this travel process of losing a day going west and gaining it back going east.

## March 22

I love the tiger
'Twill be a good change from frogs
On my hallway shelf.


2010 is the Year of the Tiger. Those who are twelve this year or multiples of twelve were born in the year of the Tiger.

## March 23

Walked to Jonathans—
Pleased with walker's functioning,
Also with my own.


I had a three-wheeled walker which I thought would be useful for my walking in Tokyo and Kyoto. It did turn out to be good for that first walk in Tokyo up to Jonathans Restaurant. I did sit down a couple times on benches on the way up–and the way down. I was pleased that I could do that much walking, though my speed is definitely diminished.

# March 24

Daughter's apartment–
I look down on cherry trees,
Tops of umbrellas.

My daughter's apartment is on the fifth floor. The median of the street that can be seen from the window is lined with cherry trees, almost in full bloom. The people walking on the median this morning on their way to work are carrying umbrellas against the chilly rain.

# March 25

The non-stop bus?
It must be a Toyota!
Non-stop? No, non-step.

I was sitting in the window of a coffee shop and noticing traffic go by on the street. My first reading of the sign on the side of a bus was 'non-stop' bus. There had been so much talk recently of Toyotas accelerating without driver choice, that I wondered if these were Toyotas. However, a closer reading turned out to be non-step. The bus could be entered at street level without the need to climb up steps.

# March 26

Sumo tournament–
Tradition and ritual
McDonald's banners!!

Pomp and ceremony are in integral part of sumo–the costumes of the referees and the wrestlers, throwing salt over the shoulder for luck, the posturing of the opponents—and following the usual short bout, a group of men walking down the aisle carrying banners. This part of the ritual involves various institutions and business which are making a contribution to the winner. The banners for the most part have signs in Japanese which indicate the business involved (if you read Japanese that is). I was tickled to see that several of the banners were decorated with McDonald's Golden Arches!! And along with all the tradition, we find McDonald's, which is now big business in Japan.

## March 27

Curry noodle soup,
Shared with my granddaughter.
I now like curry.

I had imagined that I did not like curry, but have learned it is always possible that a new day brings new taste treats.

Shinkansen Bullet—
Potato salad sandwich—
On train to Kyoto.

We took the speedy bullet train from Tokyo to Kyoto. One of the sandwiches purchased from the vendor had a potato salad filling. As I commented before, it is possible to have a new taste treat. However, I don't think potato salad sandwiches make the grade in my book.

## March 28

Bus from the station
Feels like Hogwarts Express
Hurtling through the dark.

We took a bus from the Joyo station to Purple Sanga City (the Purple Sanga is the Joyo soccer team). Because the area is so unfamiliar to me, it seemed like we were speeding through dark nothingness, like the bus in the Harry Potter book. When we got off the bus, we had just a short walk to the Iris Inn.

Joyo Iris Inn
I've slept in this bed before.
It's not on the floor!!

We had reserved the only room in the Iris Inn which had beds in it and not the usual mats on the floor. Although there is an increasing use of Western style furniture, sleeping on mats on the floor is still common–mostly because so many Japanese homes have limited space, and need to make dual use of many rooms.

# March 29

Seen from the hillside–
The snow falling on Kyoto
White cherry blossoms.

Coming into Kyoto, Mr. Okubo drove us up a zigzag hilly road, to a scenic overlook. The snow was falling in big fluffy flakes like white cherry blossom petals. I remember the beauty–and not the cold discomfort!!

Chee-toe-seh guest house–
Traditional with extras–
Heated toilet seat!!

By the time we reached our guest house, my main interest was in the heated toilet seat on a western style toilet. And the bed on the floor later on was also most welcome.

# March 30

How long does it take
To make a taxi driver?
DNA imprint?

The taxi drivers know their way around the convoluted streets and alleys of Kyoto and Tokyo. It seems impossibly complicated to me. Of course of recent years, GPS is available, as well as computer print outs of destination locations.

# March 31

The increasing dearth
Of Japanese style toilets
Sits kindly with me.

Old style Japanese toilets were floor level, and required squatting ability. These were the most common on our earliest visits to Japan 20-30 years ago. Now they are mostly replaced with western style, often more elegant than my own!! The heated seat is one nice addition.

# ABOUT THE EDITOR

Deborah Guyol, who is a lawyer and writer as well as an editor, has taught creative writing in the Mature Learning Program at Clark College since 2002. She is co-author of a book first published in 1994, *The Complete Guide to Contract Lawyering* (3rd ed. 2003). Her website, www.writingintothesunset.com, is a resource for writers of a certain age.